THE GURU
IN INDIAN CATHOLICISM

Ambiguity or Opportunity of Inculturation?

Louvain Theological and Pastoral Monographs is a publishing venture whose purpose is to provide those involved in pastoral ministry throughout the world with studies inspired by Louvain's long tradition of theological excellence within the Roman Catholic Tradition. The volumes selected for publication in the series are expected to express some of today's finest reflection on current theology and pastoral practice.

Members of the Editorial Board

The Executive Committee:

Raymond F. Collins, Catholic University of Leuven, chairman
Thomas P. Ivory, The American College, Catholic University of Leuven
Joël Delobel, Catholic University of Leuven
Lambert Leijssen, Catholic University of Leuven
Terrence Merrigan, Catholic University of Leuven, secretary

Members at Large:

Raymond E. Brown, Union Theological Seminary, New York
Juliana Casey, The Catholic Health Association of the United States
José M. de Mesa, East Asian Pastoral Institute, Manila, Philippines
Catherine Dooley, The Catholic University of America
Mary Grey, The Catholic University of Nijmegen, the Netherlands
James J. Kelly, Trinity College, Dublin, Ireland
Maria Goretti Lau, Holy Spirit Study Centre, Hong Kong
Donatus Mathenge, Nyeri Catholic Secretariat, Nyeri, Kenya
Michael Putney, Pius XII Provincial Seminary, Banyo, Australia
Ronald Rolheiser, Newman Theological College, Edmonton, Alberta, Canada
Donald P. Senior, Catholic Theological Union, Chicago
James J. Walter, Loyola University of Chicago

LOUVAIN THEOLOGICAL & PASTORAL MONOGRAPHS

6

THE GURU IN INDIAN CATHOLICISM

Ambiguity or Opportunity of Inculturation?

Catherine Cornille

PEETERS PRESS

LOUVAIN

ISBN 90-6831-309-6
D. 1991/0602/4

TABLE OF CONTENTS

ACKNOWLEDGMENTS

It is often said that to really understand the figure of the master, one must become a disciple. Rather than as a disciple, it was as a student that I conducted this study. The study of the master-disciple relationship in Hinduism, in Christianity, and in the Hindu-Christian dialogue has nevertheless led to the discovery of many a great master, to intimations of discipleship. I wish to thank those who through their example and guidance have taught me humility — my teachers and masters: Frank De Graeve, Lee Siegel, and the leaders of Catholic ashrams in India: Bede Griffiths, Francisacharya, Sara Grant, Vandana, Isvaraprasad, Mariadass, Ignatius Hirudayam, and Amalorpavadass. The personal encounter with these pioneers of inculturation and the time spent in their ashrams has been not only academically interesting, but also personally enriching.

My gratitude also goes to James Stuart, Bettina Baumer, Odette Bäumer-Despeigne, and George Gispert-Sauch for providing access to unpublished or rare materials. A special homage to Raimundo Panikkar, not only for his magistral role in the Hindu-Christian dialogue, but also for his helpful comments on this work. Thanks to Ray Collins for including this work in the series.

In India, the title of master or guru is often applied to the parents, who more than anyone are worthy of respect, reverence and gratitude. My own parents' wise and loving guidance has made them eminently deserving of this title. I finally wish to thank all those who on my journeys through India, during my stay in Hawaii, and in the years of maturation and composition of this work, have crossed my path or travelled along, and who in their friendship and truth, have often unknowingly been as masters.

INTRODUCTION

Each re-expression of the Word is a grasp of a new aspect of it
— its relevance to a new situation — so that, not the Word-in-
itself, but our perception of it becomes enriched by every new
expression of it.[1]

The process of inculturation always risks overstepping its own intention. In the course of the past few decades, considerable efforts have been taken in the African and Asian churches to become immersed in the local culture and to enter into dialogue with other religious traditions. This is in keeping with Vatican Council II which came to recognize elements of goodness and truth in non-Christian religions and cultures, and prompted Christians "while witnessing to their own faith and way of life, [to] acknowledge, preserve, and encourage the spiritual and moral truths found among non-Christians, also their social life and culture."[2] Missionaries were encouraged to "borrow from customs, traditions, wisdom, teaching, arts and sciences of their people everything which could be used to praise the glory of the Creator, manifest the grace of the saviour, or contribute to the right ordering of Christian life."[3] While symbols and rituals belonging to different religious traditions could be borrowed, they needed to be purified, elevated, restored, or, in short, adapted to the established Christian meaning.[4] The purpose was not so much to enrich or challenge Christianity as to effect an in-depth evangelization, the infusion of a particular culture in its very roots with

---

[1] Michael Amaladoss, "Indigenous Theology and Spirituality" *NBCLC Seminar Leaflet Series*, 18.

[2] *Nostra Aetate*, 2. The translation of Conciliar documents used is that of Austin Flannery, *Vatican Council II: The Conciliar and Post Conciliar Documents* (Wilmington, DE: Scholarly Resources, 1975.)

[3] *Ad Gentes*, 22.

[4] *Ad Gentes*, 3, 9; *Lumen Gentium*, 13, 17; *Gaudium et Spes*, 58.

the Gospel message. This idea also comes through in *Evangelii Nuntiandi*, the most important post-Vatican II document on evangelization, in which Paul VI states:

> The deposit is to be translated into every tongue but it must not be impaired or mutilated. It is to be clad in the symbols of each people and explained with the help of theological formulations which draw upon the models and resources of each culture, society and race, but it must remain the complete Catholic faith which the ecclesiastical magisterium has received and passed on.[5]

This statement reflects a clear awareness of the risks which exist in adopting symbols and ideas belonging to a different culture or religious tradition. Symbols and concepts cannot be isolated from their original structural context to serve a totally different semantic function. In being adopted within a different religious context, they carry along their original meaning which may transform, enlarge, and deepen or challenge the tradition in which they have been absorbed.

Inculturation thus gradually came to be understood as a two-way process. At the Bishops' Synod of 1977, on "Catechesis in our time," the term "inculturation" was used for the first time in an official document of the Church. The Message of the Synod stated: "The Christian message must find its roots in human cultures, and must also transform these cultures. In this sense we can say that catechesis is an instrument of inculturation."[6] In the same document, it is said that "the real incarnation of the faith through catechesis is not just the process of giving but also that of receiving." This implies that faith itself may be re-thought and re-interpreted in the process of inculturation.

Inculturation has thus come to be understood as a process of implantation, growth and maturation of the Gospel in a certain cultural and religious context. Practice hereby necessarily precedes reflection. The outcome of integrating customs, symbols, concepts, and ideas belonging to a particular tradition cannot be

---

[5] *Evangelii Nuntiandi*, 65, In *The Pope Speaks* 21 (1976), p. 37.

[6] "Message of Synod of Bishops to the People of God" *Osservatore Romano*, English Edition, November 3, 1977, p. 5.

predicted — the fruits of inculturation cannot be planned or foreseen. Dialogue and mutual fecundation generates a *tertium quid* which can only be assessed once it has started to take shape.

The intention of inculturation is thus that of bringing the essence of the Gospel message in touch with the very roots of a particular culture, or with the heart and essence of a particular religious tradition. Throughout the history of the Christian mission in India, the core of Hinduism has been seen to be its spiritual tradition. While folk religion was denounced as pagan idol-worship and superstition, the spiritual tradition, represented by its ochre-clad ascetics and gurus, was held in some respect, and regarded as not incompatible with Christian faith. Roberto de Nobili, one of the early Catholic missionaries to India, dressed in ochre and presented Jesus Christ as guru. Abbé Dubois, in his otherwise denigrating and unflattering account of Hinduism, refers to the theories on the guru as evidence "that even the very highest moral virtues are not unknown to the Hindus."[7] The change of attitude towards non-Christian religions, introduced by Farquhar's book, *The Crown of Hinduism*, coincided with the first translations which were made of the ancient Indian spiritual texts.[8] Brahmabandhab Upadhyaya, Jules Monchanin and others came to believe that the christianization of India would be effected only through Christian sannyasis, yogis, or gurus. Around Cuttat, the Swiss ambassador to India, a group gathered to contemplate Indian and Christian mystical texts, and discuss possibilities of encounter and dialogue between the two spiritual traditions. Pierre Johanns used categories of Advaita Vedanta to

---

[7] J.A. Dubois, *Hindu Manners, Customs, and Ceremonies* (Oxford: Clarendon Press, 1892) p. 123. This praise, however, was meant only to demonstrate the contrast with reality. Among what he considers to be the perversions of the ideal, Abbé Dubois mentions the "disgusting ceremony" in which "they solemnly pour water over the feet of their *guru* and wash them, reciting *mantras* the while; then carefully collecting the water so used in a copper vessel, they pour part of it over their head and face, and drink the rest" (p. 132).

[8] John Nicol Farquhar, *The Crown of Hinduism* (Oxford: Oxford University Press, 1913).

develop an Indian Christian theology, and many came to believe that a real theology of the Spirit would be developed only through the integration of the Indian spiritual tradition.

This was based upon — as it conversely may have influenced — the suggestion at Vatican Council II that religious institutes "should carefully consider how traditions of asceticism and contemplation, the seeds of which have been sown by God in certain ancient cultures before the preaching of the Gospel, might be incorporated into the Christian religious life."[9] At the All India Seminar on the Church in India Today in 1969, it was especially in the workshop on spirituality and in reference to the Indian spiritual heritage that the need for Indianization was mentioned.[10]

The strongest expression of the fascination with the Indian spiritual tradition has been the attempt at inculturation of ashram life in Indian Catholicism. In the course of our century, a number of Catholics have adopted the lifestyle, the dress, the eating and sleeping habits and the symbols, concepts and rituals characteristic of traditional Indian religious communities. After a few failed attempts, Catholic ashrams have achieved some success and multiplied. Though relatively few in numbers, they have exercised a considerable influence on the Church in India, and have stood as model for similar religious communities abroad.

Ashrams are generally small religious communities which emerge spontaneously around a spiritual master, in India called guru. In the traditional Hindu prototype, the guru is thus the constitutive element, the necessary and sufficient cause, the *raison d'être* of the ashram. Reflection on the Catholic version of the Hindu ashram thus naturally crystalizes around the figure of the guru in Catholic ashrams. The ambiguity involved in adopting the term guru for the spiritual master of Catholic ashrams is reflected in the intuitive resistance toward or the radical refusal of

---

[9] *Ad Gentes*, 18.

[10] *All India Seminar on the Church in India Today* (New Delhi: C.B.C.I., 1970) p. 561.

the term "Catholic guru" by some, and the willing assumption of this title by others. The purpose of this book is to elucidate the problems and possibilities involved in adopting the term guru within Christianity through a historical and comparative analysis of the figure of the spiritual master in the Hindu and the Christian traditions, reflections on Christ as guru, and field research done in the Catholic ashrams in India.

I

The Master-Disciple Relationship
in Hinduism and Christianity:
A Comparative Analysis

The master-disciple relationship is a category common to all religions, or at least to the mystical trends within religious traditions. From a phenomenological point of view, the Christian equivalent to the Hindu guru may be the figure of the spiritual father. The guru and the spiritual master answer to certain archetypical features which they also share with the spiritual masters of other mystical traditions, with the *pir* or *shaykh* in Sufism, with the *kalyana-mitra* in the Theravada-, and the *bodhisattva* in the Mahayana tradition of Buddhism.

The archetypal nature of the spiritual master may be understood from psychological or sociological points of view. Here, we merely attempt to demonstrate the universality of certain characteristics of the spiritual master on the basis of dynamics, intrinsic to the master-disciple relationship, and through juxtaposition with other universal archetypes such as the saint, the teacher, and the therapist. A certain degree of generalization and arbitrariness is inevitable. The master-disciple relationship may be regarded as the most universal, but also as the most particular dyad. Every spiritual master, every disciple, and thus every relationship between the two is unique. The examples chosen are considered to be orthodox within their particular traditions, and may thus be seen as representative of the whole. If the Christian and the Hindu traditions are less emphasized, it is because the issue at hand is extensively discussed in the following chapters.

While a phenomenological approach may throw light on certain clearly universal patterns, every master-disciple relationship remains embedded in a particular religious tradition, in a certain worldview, belief system and history. It is thus necessary to study the Hindu guru-sishya relationship, and the Catholic spiritual father-disciple relationship within their respective historical and theological or philosophical contexts. In both the Hindu and the Christian tradition, the question of the nature and function of the figure of the spiritual master is very complex. It is related to the development of different spiritualities, philosophical schools and sects, at the very origin of which are often different spiritual masters.[1]

This discussion of the archetypical and the particular characteristics of the master-disciple relationship may also be read from the perspective of this century's discussion on the sameness or difference of mystical traditions. In the beginning of the century, it was fashionable to believe that the ultimate mystical experience refers to the same reality in different religious traditions, and that all religions meet in their mystics. This was based partly on works such as *The Varieties of Religious Experience* where, from the similarities in both the accounts and the fruits of the mystical experiences, William James argues for the transcendence of mystical states and mystical classics of any particular religion:

> In mystic states we become one with the Absolute and we become aware of our oneness. This is the everlasting and triumphant mystical tradition, hardly altered by the differences of time or creed. In Hinduism, in Neoplatonism, in Sufism, in Christian mysticism, in Whitmanianism, we find the same recurring note, so that there is about mystical utterances an eternal unanimity which ought to make critics stop and think, and which brings it about that the mystical classics have, as has been said, neither birthday nor native land.[2]

From this perspective, the master-disciple relationship is regarded as essentially beyond any particular religious tradition.

---

[1] The masculine form is used in this book because the master-disciple relationship was historically developed principally in male circles. Exceptions to the rule are, consequently, even more manifest than they would otherwise be.

[2] William James, *The Varieties of Religious Experience* (London: Longmans and Green, 1952) p. 410. The same idea was developed among others by Aldous Huxley, Ananda Coomaraswamy, René Guénon, Seyyed Hossein Nasr, and Frithjof Schuon.

However, the unqualified use of the term mysticism and the belief that it constitutes a self-contained and autonomous realm of experience was criticized on epistemological grounds.[3] According to the mystical relativist approach, there is no direct experience of the world, no pure and ineffable grasping of reality.[4] All experience is mediated, and constituted by that which mediates it.[5] From this point of view, the Hindu and the Christian mystical experience, and not only the content but also the form of the master-disciple relationship, would be radically different.

The relationship between content and form and the actual experience is, however, a very complex one. The mystics themselves insist upon the radical discontinuity and ineffability of the experience. This ultimately thwarts all attempts at resolving the discussion on the sameness or the difference of mystical experiences and traditions. For those who believe that the experience is shaped or conditioned by the teaching and discipline which led to that experience, the first part of this study may provide useful material for argumentation.

[3] One of the first to re-emphasize the particularity of the different mysticisms above their universal features was Gershom Scholem who, in his introduction to *Major Trends in Jewish Mysticism* (1941), reacted against the common view by stating that "there is no mysticism as such, there is only the mysticism of a particular religious system, Christian, Islamic, Jewish mysticism and so on. That there remains a common characteristic it would be absurd to deny... But only in our days has the belief gained ground that there is such a thing as an abstract mystical religion" (p. 6).

[4] One of the strongest critics of the view of the sameness of all mysticism is Steven Katz, who edited two volumes dealing with the particularity of the different mystical traditions from a linguistic, epistemological and dogmatic point of view: *Mysticism and Philosophical Analysis* (London: Sheldon, 1978) and *Mysticism and Religious Traditions* (Oxford: Oxford University, 1983.)

[5] From this perspective, a distinction was made between love-mysticism and the dispassionate kind. Non-absorptive was distinguished from absorptive mysticism, voluntaristic from gnostic, and mysticism of personality from mysticism of infinity.

The Master-Disciple Relationship as Archetype

The figure of the wise old person, the master or teacher who represents the ultimate spiritual state to which all human life tends, is of all times, places and religious traditions. With Carl Gustav Jung, the spiritual master has generally come to be understood as archetype.[1] He or she represents the state of individuation conceptualized in a particular religion's categories of self-realization or holiness. The archetypical nature of the spiritual master cannot, however, be dissociated from that of the disciple. It is the surrender of the disciple which makes the master. In the field of mysticism, within which the master-disciple relationship belongs, surrender is regarded as the necessary means or even the ultimate end of the spiritual pursuit. The roles of master and disciple are thus mutually constitutive. This may be illustrated through examples from various mystical traditions.

The Dynamics of Surrender

Surrender as the Ultimate Goal

That life presupposes death or absolute freedom the sacrifice of personal freedom is the ultimate paradox. It is ultimate in its aim, aspiring for the ultimate end of perfection, liberation, complete detachment and peace, unity or union with the absolute. It presupposes the ultimate sacrifice: the absolute surrender of self.

---

[1] C.G. Jung, *The Archetypes and the Collective Unconscious* (London: Routledge & Kegan Paul, 1969). See also A.-M. Besnard *et al.*, *Maître Spirituel* (Paris: Cerf, 1980) p. 12.

Every religious tradition insists upon this paradox but the rationale for and the dynamics of surrender may vary. In general, theistic traditions understand surrender as to a transcendent and absolute Will, while in non-dualistic traditions it consists of the annihilation of all that is not absolute.

The spiritual path of the three monotheistic religions, Judaism, Christianity, and Islam, proceed through asceticism and self-mortification. What is considered to be obstructive of the perception of the divine Will and the metaphors used to express it may differ but the end is the annihilation of one's own will. The famous thirteenth century Jewish Kabbalist Abraham Abulafia saw the self as constituted by seals and knots formed by sense perceptions and emotions which obstruct the divine flow. He thus spoke of surrender as a process of "unsealing the soul, untying the knots which bind it."[2] In the New Testament the idea of self-mortification is expressed in Jesus' words: "If any man will come after me, let him deny himself and take up his cross and follow me."[3] It is also understood as the need to "put off the old nature with its practices."[4] One of the classical Christian treatises on ascetical and mystical theology states: "In Heaven we shall love without any need of self-immolation. Here on earth it is quite otherwise. In our present state of fallen nature, it is impossible for us to love God truly and effectively without sacrificing ourselves for him."[5] The *via purgativa*, which is one of the three ways which traditionally constitute the Christian spiritual path, involves what Evelyn Underhill calls a process of "self-naughting."[6] The penultimate step in Islamic mystical theology is called *fana* which refers to the

[2] Quoted in Gershom Scholem's *Major Trends in Jewish Mysticism* (Jerusalem: Schocken, 1941) p. 131. Scholem points out that the expression "untying of knots" also occurs in Tibetan Buddhism as a symbol of the great liberation of the soul from the fetters of sensuality. See Lamotte's translation of the *Samadhinirmocana Sutra* as "Sutra détachant les noeuds" (Louvain: Bureaux du Recueil, 1935.)

[3] Matt 16:24.

[4] Col 3:9.

[5] Adolphe Tanquerey, *The Spiritual Life. A Treatise on Ascetical and Mystical Theology* (Tournai: Desclée, 1928) p. 321.

[6] Evelyn Underhill, *The Mystic Way* (London: J. M. Dent, 1913) p. 112.

stage of "the passing away of the personal self."[7] A true Sufi is often paradoxically referred to as one who is not. The process of stripping away the lower self is powerfully evoked by the expression of the early Muslim mystic Al-Bistami: "I have shed my Ego as a serpent sheds his skin, then I regarded my essence, and I was myself, He.[8]

In the Hindu tradition, both theistic and non-dualistic forms of spirituality and approaches to surrender developed from the same Vedic sources. The principle of self-sacrifice developed with the process of internalization of the Vedic sacrifice in the Upanishads.[9] In the oldest Upanishads, self-mortification is seen to be coterminous with divinization: "That world of Brahman belongs to those who find it by abstinence."[10] The discovery of the true Self called *Atman* is the fruit of the systematic negation of false conceptions of self. Since *Atman* is regarded as not different from the ultimate ground of existence, *Brahman*, surrender, came to mean the abstinence from all that is relative and finite. This understanding of surrender was further developed by Shankara and the tradition of Advaita Vedanta.[11]

---

[7] Annemarie Schimmel, *Mystical Dimensions of Islam* (Chapel Hill, NC: University of North Carolina Press, 1975) p. 362.

[8] Quoted by Margaret Smith, *The Way of the Mystics: the Early Christian Mystics and the Rise of Sufism* (London: Sheldon, 1976) p. 242. Here, a more or less non-dualistic interpretation of the mystical experience emerges in the most monotheistic and dualistic of all traditions. (The same words led to the execution of one of the first Sufis, Al-Hallaj.) It is a tendency of mysticism in general.

[9] Early signs of this development may already be detected in the consecration ritual or *diksha* of the Vedic sacrificer: in the *Shatapatha Brahmana* (3.3.4.21) it is said that "He who consecrates himself offers himself to the deities."

[10] *Chandogya Upanishad* 8.4.3.

[11] *Advaita Vedanta* is the philosophical system, generally attributed to Shankara (788-820), which advances a non-dualistic (a-dvaita) interpretation of the Upanishads and the Brahmasutras of Badarayana. It holds that every distinction in being is an illusion, *maya*, born of the ignorance (*avidya*) of the ultimate non-duality of the true self (*atman*) and the ultimate ground of Being (*Brahman*). Only the Brahman without qualifications (*nirguna Brahman*) is seen to be a worthy expression of the ultimately Real. The experience of this reality is expressed as *saccidananda*, ultimate Being, ultimate consciousness, and ultimate bliss. For an excellent introduction to Advaita Vedanta, see Eliot Deutsch, *Advaita Vedanta: A Philosopical Reconstruction* (Honolulu: University of Hawaii, 1969.)

In the theistic Upanishads, mostly of later date, liberation may be reached "through the power of penance and the Grace of God."[12] Self-surrender comes to be understood not so much as ascetic self-mortification, but as loving abandonment to the deity. In the *Bhagavadgita*, the fountainhead of the Hindu theistic tradition and of the way of Bhakti or loving devotion, the God Krishna encourages the devotee to dedicate everything to him: "Whatever you do, whatever you eat, whatever you offer up in sacrifice or give away in alms; whatever penance you may perform, offer it up to me."[13] When all thoughts, desires, and actions are dedicated to God, no thought of self remains. This attitude of absolute self-surrender is called *prapatti*.[14] When fused with Southern forms of devotion, prapatti became the passionate abandonment of self to the Godhead. Ramanuja, who in the eleventh century provided the philosophical foundation for the Bhakti tradition, defined the *ahamkara* which must be surrendered as that which "causes the assumption of Egoity on the part of the body which belongs to the Non-self ... also designated as pride or arrogance, which causes men to slight persons superior to themselves, and is referred to by scripture in many places as something evil."[15]

Like the sixteenth century saint Caitanya, who, intoxicated with love for Krishna drowned himself in water which reminded him of the sound and call of his lover, the hagiographies of other saints are characterized by a love of God which came to be at the complete expense of their own person.

In the non-theistic tradition of Buddhism, the ultimate goal of *nirvana* or "extinction" expresses the concurrence of self-annihila-

---

[12] The *Shvetashvatara Upanishad* 7.21.

[13] *Bhagavadgita* 9.27, 3.30, 11.55.

[14] Mariasusai Dhavamony describes prapatti as "a state of readiness to pray to God, associated with the deep conviction that he alone is the saviour and that there is no other way of attaining his grace except by such self-surrender" (*Classical Hinduism* [Rome: Gregorian University, 1982] p. 487).

[15] George Thibaut, *The Vedanta Sutras with Commentary of Ramanuja*, in *Sacred Books of the East*, 48 (Oxford: Clarendon Press, 1896) p. 72. *Ahamkara* may be understood as egoism, selfishness.

tion and final liberation. It is the extinction of the five compounds of elements, or *skandhas*, which constitute every particular sentient being: material qualities, sensations, perceptions, tendencies, and consciousness. Nirvana is usually understood in negating terms as the absence of passion, destruction of pride, getting rid of thirst, freedom from attachment and destruction of all sensual pleasures. The Arhat who has realized nirvana according to the Theravada tradition of Buddhism is one who is annihilated.[16]

Self-surrender may thus be reached through the loving abandonment of self, or through strenuous self-mortification. It may be understood in terms of submission to the transcendent God, or as the annihilation of all that is not absolute and divine. It may be seen as a step on the way leading to final union with God, or as the very end itself. In any case, all traditions regard the surrender of self as the basic and indispensible condition for attaining to the ultimate religious experience.

The Spiritual Master as Means of Surrender

Very rarely does surrender occur spontaneously, without mediation. It most often proceeds through the submission of will, feelings and intellect to someone else. To be able to induce this state of surrender, the other must, however, be regarded by the disciple as a person of exceptional spiritual qualities, as a spiritual master. All traditions emphasize — for a variety of different reasons — the indispensability of the spiritual master on the path to salvation or ultimate liberation.

In ancient mystery religions, the necessity of the master was an exponent of the esoteric nature and the initiatory structure of the religion. The end was regarded as so far removed from common sight and experience that only one who had been there could

[16] Cf. R.C. Childers' remarks on the *Arhat*: "The ideas of Arhatship and of the annihilation of being are inextricably bound up together, there being no annihilation without Arhatship, and no Arhatship that does not end in annihilation..." in *A Dictionary of the Pali Language* (London: Kegan Paul, Trench, Trübner, 1872) p. 267.

testify to its existence. The way itself was, moreover, pictured as long and dangerous, full of sidetracks and precipices, unbridgeable abysses and unsurmountable heights. The energies unleashed in the course of the journey could be constructively used or dangerously misused. Only the initiation and guidance of an experienced master could guarantee a safe journey and a sure arrival.[17] This has remained the basic rationale for the indispensability of the spiritual master in the different mystical traditions.

While in the Jewish mystical tradition from Merkabah through Kabbalah, the master or rabbi fulfilled an important function in transmitting esoteric knowledge, the most explicit emphasis upon the necessity of the spiritual master came with the rise of Hasidism. Israel Friedmann, a late eighteenth century Hasid, says about the relationship between the master or Zaddik and Hasid that "Just as the letters of the alphabet are mute without the vowel signs, and just as the vowel signs are meaningless without the letters, so Zaddikim and Hasidim are bound up with one another."[18] This expression emphasizes the indispensability, not only of the Zaddik for the Hasid, but also of the Hasid for the Zaddik. Without disciple, the master's teaching remains barren.

The early Church Fathers taught that "if you see a young man ascend to heaven by his own will, grab his feet and throw him back to earth, for it will be of no avail."[19] With its emphasis on spirituality and contemplation, the Eastern Orthodox tradition has always maintained the highest respect for its spiritual masters, and the figure of the *staretz* has come to play an important role in Russian piety. Bernard de Clairvaux, one of the famous reformers within the Western monastic tradition, stated that whoever has no other master than himself, makes himself into the disciple of a fool. The protest against the possible abuse of power and the emphasis upon Jesus Christ as only mediator led the Protestant

[17] Cf. Louis Bouyer, *Mysterion: Du mystère à la mystique* (Paris: O.E.I.L., 1986.)

[18] Harry Rabinowicz, *The World of Hasidim* (London: Valentine Mitchell, 1970) p. 121.

[19] *Vitae Patrum* V, 10, 111; PL 73, 932bc.

tradition to deny the necessity of a spiritual master, as is clearly illustrated in a letter written by Calvin to the Duke of Summerset (October 22, 1548):

> That we hold God to be the sole governor of our souls, that we hold His law to be the only rule and spiritual directory of our consciences, not serving Him according to the foolish inventions of men.[20]

The strong sense of human sinfulness and the idea of the priesthood of all believers limited the authority of the spiritual master in the Protestant tradition. Nevertheless the presence of spiritual direction manifests itself through the rich correspondence in spiritual letters.

In the Muslim mystical tradition, the spiritual master is called *shaykh* (Arabic) or *pir* (Persian.) The Islamic tradition or *hadith* warns that "When someone has no Shaykh, Satan becomes his Shaykh." This illustrates the belief in the danger involved in pursuing the mystical path alone. To travel without a spiritual master is not only dangerous, but may also greatly extend the duration of the journey. As the link in the mystical chain, the *shaykh* or *pir* is, moreover, regarded as a guarantee of the authenticity of the path. This is expressed in the words of the tenth century Sufi master al-Khayr: "If any one by means of asceticism and self-mortification shall have risen to an exalted degree of mystical experience without having a *Pir* to whose authority and example he submits himself, the Sufis do not regard him as belonging to their community."[21]

In the Hindu tradition, the indispensability of the spiritual master may be seen as the only common article of faith. All traditions in India, from the absolute non-dualistic to the fully theistic, emphasize the necessity of an authentic spiritual master to reach the ultimate experience. The origin of this may be found

---

[20] Quoted in John McNeill, *History of the Cure of Souls* (New York: Harper and Row, 1951) p. 209.

[21] Robert Nicholson, *Studies in Islamic Mysticism* (Cambridge: Cambridge University Press, 1921) p. 10.

in the Upanishads, which all Hindus regard as sacred and author-itative. Here, sacred knowledge is believed to be transmitted only through the spiritual master. Desperate seekers approach the master saying: "Master, to thee be homage; teach us further. Thou art our only way; there is no other. By what method can the individual self attain to union with the Self once it is rid of this (body)?"[22] The reason why a spiritual master is necessary is said to be because "that [Self], when taught by an inferior man is not easy to be known, even though it is often thought upon; unless it is taught by another, there is no way to it, for it is inconceivably smaller than small."[23]

The famous last words of the Buddha, "Work out [your] salvation with diligence," appear to be a summon to shun all spiritual direction and to simply rely on oneself for salvation. The goal was to become a *pratyeka-buddha*, "one enlightened by himself, this is, one who has attained to the supreme and perfect insight, but dies without proclaiming the truth to the world."[24] A teacher, however, remained necessary, if only to transmit the Buddhist teaching. In *The Guide*, the question "where the Mode of Conveying actually comes into being?" is answered: "When the Master, or some respected companion in the Divine Life, teaches the True Idea to someone, then that someone, on hearing that True idea, acquires faith."[25]

The Theravada Buddhist concept of the spiritual master is that of the *kalyana-mitra*, the guiding friend or friendly guide. To teach and preach the Buddhist doctrine was — in following the Buddha himself — one of the duties of the *arhat*, the liberated one. Because of its neglect, Mahayana Buddhism introduced the new ideal of *bodhisattva*, who, with the vow not to enter into final nirvana before all beings have been liberated, reemphasized not

---

[22] *Maitri Upanishad* 4.1.

[23] *Katha Upanishad* 1.2.8.

[24] From the *Puggala-pannatti*, p. 14 in Har Dayal, *The Boddhisattva Doctrine in Buddhist Sanskrit Literature* (Delhi: Motilal Banarsidass, 1932) p. 3.

[25] From the *Netti-Ppakaranam*. See Bhikkhu Nanamoli, *The Guide* (London: Routledge & Kegan, 1977) p. 16.

only the value of compassion as against the apparent coldness, self-complacency and lack of altruism of the *arhat*, but also the need for help or mediation on the way to liberation.

With its emphasis upon tradition and lineage, the spiritual master in the Tibetan tradition of Buddhism becomes not only helpful but indispensible. sGrampo-pa, master of the Kargyüt-pa tradition stated that:

> Although you may possess the most perfect working basis, but are not urged on by spiritual friends as a contributary cause, it is difficult to set out upon the path toward enlightenment, because of the power of the inveterate propensities due to evil deeds committed repeatedly in former times. Therefore you have to meet spiritual friends. . . Spiritual friends are like a guide when we travel in unknown territory, an escort when we pass through dangerous regions and a ferry-man when we cross a great river.[26]

In banning all scriptures, the only channel of transmission and enlightenment in the Zen tradition became the Zen master, or *roshi*. Hakuin (1685-1768), one of the most famous Japanese Zen masters, severely criticized those who denounced the need for a spiritual master: "Today they end up like dead dogs and tomorrow it will be the same thing. Even if they continue this way for endless kalpas, they will still be nothing more than dead dogs. Of what possible use are such people!"[27]

While the nature and status of the spiritual master may differ radically in different religious traditions, all emphasize that he or she is indispensable in bringing about the required state of total self-surrender of the disciple on the mystical path.

The Master as Archetype

To bring about the attitude of unconditional surrender in the disciple, the spiritual master must possess certain qualities and functional characteristics which are more or less universally requir-

---

[26] Hans Guenther, *sGram.po.pa: Jewel Ornament of Liberation* (London: Shambala, 1959) p. 30.

[27] Philip Yampolsky, *The Zen Master Hakuin: Selected Writings* (New York: 1971) pp. 114-115.

ed. Their archetypical nature can be detected through juxtaposition with other archetypes: the saint, the teacher, and the therapist.

Master and Saint

Religions are often said to meet in their saints and sages. In his comparative hagiography, Jean Leclercq remarked that the saints are closer to one another than the teachings which they profess.[28] William James spoke of "a certain composite photograph of universal saintliness, the same in all religions, of which the features can easily be traced."[29] These universal features are, according to James, a sense of being in a wider life than this world's selfish little interests, of self-surrender, of freedom, and of loving and harmonious affections.[30] They are manifested in a tendency to asceticism or self-sacrifice, in detachment and equanimity, in humility, purity, moral perfection, and charity.

While sainthood may answer to certain universal characteristics, saints may also be regarded as the primary representatives of the particularity of different traditions. Within a particular tradition the saint is presented as the paradigm of orthodoxy. The commemoration of saints is part of the official liturgical life. Some hagiographies are censured and others propagated, the cult of certain saints promoted and that of others forbidden. Sainthood may thus also be seen as determined by very particular characteristics.

A saint does not automatically or necessarily become a spiritual master, nor is a master always a saint. Many saints lead hidden lives, and are never acknowledged as such during (or after) their lifetime. It is the surrender of disciples which constitutes the spiritual master. Only when sainthood is acknowledged and aspired by others, may a saint become a spiritual master.

---

[28] Jean Leclercq, "Pour une hagiographie comparative," *Studia Missionalia* 34 (1986) p. 112.

[29] William James, *The Varieties of Religious Experience* (London: Longmans, Green and Co., 1952) p. 266.

[30] William James, *The Varieties of Religious Experience*, p. 220.

Anyone who succeeds in bringing about surrender is, moreover, regarded by his disciples as a spiritual master, even when a fraud or charlatan. The authority of the spiritual master is thus purely charismatic, constituted by the persuasive qualities of the master and the surrender of disciples.[31]

The authority of the spiritual master is thus not derived from the official authority of a tradition. Nor is it dependent upon institutional prescriptions and control. This poses no problem or threat for traditions without a central body of doctrinal and institutional authority. According to the monotheistic traditions, however, all authority is derived from and must be related theologically to the sole source of absolute authority. Institutionally it must be related to its legitimate depository on earth. The non-institutional source of authority of the spiritual master always represents a potential challenge or threat to the authority of office. While sainthood may thus be defined and controlled by the institutional, the spiritual master escapes institutional control. This explains the tensions which exist between priests and prophets, and between institutional and charismatic authority in the major monotheistic traditions, Judaism and Islam.

The Torah is the fountainhead of holiness and authority in Judaism. Though saintliness was more a quality of a group, a people, than of an individual, those who transmitted and interpreted the Torah were always regarded with special reverence.[32] To establish their orthodoxy, the esoteric traditions of Merkabah, Kabbalah, and Hasidism presented themselves as the "oral

---

[31] The concept of charismatic authority developed by Max Weber emphasizes in the first place the personal qualities of the charismatic person. The trust and surrender of the disciples is not so much the basis of charismatic legitimacy as the response of believers to someone's charisma. See *Economy and Society*, part I, chapter 3, section 4. Since Weber, the term charisma has been widely used and misused. Brian Wilson offered a reification of the term: "Charisma is a relation of supreme trust in the total competence of an individual whose qualities are supernatural, superhuman, or at least specifically exceptional." See *The Noble Savages; the Primitive Origins of Charisma and its Contemporary Revival* (Berkeley, CA: University of California Press, 1975) p. 25.

[32] There were some rabbis whose names were remembered and who have remained exemplary figures: Simeon ben Yohai, Akiba, Ismaël, Abulafia, etc.

torah." Kabbalistic masters understood their function as the handing down to their disciples of the secret of God's revelation to Moses, transmitted through the unbroken chain, the *shalsheleth hakabbalah*.[33] Besides the tradition received from the ancients, however, the Kabbalistic tradition also acknowledged the grace of divine revelation as authoritative.[34] It thus came to regard the *Zohar*, a thirteenth century anonymous mystical midrash, as an authoritative scripture. While the Kabbalistic tradition saw the *Zohar* as secondary to the Torah, a heretical movement called Sabbatianism emerged from the reliance on the *Zohar* alone. Sabbatians were excluded from the Jewish community because "the rabbis felt a challenge from preachers who took their authority from a different source."[35]

Though the cult of the Zaddik almost took the place of study of the Torah in Hasidism, it remained orthodox.[36] The Zaddik was supposed to possess a perfect knowledge of the Torah, and his soul was said to be "in effect the oral Torah for his time, the bearer of the ongoing Mosaic revelation."[37] Arthur Green understands the authority granted to the Zaddik as the transference of the *axis mundi* symbolism from a particular place to a particular person:

> the dispersed community of necessity had to have within it various means of more ready access to the sacrality which its great shrine once provided; Israel wandering through the wilderness of exile was to find that it still had need of a portable Ark of the Covenant.[38]

[33] Gershom Scholem, *Major Trends in Jewish Mysticism* (New York: Schocken, 1941) p. 21.

[34] Gershom Scholem, *Major Trends in Jewish Mysticism*, p. 119.

[35] Steven Sharot, *Messianism, Mysticism, and Magic: A Sociological Analysis of Jewish Religious Movements* (Chapel Hill, NC: University of North Carolina Press, 1982) p. 123.

[36] Harry Rabinowicz, *The World of Hasidim*, p. 59. Scholem believed that the Zaddik was accepted as orthodox because his role neutralized the extreme messianic tendencies of Sabbatianism. See *Major Trends in Jewish Mysticism*, p. 329.

[37] Arthur Green, "The Zaddik as Axis Mundi in Later Judaism," *Journal of the American Academy of Religion* 45 (1977), p. 341.

[38] Arthur Green, "The Zaddik as Axis Mundi in Later Judaism," p. 329.

Every Hasidic community came to have its own *axis mundi* and every Hasid his own Zaddik who became for him the center of his own subjective cosmos.

The Zaddikim, however, did not always acknowledge the higher authority of the Torah. Nahman of Bratslav conceived of himself as the supreme Zaddik, utterly different in essence and therefore in moral and religious standards of conduct, from all other men, fellow Zaddikim and ordinary people alike. He believed that his own words were more precious than the words of the Torah and the Prophets, that the Zaddik could perform miracles in heaven and on earth, and that only through the Zaddik could a human attain to an understanding of the divine.[39] Nahman's ideas thus came to border on the blasphemous.

While the Arabic term for saint, *waliy*, referred in the Koran exclusively to God and at the most to pious people collectively, in the Sufi tradition it gradually came to be applied to "one enraptured by God."[40] To remain within the Islamic tradition, the shaykh must affirm the unique sanctity of the Koran and the primacy of Mohammed.[41] The Sufi master nonetheless derives his authority from his own lineage and tradition, called "the chain of grace," *silsilat al-baraka*. Within this tradition, he is believed to continue the esoteric function of the prophet and is described as the "theophany of the Divine Mercy which lends itself to those willing to turn to it."[42] Even though the Sufi disciple always owes, besides surrender to the shaykh, obedience to the law or *shari'a*, the absolute authority which the disciple grants to the shaykh could be seen as a threat to the *Ulama* which considers itself to be the repository and arbiter of orthodoxy, and to the basic article of faith which proclaims the unity or *tawhid* of God.

---

[39] Harry Rabinowicz, *The World of Hasidim*, p. 80.

[40] Robert Nicholson, *The Mystics of Islam* (London, Routledge and Kegan Paul, 1914) p. 123.

[41] A saint cannot claim the same authority as a prophet who is characterized by his immaculate nature, and his "particular knowledge of things unknown and unseen." Cf. Toshihiko Izutsu, *Sufism and Taoism* (Berkeley, CA: University of California Press, 1983) p. 265.

[42] Seyyed Hossein Nasr, *Sufi Essays* (London: George Allen and Unwin, 1972) p. 57.

Master and Teacher

The spiritual master may be regarded as a saint become teacher. Like the teacher, the spiritual master is one who possesses a body of knowledge or experience which he is willing to transmit to others, and which puts him in a position of authority. The basis of their authority, as well as the content and the form of their teaching differentiate, however, the spiritual master from the teacher.

In his famous article, "Master and Disciple," Joachim Wach discusses the specificity of the master in comparison to that of the teacher.[43] In the relationship between teacher and student it is the subject matter, certain crafts, skills, or a body of knowledge, which is central. The prestige and authority of the teacher and the openness and receptivity of the student are based upon the value of the object of study for the student and upon the erudition of the teacher. Time, place and duration of the relationship are in function of the object of study. The personality of the teacher is secondary to the content of the teaching. Wach points out that in the relationship between teacher and student, "everything that is primarily objective is on the foreground, and where subjectivity plays a part, it is only accidentily interwoven in this relationship between person and thing."[44]

Personal qualities become all-important in the relationship between master and disciple: "What the master is to the disciple, he is through his existence, that is, if he is to be a master, he must be himself."[45] The same applies to the disciple. Only when the disciple is touched at the core of his person does a relationship come about. While it is the objective mastery of knowledge which is the basis of the authority of the teacher, it is the subjective response of the disciple which makes the master. Whereas all who desire to acquire a certain knowledge or skill acknowledge the

---

[43] Joachim Wach, "Master and Disciple: Two Religio-Sociological Studies," *Journal of Religion* 42 (1962) 1-21.

[44] J. Wach, "Master and Disciple," p. 4.

[45] J. Wach, "Master and Disciple," p. 2.

authority of the one who is able to teach it, the same master may appeal to some and not at all to others.

The interaction between teacher and student is predominantly verbal. Both teacher and student are primarily concerned with, and attentive to, the content of what is expressed. Each teacher may have a different style, different ways of expressing the same content, but this is secondary to the subject matter itself. The teacher will attempt to avoid ambiguity by expressing himself as clearly and as precisely as possible. The teacher aims to achieve the smallest possible discrepancy between the understanding of the different disciples and what he himself attempts to communicate. The teacher does not adapt the teaching to the personality of each student, but attempts to bring every student to the same complete understanding of the teaching. There is little margin for diversity or uniqueness in the relationship between teacher and student.

Every single relationship between a master and a disciple on the other hand is particular. Language itself is used differently. The experience which the master attempts to transmit is believed to be ineffable, and language an inefficient and limited expression of reality. When the master speaks, it is often in symbolical or allegorical language which may be grasped only by those who are initiated. The vagueness of the master's speech allows for many different interpretations, and for every disciple to hear whatever is appropriate to his or her situation. While in the teacher-student relationship, language is meant to bring about discursive reasoning, in the master-disciple relationship it is meant to break through ordinary patterns of thought. The Zen koan confronts the disciple with the meaninglessness of normal verbal expression and forces him or her to a non-discursive level of understanding. Prayers and mantras are often only a means to bring about internal silence; the essence of the teaching of the master is communicated without words.

The relationship between teacher and student is completed when the latter has proven, through objectively verifiable means, to have mastered a particular body of knowledge or a certain skill. The self-realization of the disciple cannot so much be objectively verified as acknowledged by one who himself has reached that state. Wach states that while a student may in turn become teacher, "a disciple will never become a master."[46] This is true in the sense that, while the student may come to play identically the same role as the previous teacher, the disciple can never fully replace the master since "whoever comes to himself only really comes to himself."[47] Every single master, even when belonging to the same teaching tradition, is different from his predecessor and successor. While the continuity of the teaching and teachers may be guaranteed by a school, the persistence of the tradition of a master cannot be ensured. The perpetuation of a tradition depends upon the continuity of charism.

Master and Therapist

It has become commonplace to attribute the emergence of the many different forms of psychotherapy and the appeal of the figure of the therapist to the vacuum which came about with the process of secularization and the withdrawal of the figure of the priest.[48] Psychotherapy is then regarded as a substitute for religion, and the therapist a secular version of the spiritual master, hereditary to priest and shaman. Methods which were spontaneously used in the relationship between spiritual master and disciple are consciously applied in the therapist-client relationship. Even though the therapist may function as spiritual director, and vice versa, and even though there is some continuity between the two functions, the roles remain fundamentally different.

The indispensability of the therapist and a personal relationship with the patient is the common and essential characteristic of all therapies. The concrete role or behavior of the therapist may

---

[46] J. Wach, "Master and Disciple," p. 20. As model of the master, Wach refers especially to the founders of the great religious traditions such as Jesus and the Buddha. This idea, however, may apply to the spiritual master-disciple relationship in general.

[47] J. Wach, "Master and Disciple," p. 18.

[48] J. Kovel, *A Complete Guide to Therapy* (Sussex: Harvester, 1977) p. 86.

be passive or active, distant and silent or responsive, authoritarian or egalitarian, directive or not. But the absolute need of the therapist, as of the master, indicates that a profound personal transformation requires interpersonal dynamics.[49] As between master and disciple, the relationship between therapist and patient or client is unique. The therapist may belong to a particular school or tradition, but the specific problem and background of the client requires a personalized approach.

It is the need, the disposition and aspiration of the patient or disciple which is constitutive of the role of both therapist and master. A felt discrepancy between the present state and an envisioned ideal, and the desire to change is the raison d'être of both the therapeutic and the charismatic relationship, of the status of both therapist and master. Trust or confidence in the authority of the master or the therapist brings about the openness and surrender necessary for transformation. The authority of the therapist, however, is derived primarily from competence, from the skill, insight and sensitivity which is acquired mainly through study and training, while the authority of the master is based upon his personal experience and personality.

The disciple differs from the patient in the nature of the needs or aspirations which call for recourse to a higher authority. For the patient, it is the inability to function at a level of what is understood to be mental health or normal social comportment which leads to consultation with a therapist. The aim of the therapist-patient relationship is to restore or reach a level of normal mental and social functioning. In the case of the master-disciple relationship, however, this mental stability is presupposed. The specific function of the spiritual master starts where that of the therapist stops. While psychotherapy most often focusses on the past and the personal history of the client, spiritual direction is oriented towards the future, and personal history is important only in as far as it must be overcome.

---

[49] J. Kovel, *A Complete Guide to Therapy*, p. 72.

The state or condition to which the spiritual master attempts to lead the disciple is generally said to be transcendent and ineffable, but it is regarded as natural or normal in so far as it is the fulfillment of the spiritual disposition of every person. What is generally regarded as mental health is then, from this point of view, still "illness," expressed in terms of a fallen or ignorant state. This is illustrated by the Buddha whose role is often compared to that of a medical doctor. The four noble truths follow the classical medical procedure of the declaration of the symptom, diagnosis, cure, and prescription. The function of the Buddha can then be understood as that of healing, or restoring wholeness in the disciple.

From a psycho-analytical point of view, on the other hand, the state to which the master leads the disciple has been characterized as mental illness,[50] as a regression to an infantile state of dependency. Normality and illness are thus reversely defined in therapy and in the master-disciple relationship. The health to which the therapist seeks to restore the patient is still regarded as illness by the master, only a step towards full sanity, while the application of psychological categories to the ultimate state indicates a pathological condition.

Several studies have attempted a psychological analysis and interpretation of the central function of the guru in Indian society. Richard Lannoy understands it within the context of the pressures inherent in a caste society.[51] Hierarchical interdependence and ritualistic interpersonal relations introduce into every relationship an element of formal and emotional constraint.[52] The continuous need to conform to a strictly prescribed role leads to a sense of dissociation of self or alienation. The Hindu disciple

[50] Richard Lannoy describes the state of absolute surrender to which the master brings the disciple as "a condition which . . . is commonly diagnosed as psychic illness." *The Speaking Tree: A Study of Indian Culture and Society* (Oxford: Oxford University Press, 1971) p. 365. He admits that "In India, since it is redirected into an exemplary and valued pattern, it cannot be so regarded."

[51] R. Lannoy, *The Speaking Tree: A Study of Indian Culture and Society*, pp. 365-372.

[52] R. Lannoy, *The Speaking Tree*, p. 347.

thus corresponds, according to Lannoy, to a schizoid case.[53] Only in the relationship with the master or guru can an authentic meeting take place between two human beings stripped of their masks. The total surrender required from the disciple to the will of the guru, however, Lannoy regards as a "strategy of desperation," as a kind of homeopathic therapy which consists of "accentuating the incipient dissociation."[54]

Peter Brent interprets the success of the guru in terms of a "focus for the displaced love of a frustrated people."[55] He claims that in a country as puritanical as India, the affection for the guru is, besides homosexuality, the only way in which the average Indian can express his love.[56] Transference, a process familiar in psychotherapy is thus regarded as the basis of the guru-disciple relationship.[57] But while the therapist knows how to handle this process and often consciously manipulates it, the spiritual master appears to act innocently, spontaneously.[58] Thus the feelings of love for the master which may have a pathological origin may be channeled to ultimately reach the end of an authentic master-disciple relationship.[59]

The ultimate end of both master and therapist is to make themselves superfluous. While generally acknowledged standards

---

[53] R. Lannoy, *The Speaking Tree*, p. 370. He uses Laing's theory on behavior "on the borderline between mental health and illness," to analyze the master-disciple relationship in India.

[54] R. Lannoy, *The Speaking Tree*, pp. 365-369.

[55] Peter Brent, *Godmen of India* (London: Penguin, 1972) p. 291.

[56] P. Brent, *The Godmen of India*, p. 285.

[57] Brent admits that from the standpoint of the disciple, there is "no question of the emotion having been transferred. It is the emotion itself, hitherto denied an object" (p. 300.)

[58] Brent suggests that this innocence may cover unconscious sado-masochistic tendencies (one of the main functions of the master is to bring the disciple to self-control through ascetic exercises) and that spontaneity often ends in actual sexual involvement (p. 303.)

[59] Marc Porté and Jaqueline Sebeo focus upon these dynamics in "Analyste et Transfert, Maître et Transmission" in *Hermes* (Paris: Deux Océans, 1983) pp. 227-251. The feelings of the patient toward the therapist are called "amour fou" while those of the disciple toward the master "amour abandon." They argue that the love of the master allows the disciple detachment from himself.

of mental health may determine the completion of the client-therapist relationship, the end of the master-disciple relationship is based upon criteria set and judged only by the master himself.

Summary

The figure of the spiritual master and that of the disciple are interdependent and inseparable archetypes. While a disciple is born when a true master is found, it is in turn the surrender of the disciple which makes the master. The master-disciple relationship usually operates within the context of mystical or spiritual traditions which require radical self-surrender as the indispensable condition to reach the ultimate religious experience or state. The spiritual master may then be seen as the one who facilitates this surrender.

To bring about unconditional surrender in the disciple, the master must first of all possess charismatic or spiritual authority. This authority is usually based upon saintly qualities which the disciple perceives in the master and desires to acquire. Qualities which are universally regarded as signs of holiness are self-control, equanimity, freedom, selflessness, and love or compassion. The spiritual master may be seen as a saint become teacher. While the teacher is responsible for the transmission of an objective body of knowledge, the master transmits his personal religious experience, adapting it to the personality of every disciple. This personal dimension of the master-disciple relationship in turn may be compared to that of the therapist-patient relationship. Yet, while the therapist is meant to lead the patient to what is generally considered to be mental health, the state or experience to which the master leads the disciple is often said to be radically discontinuous with so called "normal" states of knowing, feeling and functioning. The figure of the spiritual master thus answers to certain universal characteristics which relate to the universalilty of the requirement and of the dynamics of self-surrender in mystical traditions.

The master-disciple relationship is, however, usually imbedded in a particular religious tradition. The status and role of the spiritual master and the meaning of the surrender of the disciple will be interpreted according to the philosophical categories and the belief content of that particular tradition. This may result in fundamental differences between theistic and non-dualistic traditions and between traditions with and those without a centralized body of authority. The similarities and the differences become clear in a comparative analysis of the master-disciple relationship in Christianity and in Hinduism, more particularly in the Benedictine tradition and in the tradition of Advaita Vedanta.

CHAPTER TWO

The Master-Disciple Relationship in Hinduism

The Master-Disciple Relationship in Hindu Scriptures

Lead me from the unreal to the real.
Lead me from darkness to light.
Lead me from death to immortality.[1]

The figure of the spiritual master has been able to flourish in its full essence, and to develop in its rich diversity within the Hindu religious tradition. The earliest holy men recorded in India were the seers or "hearers" called *rishis*. They were the ones who had heard the sacred verses or *mantras* in which all power was believed to reside. In the oldest Vedic texts, the term *guru* which means "heavy," "weighty," or "bearing much power" was used as an adjective to mantra. It was the sound rather than the meaning which was believed to have a special potency, and which called for attention and safeguarding. These mantras were activated through recitation and preserved through transmission by the rishis. They were collected and appropriated by certain families and carefully handed down from father to son. The rishi was regarded as a mere channel of the sound which needed to remain a living force in the universe. Complete self-effacement was thus required from both the rishi and from the disciple.

The priestly families became known as Brahmans. In addition to reciting hymns, they performed the Vedic sacrifice which became the locus of power. The sacrificial ritual came to be viewed as a microcosm which effected all desired results mechanically. Everything depended upon the exact execution of the ritual,

---

[1] *Brihadaranyaka Upanishad* 1.3.27.

and on the competence of the sacrificial priest. Power and authority thus gradually came to be identified with the individual. In the *Brahmanas*, the Brahman priests who conducted the ritual and recited the mantras came to be regarded as all-powerful: "The Brahmans who have studied and recited the sacred lore are the human gods."[2]

The important role and supreme status of the Brahman priest may also be seen in the puberty initiation ceremony, the *upanayana*. In the course of this ceremony, the novice is said to be reborn from the teacher: "the teacher conceives when he puts his hand on the boy's shoulder, and on the third day, the boy is reborn a brahman."[3] Insofar as the Brahman priest is able to effect the rebirth of his disciple, Jan Gonda sees evidence of the belief that the Brahman is an important and mighty person, "identified with Varuna and other deities."[4] With the Brahman as a human god, the initiation comes to be regarded as divinization. The initiate is said to be reborn among the gods, the black antelope skin on which he is seated being the ship which carries him to heaven.[5]

It is mainly with the process of internalization of the sacrifice in the *Upanishads* that the absolute status and authority of the spiritual master developed. Rather than the sacrificial fire, it is the person who now becomes the microcosm and the locus of power. This power is acquired through austerities, through self-sacrifice. Disciples called *shishyas* or *chelas* followed these ascetics into the forest and sat down at their feet to learn.[6] In the *Chandogya Upanishad* (8.15.1) the term *guru* is for the first time applied to the ascetic teacher. The power which made the mantra heavy or weighty has become incarnated in a person. While the authority

---

[2] *Shatapatha Brahmana* 2.2.2.6.

[3] *Shatapatha Brahmana* 11.15.4.12-13. An elaborate symbolism is used to enact this rebirth.

[4] Jan Gonda, *Change and Continuity in Indian Religion*, (The Hague: Mouton, 1965) p. 235.

[5] *Apastamba Srautasutra* 10.9.3.

[6] Whence the term *Upanishad* which literally means "sitting down near and respectfully lower."

of rishis and Brahmans was based on an external element, upon that which they had heard or mastered, the authority of the guru lies in personal realization. Truth, *satya*, became a quality of the guru, who is thus regarded as worthy of respect and reverence.

The divine status of the guru in the Upanishads is based on the belief that the deepest ground of one's personal being, one's true Self or *atman* is no different from the absolute, *Brahman*, and that there is nothing beyond the one who has realized this. The state of self-realization or liberation, *moksha*, moreover is, regarded not as momentary and transitory, but as permanent. This is expressed in the idea that "as water does not cling to a lotus leaf, so no evil deed clings to one who knows it."[7] The divinity of the guru becomes further manifested in the emphasis upon his indispensability. The guru is needed, it is said, because "nothing that is eternal [not made] can be gained by what is not eternal [made]."[8] Disciples are explicitly encouraged to see their guru as god: "Let thy teacher be unto thee like a god"[9] and "if these truths have been told to a high-minded man who feels the highest devotion for God, and for his Guru as God, then they will shine forth, — then they will shine forth indeed."[10] The divine status of the guru is acknowledged by the disciples in the words: "Not men, but you only, Sir, I wish, should teach me."[11]

The status of guru depends on the recognition by other gurus and the surrender of disciples. A guru cannot be self-proclaimed because all distinctions are said to disappear in the state of realization so the one who is liberated does not even "know" this:

> As bees, dear boy, make honey by collecting the juices of many trees and reduce the juice to a unity, yet (those juices) cannot perceive any distinction there [so that any of them might know:] "I am the juice of this tree," or "I am the juice of that tree," [so too],

[7] *Chandogya Upanishad* 4.14.3.
[8] *Mandukya Upanishad* 1.2.12.
[9] *Taittiriya Upanishad* 1.11.2.
[10] *Shvetashvatara Upanishad* 6.23.
[11] *Chandogya Upanishad* 4.9.11.

> my dearest boy, all the creatures (here), once they have merged into
> Being, do not know that they have merged into Being.[12]

Since the state of realization cannot be measured by normal human categories, and since even the one who has realized is not aware of this, it takes another realized person to recognize and ratify the state of realization. The authenticity and authority of a guru is thus established objectively through the recognition by another guru of a legitimate lineage. If the acknowledgment by an authentic guru is the formal cause, the surrender of disciples may be seen as the effective cause of guruhood. In the Upanishadic tradition a guru is born only when a shishya approaches a sage with fuel in the hand, expressing the desire to surrender and serve by tending to his domestic fire.

The Master-Disciple Relationship in the Hindu Tradition

The guru-shishya relationship became the kernel of the Hindu religious tradition. The guru has been described as "the centre of sacredness,"[13] as the unifying force of Hinduism. Xavier Irudayaraj states that "the chain which binds religion together is the continuity of divine awareness which runs through the succession of Gurus" and defines orthodoxy as "the attachment to a living tradition with a legitimate line of Gurus."[14] There is in the Hindu tradition no centralized hierarchy which would have the final authority in doctrinal or disciplinary matters. The only scriptures which all Hindus regard as authoritative are the Vedas. And in the Vedas, it is the guru who is the highest religious authority. The guru is thus not subjected to any higher authority or institutional control. He is absolute and autonomous.

The Laws of Manu or the *Manavadharmashastra*, which all Hindus regard as normative, regard the guru as "the image of

---

[12] *Chandogya Upanishad* 6.9.1.

[13] David Miller, "The Guru as the Centre of Sacredness," *Studies in Religion* 6/5 (1976-77) pp. 527-533.

[14] Xavier Irudayaraj, "The Guru in Hinduism and Christianity," *Vidyajyoti* 34 (1975) p. 338.

Brahman."[15] In one of the earlier lawbooks, the shishya is told to "approach his teacher with the same reverence as a deity, without telling idle stories, attentive, and listening eagerly to his words."[16] In the Laws of Manu, however, the term guru may refer to different authority figures, to various kinds of teachers:

> The pupil must know that also that man who benefits him by the instruction of the Veda, be it little or much, is called in these writings his Guru, in consequence of that benefit conferred by instruction in the Veda.[17]

In addition to the teachers of the Veda, parents may be called gurus. Mother, father and teacher are said to be the three highest gurus: "By honoring his mother he gains this [nether] world, by honoring his father the middle sphere, but by obedience to his teacher the world of Brahman."[18] The term guru may also be applied to the husband or any elder family member, the instructor of dance, music or fighting skills. With the name also came often the same expressions of reverence.

The Laws of Manu profoundly shaped the general attitude of respect and reverence towards elders and teachers in the Indian tradition, and the concrete forms in which that attitude is expressed.[19] The self-surrender of the disciple is expressed and brought about in acting humbly and with a sense of inferiority towards the guru:

---

[15] *Laws of Manu* 2.226.

[16] *Apastambha Dharmashastra* 1.2.6.13.

[17] *Laws of Manu* 2.149. Manu distinguishes two kinds of teachers: the *Upadhyaya*, who teaches only a portion of the Veda, and who teaches it for livelihood; and the *acharya*, who invests the student with the sacred thread, teaches the Veda with the Kalpasutras and the Upanishads, and who does not charge for the teaching (2.140-141).

[18] *Laws of Manu* 2.233. In another verse (2.145), it is the mother who is regarded as the highest guru.

[19] The Laws of Manu, however, were an attempt to temper the ascetic zeal which in the Upanishads gave birth to the guru-disciple relationship. It describes the duties of guru and disciple within the context of the first stage in life, that is, that of the student or *brahmacarin*. The prescriptions, however, came to apply to the guru-disciple relationship in general.

> In the presence of his teacher let him always eat less, wear less valuable dress and ornaments [than the former], and let him rise earlier [from his bed] and go to rest later. . . . Let him answer or converse with his teacher standing up, if [his teacher] is seated, advancing towards him when he stands, going to meet him if he advances, and running after him when he runs.[20]

The laws of karma and rebirth also apply to the guru-disciple relationship. While a higher or no rebirth is the reward for strictly obeying the teacher, disobedience or disrespect is regarded as a mortal sin which is severely punished and leads to the lowest rebirth:

> For violating the Guru's bed, [the mark of] a female part shall be
> [impressed on the forehead with a hot iron.][21]
> By censuring [his teacher], though justly, he
> will become [in his next birth] an ass, by falsely
> defaming him, a dog; he who lives on the teacher's
> substance will become a worm, and he who is envious
> [of his merit] a [larger] insect.[22]

While the figure of the guru may be regarded as the unifying force of Hinduism, he may also be seen as the cause for the diversity and disparity which exists within the Indian religious tradition, or, in other words, as the reason why the term "Hinduism" does not refer to a unified belief system or body of doctrines. The absolute authority which is granted to the guru also implies doctrinal autonomy. Any guru may thus start a new teaching tradition or *sampradaya*. In his introduction to Hindu textual materials, Louis Renou describes the typical genesis of a sampradaya:

> The deciding factor for the creation of a sect is the initiative of a master who preaches and explains the scriptures. The type of these founders is repeated throughout history as if by historical law. Under the influence of enlightenment, a man breaks with his past, starts preaching a new doctrine, and after many ordeals succeeds in

---

20 *Laws of Manu* 2.194-196; see also 2.177-178.
21 *Laws of Manu* 9.237.
22 *Laws of Manu* 2.201.

gathering around himself a body of disciples from among whom shall be found his successor. After his disappearance, his biography is shrouded with legends: here lies the great influence of the guru on the Indian mind.[23]

Every founding guru of a teaching tradition may thus be regarded as a founder of a different Hindu tradition. Various gurus have been at the origin of different philosophical schools and belief systems which in turn shaped the understanding of the status and role and the practice of veneration of the figure of the guru.

The methods used to lead the disciple differ according to the school to which the guru belongs. Three forms of *yoga*, or discipline are usually distinguished and may be understood as different ways by which the disciple can be led to the end: *karma* or works, *jñana* or knowledge, and *bhakti* or loving devotion. These different ways, or *margas* are based upon different philosophies which themselves condition the understanding of the status and nature of the guru.

In *Advaita Vedanta*, the philosophical school of non-dualism developed by Shankara (8th century C.E.), the guru is regarded as ontologically absolute. The oldest Upanishads, upon which this tradition is based, state that "he who knows that highest Brahman, becomes even Brahman."[24] There is thus no difference between the absolute and the one who has realized the absolute. The state of liberation or *moksha* is understood as the experience in which "the pure light of Brahman as the identity of pure intelligence, being, and complete bliss shines forth in its unique glory, and all the rest vanishes as illusory nothing."[25] The one who has reached this stage is called *jivanmukta*, emancipated while living. Beyond the jivanmukta, there is nothing.

According to Ramanuja (11th century C.E.), who constructed a theistic form of advaita which became the philosophical base of the Bhakti or devotional tradition, the state of liberation is

[23] Louis Renou, *Hinduism* (New York: Washington Square, 1963) p. 29.

[24] *Mundaka Upanishad* 3.2.9.

[25] Surendranath Dasgupta, *A History of Indian Philosophy* (London: Cambridge University Press, 1922) p. 491.

understood in relational terms as a union with God in which the difference between God, who is understood as personal, all-pervasive, powerful, merciful, knowing, and independent, and man is preserved. The status of the guru is thus one of dependency upon God. Rather than knowledge, it is loving devotion or *bhakti* which leads to liberation. The guru is then seen as a perfect lover of God. This attitude of loving devotion is in the bhakti tradition directed towards one of the *avataras* or "descents" of God.[26] Through the avatars, the deity was personalized in the popular theistic tradition. Figures such as Krishna and Rama acquired distinctly human traits. This in turn allowed for the human gurus to be deified. Some of the bhakti gurus even became worshipped as avatar. The sixteenth century Bengali saint Caitanya, for example, was regarded as an incarnation of both Krishna and his consort Radha. As Jan Gonda points out, the veneration of the guru did not diminish, but on the contrary increased in the Bhakti tradition:

> The tradition of profound respect for the guru did not only continue throughout the whole history of Hinduism, this reverence grew, not rarely to exaggerated dimensions. The guru was worshipped and even recognized as God, and so devotion to this man who replaces the great avatars often became the vital centre of the religion.[27]

While the avatar doctrine forms part of Vaishnava theology, the Shakta and Shaivite traditions developed their own conception of the status and the role of the guru. Shiva or God is usually understood to be the only Guru. He operates in the world

---

[26] The term avatar may best be explained through its first mention and explanation by Krishna in the *Bhagavadgita*:

> For the protection of the good
> For the destruction of the evildoers,
> for the setting up of righteousness,
> I come into being, age after age (4.8).

> For that a human form I have assumed,
> Fools scorn Me,
> Knowing nothing of my higher nature,
> Great Lord of (all) contingent beings (9.11).

[27] Jan Gonda, *Change and Continuity in Indian Religion*, pp. 280-281.

through the divine energy or grace, *shakti*. Human gurus channel this grace, and are thus regarded as *upaya-guru*, instrumental guru and manifestation of Shiva.[28] The main function of the guru is here to impart *diksha*, or the initiation which opens the disciple to God's grace. According to Agehananda Bharati, the famous Tantric scholar, diksha forms the essence of guruhood:

> The notion of diksha provides us, as a semantic by-product so to speak, with a definition of a guru — for a guru is one who has received diksha from one or more gurus, is capable of conferring and has actually conferred diksha on another person or persons. All other qualifications — spiritual maturity, age, renown, learning, etc. are marginal to guruhood.[29]

While in theory the human guru is distinguished from God, in the Tantric ritual practice the guru is treated with utmost reverence and worshipped as God. Gonda remarks that often no distinction is made between the one who initiates to God, and God himself: "the earthly guru through whom speaks the One Guru God, is not different from the Supreme Being; he is 'the root of initiation.'"[30] In his translation of the *Tantra of the Great Liberation*, Arthur Avalon also points out that "the Guru is not to be thought of as mere man. There is no difference between Guru, mantra, and Deva."[31] In some cases, the guru even came to be regarded as superior to God since it is he who leads the soul to God,[32] and since "the guru can save from the wrath of Shiva, but no one can be saved from the anger of the guru."[33]

[28] Xavier Irudayaraj emphasizes the distinction which exists in the Shiva-Siddhanta tradition between "the *Sar-Guru*, who is Shiva manifesting himself immediately, as he shines in the realized Jñani, and the *Nar-Gurus* through whom Shiva mediately prepares the soul for the gift of *Pati-jñana*." See "The Guru in Hinduism and Christianity" *Vidyajyoti* 34 (1975) p. 345.

[29] Agehananda Bharati, *The Tantric Tradition* (New York: Samuel Weiser, 1975) p. 186.

[30] Jan Gonda, *Change and Continuity in Indian Religions*, p. 278.

[31] Arthur Avalon, *Tantra of the Great Liberation* (New York: Dover, 1972) p. llxxii.

[32] "A guru is considered to be worthy of more reverence than is due to Shiva, the Supreme, because it is he who leads the soul to unity with Shiva." S.C. Nandimath, *A Handbook of Virashaivism* (Bangalore: Basel Mission Press, 1942) p. 54.

[33] A. Avalon, *Shakti and Shakta* (Madras: Ganesh, 1951) pp. 491-492.

Although the term guru has been applied to any figure in a position of power and authority, it originally (in the Upanishads) and generally (in all philosophical systems) refers to one whose status and authority is believed to be absolute. Within a lineage or teaching tradition, every guru is believed to incarnate the full authority of the original guru and of the tradition itself. In the chain or tradition of gurus, the *guruparampara*, it is usually the guru who appoints a successor. It is, however, only the acceptance of the new guru by the disciples that ensures the continuity of the lineage. Teaching traditions may dissolve, and new ones, based on the surrender of disciples to a guru who does not belong to an established lineage, emerge.

Within some established traditions, the guru-shishya relationship has been more or less systematized or even institutionalized. The qualities which the guru must possess are delineated, the conditions for discipleship outlined, and the interaction between guru and disciple prescribed. Especially in Tantric texts, which may be seen as manuals of initiation, the requirements and roles of guru and disciple are elaborately developed. The *Kularnava Tantra*, for example, lists about seventy characteristics necessary to qualify as a perfect guru.

A classic reflection on the guru-disciple relationship outside the Tantric tradition is Shankara's *Upadesasahasri* or *Thousand Teachings*.[34] This presentation of the guru-disciple relationship may be regarded as idealistic, but it remains the ideal to which every relationship between guru and disciple tends in the tradition of Advaita Vedanta.[35] It consists of a metrical part, which may be regarded as a textbook for disciples, in which Shankara discusses the basic philosophical problems of Advaita, and a

---

[34] This work occupies an important position in the history of Advaita Vedanta, and is the only work which is not a commentary, which can safely be attributed to Shankara.

[35] Within the tradition of Advaita Vedanta, the guru-disciple relationship became institutionalized partly through the foundation of the four monasteries or *mathas* in the four directions, (in the South the Sringerimatha, East the Govardhanamatha, West Saradmatha, and North Jyotirmatha) and through the creation of the orders or *darshanas*.

prose part, which presents itself as a guide for teachers, explaining how to teach the means of final liberation.[36]

The Master-Disciple Relationship
in the Thousand Teachings of Shankara

The Disciple

The qualifications for discipleship are very demanding in the *Thousand Teachings* of Shankara. The disciple is expected to be completely "dispassionate toward all things non-eternal which are attained by means (other than knowledge)."[37] This implies that he has "abandoned the desire for sons, wealth and worlds and reached the state of a *paramahamsa* wandering ascetic."[38] In the oldest Upanishads, which are the main source of inspiration for Shankara, *sannyasa,* or the state of the ascetic, is seen as the transcendence of those very desires which tie a person to the world and thereby prevent final liberation.[39] The *paramahamsas* are traditionally regarded as ascetics of the highest order.[40] They

[36] Sengaku Mayeda, trans., *A Thousand Teachings. The Upadesasahasri of Sankara* (Tokyo: University of Tokyo Press, 1979.)

[37] *A Thousand Teachings* 2.1.2.

[38] *A Thousand Teachings* 2.1.2. In the metrical part of the work it is also pointed out that "the meaning of the *Veda* herein determined, which has been briefly related by me, should be imparted to serene wandering ascetics by one of disciplined intellect."

[39] The *Brihadaranyaka Upanishad* 4.4.22 states: "And they, having risen above the desire for sons, wealth, and the new worlds, wander about as mendicants." *Sannyasa* is the state of total renunciation of the world. It came to be regarded as the fourth and ultimate *ashrama* or stage in life, which could only be acquired after the other stages of student, householder, and forest hermit had been completed.

[40] Ascetics are often classified in four groups in ascending order: *kuticaka, bahudaka, hamsa,* and *paramahamsa.* One of the marks which distinguishes the different kinds of ascetics is who they are allowed to beg from. The first begs only from his sons, the second begs from brahmans and "well-conducted men," the third begs from village people, and the paramahamsas beg from people of all castes. They have thus transcended all purity rules. Cf. P.V. Kane, *History of Dharmasastra,* II-II (Poona: Bhandarkar Oriental Research Institute, 1974) p. 930 ff.

are described as the kind of sannyasis who "always stay under a tree or in an uninhabited house or in a burial place, and either wear a garment or are naked. They are beyond the pairs of dharma and adharma, truth and falsehood, purity and impurity. They treat all alike, they regard all as the Self, to them a clod of earth or gold is the same and they beg alms from persons of all varnas."[41] There are two kinds of paramahamsas: those who have already realized Brahman, called *vidvat*, and those who are eager seekers after realization, the *vividishu*. The shishya belongs to the latter category.

The qualities associated with discipleship are specified as "tranquility, self-control, compassion, and so forth."[42] Shankara mentions that the qualities of the pupil are well known from the scriptures. He probably refers to the *Brihadaranyaka Upanishad*, which declares: "He who knows thus becomes tranquil, self-controlled, withdrawn, patient, and collected..."[43] In another text traditionally attributed to Shankara, the qualities of the shishya are said to be discrimination between the Real and the unreal, disregard for enjoyment now or after death, the possession of six perfections: calmness, control of senses, self-settledness, fortitude in enduring opposites like heat and cold or pleasure and pain, concentration of mind, and faith in the teaching of Vedanta, and finally the longing for liberation.[44] The desire for liberation is the only legitimate one.

Another requirement is that the disciple "approaches the teacher in the prescribed manner."[45] This means that the disciple must approach the teacher carrying fuel which expresses his desire to serve. Obedience to and service of the guru are an essential part of discipleship. This is explicitated in the metrical part of the *Thousand Teachings*:

---

[41] P.V. Kane, *History of Dharmasastra*, p. 940.

[42] *A Thousand Teachings* 2.1.2.

[43] 4.4.23.

[44] *Vivekacudamani* 19-27, Cf. S. Dasgupta *A History of Indian Philosophy*, 1 (Cambridge: Cambridge University Press, 1969, vol. I) pp. 436-437.

[45] *A Thousand Teachings* 2.1.2.

> This [highest means of purification] should be always taught to a seeker after final release whose mind has been calmed, whose senses have been controlled, whose faults have been abandoned, who is acting as prescribed [in the scriptures], who is endowed with virtues, and who is always obedient [to his teacher].[46]
> This secret and supreme knowledge should not be given to [a student] who is not tranquil but should be taught to a student who is dispassionate and obedient.[47]

Obedience and service bring about self-surrender, self-purification and humility which are necessary for acquiring knowledge. Service itself may, moreover, lead to important insights. This is allegorized in the *Chandogya Upanishad* where a student who has become completely exhausted from serving the guru and tending his fires for twelve years is finally taught by the fires themselves:

> Thereupon the fires said among themselves: "This student, who is quite exhausted, has carefully tended us. Well, let us teach him."[48]

Service is here understood as both means and end. The elimination of a false sense of self is necessary to acquire knowledge, but may also result from knowing the true self.

A last requirement of discipleship in the *Thousand Teachings* is that the disciple is "a Brahmin who is (internally and externally) pure;" and that "his caste, profession, behavior, knowledge (of the Veda), and family have been examined."[49] Shankara thus appears to set social conditions to discipleship. This may seem to be in contradiction with the further teaching which denies any sense of identity formed by caste.[50] Shankara may, nonetheless, be seen as an exponent of Brahmanical orthodoxy. He insists upon the knowledge of the Veda before embarking upon the path

---

[46] *A Thousand Teachings* 1.16.72.

[47] *A Thousand Teachings* 1.17.85.

[48] 4.10-14. Service of the teacher also often implies begging for him and looking after his cows. Cf. *Chandogya Upanishad* 4.4.5-9. After the disciple had brought the number of cows from a hundred to a thousand, it is the bull of the herd who starts the teaching saying "We have become a thousand, lead us to the house of the teacher; and I will declare to you one foot of Brahman,"

[49] *A Thousand Teachings* 2.1.2.

[50] *A Thousand Teachings* 2.1.10 ff.

to liberation, and believed that the Veda could be read only by Brahmans.[51]

Even though it is emphasized that no amount of material goods can repay the treasure of knowledge which is received from the guru, the disciple is expected to offer a gift, or *dakshina*, to the teacher.[52] Respect is expressed in India by bowing or prostrating, and touching the master's feet. Even a king humbles himself for the guru: "Janaka Vaideha, descending from his throne, said: 'I bow to you, O Yajnavalkya, teach me.'"[53]

The Master[54]

The teacher must first of all possess the qualities required of the disciple. Those explicitly mentioned in the *Thousand Teachings* are "tranquility, self-control, ... not [being] attached to any enjoyments, visible or invisible..."[55] While the disciple is in search for liberation or *moksha*, the teacher is one who has reached that end through the knowledge of Brahman. This is understood not as a momentary experience, but as a permanent state: "a knower of Brahman, he is established in Brahman."[56] The teacher is thus regarded as a *jivanmukta*, or one who is liberated while still alive. Athough he must live out the present existence, the Upanishads teach that no new karma is accumulated, since "as water does not cling to a lotus leaf, so no evil clings to one who knows it."[57] Once the previously stored karma is

---

[51] There were different opinions on whether only Brahmans, or also *kshatriyas* and *vaishyas* could become sannyasis. Shankara takes the saying of the *Brihadaranyaka Upanishad* 3.5.1 that "When Brahmanas know that Self, and have risen above the desire for sons, wealth and worlds, they wander about as mendicants" to mean that the state of sannyasa is reserved only for Brahmans. Cf. P.V. Kane, *History of Dharmasastra*, II-II (Poona: Bhandarkar Oriental Research Institute, 1974, vol.) p. 943.

[52] *Chandogya Upanishad* 4.2.1-5.

[53] *Brihadaranyaka Upanishad* 4.2.1.

[54] Rather than guru, Shankara uses the term *acharya*, which means teacher in the larger sense of the word, but is used by him as an equivalent of the term guru.

[55] *A Thousand Teachings* 2.1.6.

[56] *A Thousand Teachings* 2.1.6.

[57] *Chandogya Upanishad* 4.14.3.

exhausted, the body is lost and the *jivanmukta* is liberated forever.

As Shankara taught the way of knowledge, the qualities of reasoning and understanding of the teacher are emphasized: "the teacher is able to consider the pros and cons [of an argument], is endowed with understanding, memory, ... versed in the traditional doctrines."[58] A teacher must be able to understand and remember the questions posed by disciples and be able to engage in dialectical discourse. The traditional doctrines in which he must be versed are, first of all, the revealed sources of the teaching of Shankara: the *Upanishads* — mainly the oldest ones which are non-dualistic — the *Bhagavadgita*, and the *Brahmasutras*, aphorisms about Brahman, traditionally attributed to Badarayana.[59] In addition the teacher was also expected to be acquainted with the other philosophical systems, if only for the sake of argument or refutation.

It is not so much conceptual or rational, but experiential knowledge of the scriptures which is required from the teacher. Throughout the Upanishads and the tradition of Advaita Vedanta the radical discontinuity between normal, rational grasping and real knowledge or *jñana* is emphasized. While normal understanding is gathered conceptually, the knowledge of the Self, or *atman*, can only be attained through the negation of what it is not, as expressed in the celebrated "*neti, neti.*"[60]

The acquisition of liberation through knowledge also implies that the teacher must have "abandoned all the rituals and their requisites."[61] Shankara points out that rituals may be performed prior to liberation as a way of purifying the mind:

> When the mind becomes pure like a mirror, knowledge shines forth; therefore the mind should be purified. The mind is purified by abstention, the permanent rites, sacrifices, and austerities.[62]

[58] *A Thousand Teachings* 2.1.6.

[59] The latter scripture does not traditionally belong to what is regarded as shruti, but it plays a very important role in Advaita Vedanta.

[60] "And he [the atman in that state] can only be described by No, no! He is incomprehensible, for he cannot be comprehended..." *Brihadaranyaka Upanishad* 4.2.4, also 4.4.22, 4.5.15, 3.9.26, 2.3.6.

[61] *A Thousand Teachings* 2.1.6.

[62] *A Thousand Teachings* 1.17.22.

But with the realization of the non-duality of atman and Brahman, the need for ritual practice dissolves. Rituals are based on a sense of duality between the one who performs the ritual on the one hand and the God for whom and/or the goal for which it is performed on the other.[63] The one who is realized naturally abandons all ritual life.

Because of this idea that the one who is realized has transcended all ritual life and action, Shankara has been accused of advocating an immoral, or at least an a-moral teaching. One of the main requirements of the teacher, however, is that he leads a "blameless life," understood as a life "free from faults such as deceit, pride, trickery, wickedness, fraud, jealousy, falsehood, egotism, self-interest, and so forth."[64] Shankara may thus not deal with ethics because he considers it self-evident, a matter of course which need not be elaborated upon.[65] Moreover, the sense of non-differentiation and interconnection in the "Self who is within all"[66] spontaneously leads to compassion and the desire to help others.

In naming the characteristics of the spiritual master, Shankara explicitly mentions the qualities of "compassion, favor, and the like."[67] He points out that it is "with the only purpose of helping others [that the teacher] wishes to make use of knowledge."[68] The one who has attained *moksha* has no interest whatsoever in teaching others. It neither adds to nor distracts from the state of realization. It is thus purely out of pity with those who are still in the wheel of transmigratory existence and dependent upon him that the spiritual master teaches.

[63] This is explained in *A Thousand Teachings* 2.1.30.

[64] *A Thousand Teachings* 2.1.6.

[65] This is also the opinion of Sengaku Mayeda, *A Thousand Teachings. The Upadesasahasri of Sankara*, p. 93.

[66] *Brihadaranyaka Upanishad* 3.4.2.

[67] *A Thousand Teachings* 2.1.6.

[68] *A Thousand Teachings* 2.1.6.

The Master-Disciple Relationship

> If the student is disciplined and properly qualified, the teacher should immediately transport him over this great interior ocean of darkness in the boat of the knowledge of Brahman.[69]

A person desiring liberation must first of all seek an authentic and suitable teacher. This may be done on the basis of the qualities of a teacher, through the recommendation of other disciples and/or on the grounds of the authenticity of the lineage. A master-disciple relationship develops only when one or more disciples surrender to someone who is believed to have reached liberation. Within the tradition of Shankara, the master-disciple relationship is concerned mainly with the acquisition of right knowledge.

Before the process of learning begins, the master must verify whether the disciple possesses all the necessary qualifications. The flaws which may need correction are "demerit, worldly laxity, absence of firm preliminary learning concerning the discrimination between things eternal and non-eternal, care about what other people think, pride of caste, and the like."[70] The qualities of the disciple thus seem to be not so much presupposed as acquired in the master-disciple relationship. When all conditions of discipleship are fulfilled, however, the guru is encouraged to teach without holding anything back.

The ancient Upanishadic way of learning as reflected in the *Brihadaranyaka Upanishad* followed three successive stages. First the disciple listens humbly and carefully to what the teacher says (*shravana*); then he contemplates this teaching through reasoning (*manana*); lastly, he meditates upon the truth so as to realize it (*nididhyasana.*)[71]

In the *Thousand Teachings*, the *shravana* stage is that of Shankara expounding his understanding of atman and Brahman, and

---

[69] *A Thousand Teachings* 1.17.52.

[70] *A Thousand Teachings* 2.1.4.

[71] Cf. R.K. Mookerji, *Ancient Indian Education* (London: Macmillan, 1951) p. 144.

explaining the characteristics of Brahman by means of the *shruti*, mainly the oldest Upanishads, and through the *smriti* or traditional texts which advocate non-dualism. *Manana*, or reflection is then induced by asking the disciple the question "who are you, my dear?"[72] The Self-discovery is of an existential rather than an intellectual nature and must be conducted by the disciple himself. This is necessary and possible because, according to Shankara, atman is eternally one with Brahman:

> But it may be asked, is Brahman known or not known [previously to the enquiry into its nature]? If it is known we need not enter on an enquiry concerning it; if it is not known we can not enter on such an enquiry. We reply that Brahman is known.... Moreover the existence of Brahman is known on the ground of its being the Self of every one.... And the Self [of whose existence we are conscious] is Brahman.[73]

Self-discovery proceeds by stripping oneself from ignorance (*avidya*) caused, according to Shankara, by the process of superimposition which identifies the Self with what it is not.[74] The teacher helps the disciple by rejecting the false self-conceptions of the disciple. In the *Thousand Teachings* the disciple first identifies with caste and its correlates: family, body, purifying ceremonies, the worship of a personal god.[75] The master then teaches the disciple that all this is name-and-form, *namarupa*. Since rituals also belong to the world of names and forms, particular emphasis is laid upon the idea that "the seeker after final release should abandon the ritual together with its requisites."[76] The disciple actively participates in the learning process. Questions are asked and arguments based upon other philosophical systems advanced. In this way the superiority of the system of Advaita Vedanta is

---

[72] *A Thousand Teachings* 2.1.9.

[73] George Thibaut, *Sacred Books of the East* 34, p. 14.

[74] Superimposition is defined by Shankara as "The apparent presentation, in the form of remembrance, to consciousness of something previously observed in some other thing." *Vedanta-Sutras with the Commentary by Sankaracarya*, in George Thibaut, *Sacred Books of the East* 34, p. 4.

[75] *A Thousand Teachings* 2.1.10-40.

[76] *A Thousand Teachings* 2.1.32.

emphasized.[77] Through psychological and epistemological argument, the disciple is then led to the realization that he himself is Brahman. This may take many years of reflection and contemplation. The god Indra is said to have lived one hundred and one years with his guru Prajapati before attaining to the final truth or liberating knowledge.[78]

The stage of *nididhyasana* is that of the profound meditation upon and integration of the teaching. The realization of the non-duality of atman and Brahman brings about the disappearance of all pain and fear associated with transmigration. It is ultimately up to the master to acknowledge the state of realization of the disciple:

> Exactly it is so. It is nescience that is the cause of transmigratory existence which is characterized by the waking and dreaming states. The remover of this nescience is knowledge. And you have reached fearlessness. From now on you will not perceive any pain in waking and dreaming states. You are released from the sufferings of transmigratory existence.[79]

When the master acknowledges the ultimate realization of the disciple, the master-disciple relationship dissolves.

---

[77] To the question of the ultimate cause of *avidya* (2.2.84-85) the guru does not answer. This remained the unresolved problem of Advaita Vedanta.

[78] *Chandogya Upanishad* 8.11.3.

[79] *A Thousand Teachings* 2.2.110.

CHAPTER THREE

The Master-Disciple Relationship in Christianity

The Master-Disciple Relationship in Christian Scripture

> But you are not to be called Rabbi for you have one teacher, and you are all brethren. And call no man your father on earth, for you have one Father, who is in heaven. Neither be called masters, for you have one master, the Christ.[1]

In the Christian tradition, the figure of the spiritual master operates within clearly defined limits of orthodoxy regarding both form and content. While the term "spiritual master" may be applicable to any office within the church, it strictly speaking refers to the relationship between "a master knowledgable of and experienced in the voices of the spirit, and a disciple desirous of profiting from that knowledge and experience."[2] Characteristic of Christian spiritual masters from the early desert fathers through the founders of monastic orders, the medieval monastic reformers, and the famous directors of the seventeenth and eighteenth centuries is the reference to Christ as the only or ultimate master: "For God is one, and there is one mediator between God and humanity, the person Christ Jesus, who gave himself as a ransom for all, the testimony to which was borne at the proper time."[3]

---

[1] Matt 23:8-10.

[2] Irenée Hausherr, *Direction spirituelle en Orient autrefois* (Rome: Pont. Institutum Orientalium Studiorum, 1955) p. 10.

[3] 1 Tim 2:5-6. Though this letter has come to be considered with Ephesians, Colossians, 2 Thessalonians, 2 Timothy, and Titus as "pseudoepigraphic," it powerfully expresses the belief in the uniqueness of Christ which came to determine the attitude toward the spiritual father.

The sovereignty of Jesus Christ is expressed throughout the New Testament and is condensed in the confession: "Jesus Christ is Lord of all" (Acts 10:36). This became manifest in Jesus' relationship with the established authority of his day. He not only distances himself from the scribes and Pharisees, but also feels that he has the authority to judge them (Matt 23:13-36). People said that "he taught them as one who has authority, and not as the scribes" (Mark 1:22).[4] This authority is manifested in priority to the sacred laws of the sabbath,[5] and in the divine prerogative to show mercy and forgive sins.[6] It has been expressed in terms of the uniqueness and radical discontinuity of Christ: "All things have been delivered to me by the Father; and no one knows the Son except the Father, and no one knows the Father except the Son and any one to whom the Son chooses to reveal him" (Matt 11:27) and "I am the way and the truth and the life; no one comes to the Father, but by me" (John 14:6).

Jesus delegates his authority to the apostles. The term apostle has been defined as one "chosen and sent with a special commission as the fully authorized representative of the sender."[7] Jesus sends the apostles with the words: "Truly, I say to you, whatever you bind on earth shall be bound in heaven, and whatever you loose on earth shall be loosed in heaven" (Matt 18:8), and "He who hears you hears me, and he who rejects you rejects me, and he who rejects me rejects him who sent me" (Luke 10:16). The one who is sent can, however, only speak in the name and by the grace of the one who sends. The apostle cannot become Christ or personally assume authority. In sending the disciples, Christ

---

[4] Cf. Luke 4:32 and Matt 7:28-29, where the expression becomes even more emphatic as it is used as a conclusion to the Sermon on the Mount.

[5] "The sabbath was made for man, not man for the sabbath; so the Son of man is lord even of the sabbath" (Mark 2:27-28). Matthew and Luke omit Mark 2:27.

[6] "That you may know that the Son of man has authority on earth to forgive sins" (Mark 2:10).

[7] Norval Geldenhuis, *Supreme Authority* (Grand Rapids, MI: Eerdmans, 1953) p. 54.

reminds them that they are always to remain in relationship to him as the ultimate reference and source of life:

> As the branch cannot bear fruit by itself, unless it abides in the vine, neither can you, unless you abide in me. I am the vine; you are the branches. He who abides in me and I in him, he it is that bears much fruit, for apart from me you can do nothing. If a man does not abide in me, he is cast forth as a branch and withers; and the branches are gathered, thrown into the fire and burned (John 15:4-6).[8]

The possibility that the followers of Christ assume individual authority and power is precluded through reference, not only to the words and example of Jesus Christ, but also to the inspiration of the Holy Spirit. In the absence of the historical Jesus, it is the Spirit which is the ultimate source of power and inspiration as is expressed in Jesus' words: "These things I have spoken to you while I am still with you. But the Counselor, the Holy Spirit, whom the Father will send in my name, he will teach you all things, and bring to your remembrance all that I have said to you" (John 14:25-26).[9]

With his image of the Church as the mystical body of Christ, in which all parts, inspired by the Spirit, fulfill an indispensible and irreplaceable role in the functioning of the whole, Paul emphasizes the fundamental equality of all Christians, and the role of the Spirit as guide. Christians are directed by the "law of the Spirit" (Rom 8:2) which "dwells in [them]" (1 Cor 3:16). The function of the preacher, nevertheless, remains necessary because:

> how are men to call upon him in whom they have not believed? And how are they to believe in him of whom they have never heard? And how are they to hear without a preacher? And how can men preach unless they are sent? As it is written, "How beautiful are the feet of those who preach the good news!" (Rom 10:14-15).

---

[8] Cf. also Jesus' warning that "a servant is not greater than his master; nor is he who is sent greater than the one who sent him" (John 14:16).

[9] See also Acts 1:7-8: "It is not for you to know times or seasons which the Father has fixed by his own authority. But you shall receive power when the Holy Spirit has come upon you; and you shall be my witness."

The apostles or preachers, like the prophets, teachers, healers, administrators, and so forth, are in the first place members of the church which as a whole possesses the Spirit of Christ.

In continuity with the prophetic and wisdom traditions, Paul understood his role as that of a father. In Israel, it was originally the natural father who was responsible for the transmission and the preservation of the sacred tradition as in the command: "you shall teach [the words] diligently to your children, and shall talk of them when you sit in your house, and when you walk by the way, and when you lie down, and when you rise" (Deut 6:7). As society became more complex, different teaching functions were delegated to specialists, but the one who transmitted or mediated the sacred knowledge continued to be called father. Elisha addressed the prophet Elijah as "my father."[10] In wisdom circles the teacher referred to his disciple as son:

> My son, do not forget my teaching, but let your heart keep my commandments; for length of days and years of life and abundant welfare will they give you (Prov 3:1-2).[11]

The teacher was called father because the teaching itself was regarded as a source of life: "The teaching of the wise is a fountain of life, that one may avoid the snares of death."[12]

Paul similarly regarded the gospel which he preached as a source of new life and his own role as that of a father: "You know how, like a father with his children, we exhorted each one of you and encouraged you and charged you to lead a life worthy of God" (1 Thess 2:11-12). He understood his role as a father in a derived, participatory, and instrumental sense, as that of a "workman for God" (1 Cor 3:9), who lays foundations and creates children "in the Lord" (1 Cor 4:17). He regards himself as "father in Jesus Christ through the gospel" (1 Cor 4:15) and sees his own disciples as "in Christ Jesus [you are] sons of God,

---

[10] 2 Kings 2:12.

[11] Characteristic of Proverbs is that "tora does not have a legal sense but usually refers to the teaching of a teacher/parent." Dermot Cox, "Learning and the way to God," *Studia Missionalia* 36 (1987) p. 15.

[12] Prov 13:14, and also 3:1, 7:2, 4:13, 8:14, etc.

through faith" (Gal 3:26). Paul therefore rages against those teachers who attach their disciples to themselves, and against those disciples who claim to belong to the one who communicated Christ rather than to Christ himself (1 Cor 1:12-17). In reaction to those who claim personal authority and credit over their disciples, he states: "I planted, Apollos watered, but God gave the growth. So neither he who plants, nor he who waters is anything, but only God who gives the growth" (1 Cor 3:6-7).

On the other hand, Paul does see his own role as father as indispensible and irreplaceable. The seed needs to be planted and fertilized, and the one who does this may be seen as father of which, according to Paul, there can be only one: "For though you have countless guides in Christ, you do not have many fathers. For I became your father in Christ Jesus through the Gospel. I urge you, then, be imitators of me" (1 Cor 4:15-16). Paul's understanding of the uniqueness of his role is thus based on his sense of responsibility as example and mediator of the Gospel. This becomes clear in the expression: "My little children with whom I am in travail until Christ be formed in you" (Gal 4:19). In Paul, it thus becomes clear that the spiritual father must continuously walk a fine line between self-effacement in Christ and self-consciousness as model and representative of Christ.

The Master-Disciple Relationship in the Christian Tradition

In the early Church, Paul's conception of spiritual fatherhood was developed in a sacramental direction which further developed into the institutional hierarchy, and in a purely spiritual direction. The former was expounded in the *Didascalia Apostolorum* where, by virtue of his giving rebirth from water, the bishop is regarded as father after God. It is thus the administration of the sacrament of baptism, then a function of the bishop, which confers the title "father" and the honor and veneration which come with his participation in the divine fatherhood.

It is, however, outside — and often in reaction to — the sacramental, institutional context that the notion of spiritual father entered the Christian tradition. During the first centuries of the Christian era, individuals fled into the desert in search of perfection. Far away from the distractions and temptations of society, and from the compromises of the developing institution, these anchorites or recluses dedicated themselves completely to contemplation, prayer, and ascetic exercises. Their charismatic qualities soon attracted others who came from the cities and towns to ask advice on prayer and self-discipline, or who had decided to follow in their footsteps. The teachings and lives of these masters are recorded in the *Apophthegmata Patrum* and the *Vitae Patrum*, and the term Desert Fathers became their common appellation. Anthony, the most famous of the earliest ascetics told those who came to him: "You must conduct yourselves like children, telling your father what you know; and I will share with you what I know in return, and the struggles I have lived through."[13]

The early Desert Fathers were most often not ordained. Yet, because of Origen's understanding of the Christian as in a process of continuous generation through every meritorious deed and reflection, the term father could be extended to the desert fathers.[14] The council of 494 did not object to the use of the term father for hermits, thereby affirming that no ordination was necessary to receive this title.[15] A non-sacramental and non-hierarchical tradition of authority thus developed parallel to the official authority within the early Church.

The role and authority of the spiritual father developed along different lines in the cenobitic communities which emerged in the third and the fourth centuries in Egypt and in Cappadocia. In Egypt, the *cenobia* was a spontaneous outgrowth of anchoritic

[13] Translated quotation from the *Vita Antonii*, 16, by Philip Rousseau, *Ascetics, Authority and the Church* (Oxford: Oxford University Press, 1978) p. 24.

[14] *In Jeremiam* IX, 4; PG 13, 356 C ff. Quoted in I. Hausherr, *Direction Spirituelle en Orient Autrefois* (Rome: Pontifica Universitas Gregoriana, 1955) pp. 31-32.

[15] "Vitas Patrum, Pauli, Antonii, Hilarionis et omnium eremitarum quas tamen vir beatus scripsit Hieronymus, cum omni honore suscipimus." *Gratiani Decret. dist.* 15, cap. *Sancta Romana Ecclesia.*

and semi-anchoritic life.[16] It emerged from the need to organize and structure the life of the many disciples who gathered around a spiritual father. Although the communal dimension came to play an important role, the relationship between spiritual father and disciple remained the constitutive element of the community. The cenobite was in the first place a disciple of the spiritual master, and only secondarily a member of a social body. Pachomius (290-346) is often regarded as the founder of the Egyptian cenobitic tradition. Theodore, Pachomius' most faithful disciple and successor, points out to the other disciples that they have formed a community, not so much because of a particular form of life, but to find salvation through the guidance and mediation of Pachomius.[17]

The Desert Fathers had a strong sense of their own sinfulness. They always referred beyond themselves to Christ and to the scriptures. Nevertheless they often became an object of veneration. Reflecting upon Jeremiah's prohibition to put faith in a man (Jer 18:5), Theodore exclaims: "some of you may be of the opinion that we glorify the flesh. Not at all. Or that we put our hope in a man. That is neither true. We bless and glorify the Spirit of God which resides in this man. But in fact, even if we did bless his flesh, it would not be illegitimate since it was the temple of God."[18] The term "*apa*" or father was thus applied to the head of the community with strong reverential connotations. Pachomius himself referred to those to whom he delegated the authority of spiritual father as "father after God:"

[16] This is the dominant theory on the development of the cenobitic communities in the early church. See Philip Rousseau, *Ascetics, Authority and the Church* (Oxford: Oxford University Press, 1978) and Adelbert De Vogüé, *La communauté et l'abbé dans la Règle de Saint Benoît* (Paris: Desclée De Brouwer, 1961.)

[17] "Listen to me, my brothers, and remember what I say to you. The man we celebrate is in fact, after God, our Father. God has convened with him to save a mass of souls through his mediation." Translated from Louis-Théophile Lefort, *Les Vies Coptes de saint Pachôme et de ses premiers successeurs*, 16 (Louvain: Muséon, 1943) p. 211.

[18] Translated from L.-T. Lefort, *Les Vies Coptes de saint Pacôme et de ses premiers successeurs*, 16, p. 211.

> After God, this is your father. You will do everything you see him do; if he fasts, you will fast with him, and whatever he does, you will do like him... and you will do nothing without him, and you will go nowhere without his permission.[19]

Radical obedience to and imitation of the spiritual father was thus expected from the disciple. With the institutionalization of charisma in monastic orders, the authority of the spiritual father becomes replaced or at least balanced by that of the Rule.

Instead of as a group of disciples gathered around the same spiritual father, the cenobitic tradition in Cappadocia emerged among Christians who decided to lead an ascetic life in group rather than in solitude. It was the requirements of community life which called for some form of leadership. While in Egypt the spiritual father-disciple relationship was constitutive of the community, here the community engenders the figure of the spiritual master. Basil called the head of the community *proestos*, "he who presides," rather than father. He was first of all a member of the community, subject to the common rules and to control by others.[20] Although the head of the community was thus strictly speaking not regarded as "superior" to the others, he was still chosen on the basis of spiritual qualities. Despite the diversity of situation and approach, it has been pointed out that "in practice the difference between the functioning of a Basilian *proestos* and that of a Pachomian *apa* was perhaps not very marked, simply because both had independently drunk from the pure source of the Gospel."[21]

For Augustine, it was likewise the group modelled after the first Christian communities, rather than the spiritual father-disciple relationship which constituted the community. The head of the community is called *praepositus*, "put ahead," and his role is discussed only at the very end of Augustine's rule. The authority

[19] Translated from L.-T. Lefort, *Les Vies Coptes de Saint Pachôme et de ses premiers successeurs*, 16, p. 261.

[20] I. Hausherr, *Direction Spirituelle en Orient Autrefois*, p. 113.

[21] "The Abbot," appendix to Timothy Fry's *The Rule of St. Benedict (RB 1980)* (Collegeville, MN: Liturgical Press, 1981) p. 345.

of the *praepositus* is strongly limited by the authority of office. Although the head of the community is to be respected and obeyed, Augustine insists in the *Regula tertia*, that this applies all the more to the priest who holds final authority over the monastery.[22] Charismatic or monastic authority has thus become strictly subject to the hierarchical authority in the Church.

No general theology of the spiritual director was developed in the Catholic tradition, and official documents have not dealt explicitly with this question. Different forms of the spiritual master-disciple relationship were implicitly accepted or rejected with their respective spiritualities. Both belief in the dispensibility and belief in the self-sufficiency of the spiritual master were condemned. The Brothers of the Free Spirit in the thirteenth century were accused of attaching too much value to their mystical experience, without recourse to a higher authority.[23] The Quietist movement was condemned because it propagated refuge in the spiritual master alone without need for other practices and without reference to ecclesiastical authority.[24] According to famous quietist master, Miguel Molinos, for example, the disciple had no right to call upon any other considerations such as moral principles, divine commandments, recommendations of the church, or even his own conscience to oppose obedience to the spiritual father.[25]

The three spiritual giants, John of the Cross, Teresa of Avila, and Francis de Sales, whose works on spiritual direction have become classics, severely warned against false or blind masters. John of the Cross describes blind masters as those who are ignorant and jealous, who transmit their own deficiencies onto

---

[22] "Praepositae tanquam matri obediatur, honore servato, ne in illa offendatur Deus: multo magis presbytero qui omnium vestrum curam gerit" *Epistola CCXI*, 15; PL 33, 964.

[23] It is blasphemous to state that man "non debere quaeri consilium a viris litteratis, sive de devotione, sive de aliis." Quoted from *Documenta*, 201 in *Dictionnaire de Spiritualité*, 3, p. 1175.

[24] Leszek Kolakowski, *Chrétiens sans Eglise. La conscience religieuse et le lien confessionnel au XVIIe siècle* (Paris: Gallimard, 1969) p. 494.

[25] Leszek Kolakowski, *Chrétiens sans Eglise*, p. 511.

their disciples. He attacks the possessiveness of some spiritual masters who, when their disciple decides to seek council from another master, "behave like a husband who is jealous of his wife."[26] While Teresa of Avila believes that only one in a thousand may be a good spiritual director, Francis de Sales speaks of one in ten thousand. The only provision which Teresa made to her famous vow of obedience to the spiritual director was that it would "not be against God or against the prelacy, for one is held to obey them, more than any others."[27] Characteristic of a true spiritual father or mother within the Church was his or her surrender to the primacy of institutional authority.

The first important formal statement about the role of the spiritual father is the document *Testem Benevolentiae* of Leo XIII to Cardinal Gibbons (Jan. 22, 1899). Here, the pope warns against those who oppose docility to the Holy Spirit and docility to the counsel of the spiritual father.[28] He first emphasizes that faith in the workings of the Holy Spirit is an essential part of Christian orthodoxy. Yet experience tells us that the promptings of the Spirit can only be discerned by means of the help of the external magisterium. Leo explicitly states that this is even more the case on the path to perfection which is dangerous and full of pitfalls. The magisterium to which the pope refers, however, fits strictly speaking into the power of neither order nor jurisdiction. Although the spiritual direction of the laity developed in the form of confession, which could only be administered by priests,[29] spiritual direction was neither originally nor essentially a preroga-

---

[26] *Living Flame of Love*, III, 59, in *The Complete Works of Saint John of the Cross* (London: Burns & Oates, 1943.)

[27] Quoted from *Relations*, p. 129-131 in *Direction Spirituelle et Psychologie* (Tournai: Desclée de Brouwer, 1951) p. 134.

[28] In *Acta Sanctae Sedis*, t. 31, 1898-9, pp. 474-476.

[29] On this development, in which the celtic penitential manuals exercised a great influence, John McNeill points out that in the beginning "confession to laymen was not uncommon in the Eastern Church and was occasional in the West; . . . In Ireland women occasionally acted as confessors." It was Columbanus (d. 615), the most important promotor of the penitentials and the practice of confession who "requires laymen guilty of certain offenses to confess to a priest." See *History of the Cure of Souls* (New York: Harper & Row, 1951) pp. 118-125.

tive of the ordained ministry. Some of the most famous spiritual directors in Christian history were women and lay men: Gaston de Renty and Henry Michel Buch, Catherine of Genoa, Catherine of Sienna, Teresa of Avila, Madame Acarie. It was only within the area of spiritual direction that women could acquire authority in the Church as abbess or superior.

While no general theology of spiritual direction has been developed, the nature and function of the spiritual master may be deduced from the Christian economy of salvation. Within its trinitarian structure, the relationship between spiritual master and disciple may be understood as toward the Father, in Christ and through the Spirit. The figure of the spiritual master may then be seen as witness to God, representative of Christ and instrument of the Spirit. The spiritual master realizes the aspect of witnessing to the presence of God in the world through his or her saintly qualities. As representative of Christ, he or she possesses the authority to bring about unconditional surrender in the disciple. As instrument of the Spirit, the spiritual master participates in its sanctifying function. John of the Cross strongly insists upon this instrumental function of the spiritual father:

> the principal agent and guide and mover of souls in this matter is not the director, but the Holy Spirit, Who never loses His care for them; and that they themselves are only instruments to lead the souls in the way of perfection by the faith and the law of God, according to the spirituality that God is giving to each one.[30]

As instrument of the Spirit, the main function of the spiritual father consists in the discernment of Spirits, the *diacrisis*. From the very beginning of the Christian spiritual tradition this has been regarded as the quintessence of spiritual direction. The indispensability of the spiritual master is based upon the inability of the disciple to discern the will of God. One of the most important requirements of the disciple is then a complete manifestation of thoughts.

---

[30] *The Living Flame of Love*, III, 46.

The absolute and unique sovereignty of Christ is the ultimate reference which both legitimizes and limits all forms of authority within the church. Since it is the church as a whole which bears the Spirit of Christ, no individual can lay claim to absolute authority whether over a group or over another individual. The Christian character of spiritual authority is then situated in its refusal of all ultimacy, in its free reference beyond itself to Christ and the church. This is expressed in the Catholic tradition in the free submission of the spiritual master to institutional control.

While the figure of the Christian spiritual master answers to certain general characteristics, its particular status and function may differ according to the particular spirituality and Rule of the different orders. By means of its Rule, the Benedictine notion of the spiritual father-disciple relationship has been formative in the Western monastic tradition. The rule was an attempt to reconcile the idea of the spiritual father which developed in Egypt with that which developed in Cappadocia.[31] The Benedictine Rule thus provides a comprehensive and standard approach of the spiritual father-disciple relationship in the Christian tradition.

The Master-Disciple Relationship in the Rule of Saint Benedict[32]

The Disciple

The Benedictine Rule does not set out any explicit requirements for discipleship. A candidate must possess the desire for a spiritual life, the disposition to live in a community, and the willingness to surrender to the authority of a superior. Humility is not so much the condition as the goal of discipleship, as is illustrated in the image of the twelve steps of humility: "We may call our body and soul the sides of the ladder, into which our

[31] The Egyptian tradition was spread by Cassian and taken over in the *Regula Magistri*, which had the strongest influence upon the Benedictine Rule. Cf. Adelbert De Vogüé, *La Communauté et l'Abbé dans la Règle de Saint Benoît* (Paris: Desclée de Brouwer, 1961) p. 528.

[32] The text used is *The Rule of St. Benedict (RB 1980)* (Collegeville, MN: Liturgical Press, 1981.)

divine vocation has fitted the various steps of humility and discipline as we ascend."[33]

The first step of humility relates the desire to abandon one's own will to the fear of God and his judgment. Extensive reference is made to the Psalms, to the theme of the omniscience of God and to his severe judgment. The second step refers to the example of Christ and to his words: "I have come not to do my own will but the will of him who sent me" (John 6:38). In the third step, the disciple "submits to the superior in all obedience for the love of God, imitating the Lord of whom the apostle says: 'He became obedient, even unto death'" (Phil 2:8).[34] The need for a superior is grounded in the fourth step in the scriptural saying: "You have placed men over our heads" (Ps 65:12). To the superior, the disciple must obey under all, even difficult, unfavorable or unjust conditions.

The fifth step of humility concerns the manifestation of thoughts and the confession of sins. The disciple must be prepared to open himself completely. This presupposes absolute trust in the superior. A humble self-esteem and composure is expected from the disciple in the sixth, seventh, and twelfth steps of humility. Steps nine to eleven deal with the control of speech and laughter. And the eighth step of humility summarizes the different steps in the requirement to do "only what is endorsed by the common rule of the monastery and the example set by superiors."[35]

The Christian emphasis upon humility is based upon the Gospel saying "Whoever exalts himself shall be humbled, and whoever humbles himself shall be exalted" (Luke 14:11; 18:14). This is related to the conception of human nature as finite, limited and sinful:

> Judging himself always guilty on account of his sins, he should consider that he is already at the fearful judgment and constantly say in his heart what the publican in the Gospel said with downcast

[33] *The Rule of St. Benedict* 7.9.
[34] *The Rule of St. Benedict* 7.34.
[35] *The Rule of St. Benedict* 7.55.

eyes: "Lord I am a sinner, not worthy to look to heaven" (Luke 18:13).[36]

The Master

In the Benedictine Rule, the role and authority of the spiritual father are concentrated in the abbot, who is essentially a spiritual father, related to a large number of disciples. The particularities of the communal structure came to demand from the abbot, in addition to purely spiritual qualities, certain administrative skills. These and other responsibilities were often delegated to cellarers, deans and priors. The abbot remained, nonetheless, the one ultimately responsible for all those who have surrendered to his authority.

The abbot is said to "hold the place of Christ in the monastery," *Christi agere vices*.[37] He is thus expected to answer to the highest moral and spiritual standards. From Pachomius to Benedict, and throughout the Western monastic tradition, the qualities of the spiritual father, superior or abbot seem to have hardly changed.[38] These qualities revolve around "goodness of life and wisdom in teaching."[39] A good life is described as being not "excitable, anxious, extreme, obstinate, jealous, or oversuspicious,"[40] but "chaste, temperate, and merciful,"[41] loving and charitable.[42] Discretion is regarded as the "mother of virtues." It is understood as the abbot's ability to adapt to the disposition and the needs of every disciple: "He must so arrange everything that the strong have something to yearn for and the weak nothing

[36] *The Rule of St Benedict* 7.64-65.

[37] *The Rule of St. Benedict* 2.2.

[38] Cf. A. De Vogüé, *La Communauté et l'abbé dans la Règle de Saint Benoît*, p. 111.

[39] *The Rule of St. Benedict* 64.2.

[40] *The Rule of St. Benedict* 64.16.

[41] *The Rule of St. Benedict* 64.9. These are qualities which in the pastoral epistles are required from bishops. See 1 Tim 3:2-4; Tit 1:7-9; 2:2-5.

[42] This is in contrast with the Rule of the Master where the abbot is regarded as more omnipotent and infallible and where severe discipline is emphasized. Cf. A. De Vogüé, *La Communauté et l'abbé dans la Règle de Saint Benoît*, pp. 78-186.

to run from."[43] This involves an equal love for all disciples. The Rule emphasizes that not social difference but only excellence in obedience may justify the stronger affection which the abbot may feel for a disciple:

> The abbot should avoid all favoritism in the monastery. He is not to love one more than another unless he finds someone better in good actions and obedience.[44]

Since monastic life may easily revolve around concerns for practical and material matters, the Rule stipulates that the abbot must remain detached from temporal worries and be focussed only upon the spiritual growth of the members of the community:

> Above all, he must not show too great concern for the fleeting and temporal things of this world, neglecting and treating lightly the welfare of those entrusted to him.[45]

While the spiritual fathers in the Egyptian desert were conspicuous for their reluctance to speak, the abbot of the monastic communities is expected to teach. He must therefore be "learned in divine law" and have mastered the *doctrina*, the whole of doctrinal and practical ordinances which apply to monastic life.[46] The abbot must be thoroughly versed in the scriptures, and never "teach or decree, or command anything that would deviate from the Lord's instructions."[47] This presupposes not so much biblical expertise as a personal integration of the gospel or of the experience of Jesus Christ.

While the abbot may be aware of his responsibility and authority, the Rule of St. Benedict emphasizes that he must also remain conscious of his own weakness.[48] Humility is a quality required

---

[43] *The Rule of St. Benedict* 64.19.

[44] *The Rule of St. Benedict* 2.16-17.

[45] *The Rule of St. Benedict* 2.33. He is here reminded of the scriptural passages "Seek first the kingdom of God and his justice, and all these things will be given to you as well" (Matt 6:33) and "Those who fear him lack nothing"(Ps 33:10).

[46] *The Rule of St. Benedict* 64.9.

[47] *The Rule of St. Benedict* 2.4.

[48] *The Rule of St. Benedict* 64.13.

not only of the disciple, but also of the spiritual father. The abbot must first of all himself submit to the stipulations of the Rule. The admonition of Jesus to his disciples "not to be called rabbis" was in reaction to the pride and hypocrisy of "scribes and Pharisees who sit on Moses' seat" and to "blind guides" (Matt 23:2-36). Both the teaching and the example of Christ emphasize that the one who is highest of all should behave as the most humble of all. Spiritual authority within the Christian tradition is, moreover, always derived and related to the Father as the absolute source of all authority. Terrence Kardong points out that "just as Christ claims no absolute authority apart from the Father, so too, the abbot, as represented by Benedict, has no independent claim to power and wisdom."[49] As shepherd, the abbot is not the owner, but merely the caretaker of the sheep. This is expressed in the account which he must give of his deeds to God:

> Once in office, the abbot must keep constantly in mind the nature of the burden he has received, and remember to whom he will have to give account of his stewardship (Luke 16:2).[50]

The Benedictine Rule took over the theology of the abbot based on the double hierarchy of church and monastery which was developed in the Rule of the Master. The title of *doctor* which applies automatically to the ordained minister was here extended to include the non-sacramental tradition of authority. The charismatic and the sacramental authority were regarded as two complementary lines of development, based upon the same source. Scriptural texts dealing with apostolic succession were then applied to the abbot just as they were to the bishop.[51]

In the Rule of St. Benedict, the sacramental and the charismatic authorities became more intertwined. While a sacramental ordination was not required to be elected abbot, the local bishop

---

[49] Terrence Kardong, *The Benedictines* (Wilmington, DE: Glazier, 1988) p. 124.

[50] *The Rule of St. Benedict* 64.7.

[51] Matt 16:19, 18:8; Luke 9:1, 10:16.

is called upon to oversee the electorial process, to interfere in case of conspiracy, and, eventually, to install a new abbot.[52] This increased the dependence of the abbot upon the authority of office and somewhat curtailed the freedom which is essential to the function of the spiritual father and which the early Desert Fathers sought to safeguard. Ordained ministers, however, can lay no claim upon a special rank in the monastery. They are in the first place monks, subject to the authority of the abbot.

The Master-Disciple Relationship

> Furthermore, anyone who receives the name of abbot is to lead his disciples by a twofold teaching: he must point out to them all that is good and holy more by example than by words, proposing the commandments of the Lord to receptive disciples with words, but demonstrating God's instructions to the stubborn and the dull by living example.[53]

Despite the communal structure, the spiritual relationship between the abbot and disciples remained, according to de Vogüé, constitutive of Benedictine communities and the core of Benedictine life and spirituality.[54] While liturgical services came to occupy an important role in monastic life — chapters eight to twenty of the Rule deal with the liturgy, — the main discipline of the monk consists of obedience to the abbot. The entire Rule has been regarded as a classic work on obedience.[55] It is both the cause and the expression of the essential quality of the disciple, humility: "The first step of humility is unhesitating obedience."[56] The desire to follow the will of another rather than one's own is based upon the fear of deviating in the face of the all-knowing

[52] *The Rule of St. Benedict* 64.3-6.

[53] *The Rule of St. Benedict* 2.11-12.

[54] Adelbert De Vogüé, *La Communauté et l'abbé dans la Règle de Saint Benoît*, p. 533.

[55] Jean Leclercq, "Religious Obedience According to the Rule of St Benedict" *The American Benedictine Review* 16 (1965) 183-189.

[56] In chapter seven, verse ten, however, it is said that "the first step of humility, then, is that a man keeps the fear of God always before his eyes"

God. It requires, however, absolute trust in the abbot as the representative of Christ. Hence the abbot is directly responsible for the obedience of the disciples:

> Let the abbot always remember that at the fearful judgment of God, not only his teaching but also his disciples' obedience will come under scrutiny.[57]

The understanding of obedience in the Benedictine tradition is Christocentric. Obedience to the abbot may be as *to* Christ, and *as* Christ to the Father. Christ may thus be seen as the one who must be obeyed or as the model of obedience. In the first case the abbot is seen as the representative or the vicar of Christ, his commands being in conformity with the message of Christ and with the will of God.[58] In the second, the emphasis is upon Christ as the model of unconditional obedience.[59] For the disciple, the abbot or spiritual master may thus be seen, on the one hand, as the objective authority who must be obeyed (in transmitting the word of God) and, on the other hand, as the subjective model of obedience (in representing Christ).

The Benedictine Rule discusses not only the principle of obedience, but also the manner in which the disciple is to obey. The orders of the abbot are to be followed "promptly as if the command came from God himself."[60] The disciple must obey swiftly and without hesitation because "if the disciple obeys grudgingly and grumbles, not only aloud but also in his heart, then even though he carries out the order, his action will not be accepted with favor by God, who sees that he is grumbling in his heart."[61] Unless obedience is given freely and gladly, it has no

[57] *The Rule of St. Benedict* 2.6.

[58] This objective view of obedience is based upon the words "whoever listens to you hears me" (Luke 10:16).

[59] The New Testament passages referred to in this context are John 6:38, "I have come not to do my will but the will of him who sent me," and Phil 2:8, "He became obedient even to death."

[60] *The Rule of St. Benedict* 5.4.

[61] *The Rule of St. Benedict* 5.18.

value, and may even generate the opposite effect.[62] Of those who obey with the right attitude, however, the Rule says:

> They no longer live by their own judgement, giving in to their whims and appetites; rather they walk according to another's decisions and directions, choosing to live in monasteries and to have an abbot above them. Men of this resolve unquestionably conform to the saying of the Lord: "I have come not to do my own will but the will of him who sent me" (John 6:38).[63]

The second, and more important way of teaching prescribed in the Benedictine Rule is through example. The abbot must live in accord with his own teaching. He must not keep himself separate from or beyond the monks, but live and work with the other monks, so that there is always an example to follow. Imitation was believed to be the most effective way of learning. In the Rule of St. Benedict obedience is regarded as a form of imitation of Christ: "The third step of humility is that a man submits to his superior in all obedience for the love of God, imitating the Lord of whom the Apostle says: He became obedient even unto death (Phil 2:8)."[64] The disciple is told to do nothing but follow the example set by superiors.[65] This imitation was understood not as mere copying or reproducing, but as personal integration and assimilation of the example and the teaching of the abbot.

Paul's expression "Be imitators of me just as I imitate Christ" (1 Cor 11:1), on the one hand, emphasizes the necessity of the spiritual father — the imitation of Christ is necessarily mediated — and, on the other hand, relativizes his role. The disciple is invited to imitate the spiritual father only in so far as he imitates Christ. The end or purpose of obedience is the personal discovery of the will of God as manifested through the Spirit. An important responsibility of the spiritual master is then the adaptation of the

---

[62] "He will have no reward for service of this kind; on the contrary, he will incur punishment for grumbling, unless he changes for the better and makes amends." *The Rule of St. Benedict* 5.17-19.

[63] *The Rule of St. Benedict* 5.12.

[64] *The Rule of St. Benedict* 7.34.

[65] *The Rule of St. Benedict* 7.55.

teaching to the different dispositions and needs of the particular disciples:

> This means that he must vary with circumstances, threatening and coaxing by turns, stern as a taskmaster, devoted and tender as only a father can be. With the undisciplined and the restless he will use firm argument; with the obedient and docile and patient, he will appeal for greater virtue; but as for the negligent and disdainful, we charge him to use reproof and rebuke.[66]

Once the disciple has become capable of discerning and surrendering to the direction of the Spirit, the guidance of an external authority becomes superfluous, and the disciple may become a hermit or a spiritual father in his own right.[67] Within the Christian tradition, however, the state of perfect obedience is believed to be unattainable in this life. There is always the risk of relapsing.[68] In the Rule of St. Benedict, therefore, there is no mention of a term or an end to the spiritual father-disciple relationship. Obedience is regaded as a lifelong commitment, an end in itself.[69]

[66] *The Rule of St. Benedict* 2.24-25. This resonates Paul's admonition: "and we would urge you, brothers, to admonish the careless, encourage the faint-hearted, support the weak, and to be very patient with them all" (1 Thess 5:14). If all else fails, the Rule does not hesitate to prescribe even physical punishment: ". . . but those who are evil or stubborn, arrogant or disobedient, he can curb only by blows or some other physical punishment at the first offence" (2.28).

[67] De Vogüé points out that in understanding cenobitic life as a preparation for the life of a hermit, Cassian saw the master-disciple relationship and the discipline of obedience to the spiritual father as a means (*Inst.* 5,4,1). See *La Communauté et l'abbé dans la Règle de Saint Benoît*, pp. 278-279.

[68] "We are in this participation in the obedience of Christ, beneficiaries as much as cooperators. Hence, we may never completely isolate ourselves of what we have called 'the obedience of the perfect,' as if it would concern a free and disinterested imitation of the pure love of Jesus for his Father and for the people. The consideration of an illness to be healed, of a possible return to the evil which must be conjured must be part of the *bonum obedientiae*." See Adelbert De Vogüé, *La communauté et l'abbé dans la Règle de Saint Benoît*, p. 284.

[69] The vow of obedience to a spiritual director of people far advanced on the spiritual path, such as Teresa of Avila and Madame de Chantal, may also be understood within this context.

The originality of the Rule of St. Benedict is that not only the abbot, but any other brother of the community is to be respected and obeyed:

> Obedience is a blessing to be shown by all, not only to the abbot, but also to one another as brothers, since we know that it is by way of obedience that we go to God.[70]

The principle of mutual obedience was based upon the belief in the salutary function of the mortification of one's own will, but also on the belief that God may reveal his will through any channel: "the Lord often reveals what is better to the younger."[71] It thus enlarged the possibility of enjoying the fruits of obedience, not only in a subjective sense, but also objectively by multiplying the voices through which God may be heard. Though mutual obedience in principle applied to all, it was in practice organized in terms of a hierarchy of seniority. The younger monks obeyed their elders.

Not only the monks, but also the abbot himself was called to listen to the suggestions of other monks in matters of importance.[72] It is here that the influence of Basil and Augustine becomes apparent. Compared to the Rule of the Master, the authority of the abbot seems to wane. The need for humility of the abbot is emphasized, not so much as a sign of superiority, but as the expression of real fallibility. The abbot is no longer regarded as omniscient, all-powerful, infallible, and independent of the official authority. He must be open to learn and to submit to the possible manifestation of the will of God through the whole community or through any member of it. While in the Rule of the Master it was the dying abbot who appointed his successor, the right or duty to elect and install a new abbot came to fall upon the community and the official hierarchy in the Benedictine Rule.[73] The abbot is thus placed not so much above

---

[70] *The Rule of St Benedict (RB 1980)* p. 293.

[71] *The Rule of St. Benedict* 3.3.

[72] *The Rule of St Benedict* 3.

[73] The Benedictine Rule is vague on the exact procedure of election. It is said

as ahead of his monks. Although it is still the relationship between spiritual father and disciple which constitutes the monastic community, the Benedictine Rule allowed more institutional control, and the community came to be regarded as a society of brothers where each plays a role in the sanctification of the other.

Conclusion

The juxtaposition of the master-disciple relationship in the Hindu and the Christian traditions points to a number of formal and functional equivalencies. The qualities which characterize the spiritual master are in both traditions self-control, tranquility or equanimity, and charity or compassion.[74] A "blameless life" (Shankara) or "goodness of life" (St. Benedict) is the absolute moral prerequisite. The role of the spiritual master is also similar in the two traditions. It is not so much explicitly directive as corrective. It consists of discerning the thoughts and the state of spiritual development of the disciple and of guiding the disciple to the discovery of the inner guide. The self-surrender which is the goal of discipleship is brought about in both the Hindu and the Christian tradition through unconditional obedience to and unswerving service of the master.[75] From the similarities in the qualities of the spiritual master, in the requirements from the

---

that he should be "selected either by the whole community acting unanimously in the fear of God, or by some part of the community, no matter how small, which possesses sounder judgement" (64.1). The ecclesiastical authority is called upon to interfere only if an unworthy person has been appointed. Later, other measures against the possible abuse of power, or appointment of a wrong person were taken. While originally the status and office of abbot was permanent and perpetual, a system of visitators and the possibility of temporary abbots came to be implemented.

[74] Compare the *Thousand Teachings* 2.1.6, which states that the guru must be "free from faults such as pride, deceit, trickery, wickedness, fraud, jealousy, falsehood, egotism, self-interest, and so forth" with the *Rule of St. Benedict* 64.16 where the abbot must not be "excitable, anxious, extreme, obstinate, jealous or oversuspicious."

[75] Although the latter is more emphasized in the Hindu tradition.

disciple, and in the ways of transmission, it may be concluded that the spiritual master-disciple relationship is an archetype which transcends all particular religious traditions. This argument may be strengthened by the fact that spiritual masters seem to manifest a certain degree of independence with regard to their respective traditions. Disciples from one tradition, moreover, often feel attracted toward masters from a different religious tradition, and there seems to exist a profound understanding among spiritual masters of different religions. From this perspective, the term guru may be applied to the Christian as well as to the Hindu spiritual master.

The understanding of the nature of the spiritual master and of the meaning of surrender differ, nonetheless, in the Hindu and Christian traditions. In the Christian tradition the need for humility and self-effacement is based upon a sense of human sinfulness and finality while in the tradition of Advaita Vedanta, it is based upon the idea of the illusory nature of a separate and self-subsistent ego. While in Christianity humility is the answer to the absolute transcendence of God, humility has no referent or object in Advaita Vedanta. It has been emphasized that in Christianity, surrender "is not the means to contemplation, but the labor of faith."[76]

The ultimate religious experience which the master represents and to which the disciple aspires is also understood in very different terms in the Advaitic and in the Christian tradition. In Advaita Vedanta, the experience is expressed in terms of the not-twoness of atman and Brahman, as the realization of one's own divinity, of the transcendence of all dualism between good and evil, God and man, and so forth. The outcome is a sense of absolute autonomy. In the Christian tradition, on the other hand, the experience is understood in relational terms as the experience of union with God in which the radical transcendence of God

---

[76] Antoon Vergote, "A Psychological Approach to Humility in the Rule of St. Benedict," *The American Benedictine Review* 39 (1988) p. 417. In the same article, however, he defines humility as "a universal virtue identical with detachment from self in all domains" (pp. 406-407).

and the uniqueness of the experience of Christ are maintained. Following this experience, the sense of personal fallibility and dependence upon God's grace persists.

Both the Hindu and the Christian spiritual master are said to lead the disciple to the inner master. But this inner master is in the tradition of Advaita Vedanta understood as the *atman*, the real Self, which is not different from the absolute, while in the Christian tradition, the inner guide is believed to be the Holy Spirit, which, though working in the individual, remains transcendent.

With the conception of the ultimate religious experience and realization, the understanding of the nature and status of the spiritual master differs in the Hindu and Christian tradition. Within the tradition of Advaita Vedanta, the master is not different from the absolute. There is no authority beyond that of the one who has attained realization. The spiritual master is thus totally autonomous. In the Christian tradition, the spiritual master is understood to be no more than a representative of Christ and an instrument of the Spirit. He does not operate on the basis of his own power or perfection. Absolute authority is concentrated in Jesus Christ and in the Church as the continuation of Christ on earth. While the absolute authority necessary to bring about total surrender is ontological in the Hindu tradition, it is understood as merely functional in Christianity.[77] While the Hindu master-disciple relationship operates between the shores of total dependency and absolute autonomy, the Christian spiritual master and disciple find themselves on the same shore, moving, one maybe ahead of the other, toward the absolute. Since the state of perfection is never fully attained, the Christian spiritual master always remains in the first place a disciple, and the need for obedience is never completely overcome. Both spiritual master and disciple are, moreover, held to obedience to the authority of office.

---

[77] This means that in the Christian tradition, the spiritual father never assumes the authority which he exercises.

While the formal and functional equivalencies between spiritual masters in different traditions are obvious, the philosphical or doctrinal differences are equally clear. The comparison makes possible further reflection upon the theological and institutional implications of introducing the Hindu conception of guru within Christianity.

II

To Jesus Christ through the Guru:
The Experience and Reflections of Abhishiktananda

> The real religious or theological task, if you will, begins when the two views meet head-on inside oneself, when dialogue prompts genuine religious pondering, and even a religious crisis, at the bottom of man's heart; when interpersonal dialogue turns into intrapersonal soliloquy.[1]

The texts from the Advaita Vedanta tradition of Shankara and from the Benedictine tradition have been discussed, not only because of their eminent position within Hinduism and Christianity respectively, but also because of the role which they have come to play in the Hindu-Christian dialogue. Several of the pioneers of Catholic ashrams were Benedictine monks. It is the tradition of Advaita Vedanta that they sought to integrate and the first Catholic ashram attempted to represent a synthesis of the Benedictine Rule and the way of life and thought of Advaita Vedanta. It is from the surrender of a Benedictine monk to gurus of the tradition of Advaita Vedanta that the most radical reflections on Christ as guru have emerged.

One of the great pioneers of the inculturation of Christianity in India is the French Benedictine monk Henri Le Saux, or the Hindu-style sannyasin Abhishiktananda (1910-1973.) Long before the Second Vatican Council and the development of theories on inculturation, he came to the realization that Christianity urgently needed to integrate the Indian spiritual tradition, not only formally, but also philosophically, and not only to appeal more to the Indian soul, but also to become itself enriched. So he attempted to return to the very source of the Indian spiritual tradition, to the experience of the ancient seers and of the Hindu

---

[1] Raimundo Panikkar, *The Intrareligious Dialogue* (New York: Paulist, 1978) p. 10.

gurus whose lineages link the present with that originating experience. The only traditional access to that experience is through the Hindu guru.

He came to believe that personal experience was not only the only way to understand the figure of the guru, but also that it could become a hermeneutical key for understanding the mystery of Christ:

> In fact nobody can know what a guru is, or have an understanding of the mystery of Christ and of his intimacy with him, which may be a spiritual aid, unless he had himself the experience of the guru-shishya relationship.[2]

His life struggle to reconcile his understanding of Advaita Vedanta with Christian theology and his experience of Hindu gurus with his faith in Jesus Christ reflects the theological difficulties involved in using the Hindu notion of the spiritual father within a Christian context.

Abhishiktananda's approach was not systematic or methodical; it was not so much an intellectual exercise as an existential struggle. Hence, it is his *Journal* which, as the reflection of this struggle, remains of particular relevance for the Hindu-Christian dialogue.[3] As Raimundo Panikkar, the leading theologian in the Hindu-Christian dialogue and personal friend of Abhishiktananda, pointed out in his last letter to Abhishiktananda: "the internal contradictions and rending conflicts (*'déchirements'* you called them) that beset you for decades helped us to see and to discern far more than any cheap synthesis or stubborn refusal could possibly have done. . . Our gratitude is for your life, more than anything else."[4] Abhishiktananda knew that his reflections

---

[2] Henri Le Saux, *Intériorité et révélation*, p. 246.

[3] H. Le Saux, *La montée au fond du coeur. Le journal intime du moine Chrétien - sannyasi Hindou 1948-1973*. (Introduction and notes by Raimundo Panikkar). (Paris: O.E.I.L., 1986). This work will be further abbreviated as *Journal*, with mention of the year in which the citation appears (so as to follow the development in his thought.)

[4] R. Panikkar, "Letter to Abhisiktananda — On Eastern-Western Monasticism" *Studies in Formative Spirituality* 3 (1982) p. 430.

or statements were daring and often hard to reconcile with traditional theology and Christian orthodoxy. In his journal's entry to the year 1952 he writes: "May any theologian who happens to read these pages kindly look at these 'statements' as no more than working hypotheses." But he saw his role, as James Stuart points out, in "pursuing a given hypothesis to its conclusion, however strange it may seem, in the hope that in the darkness light might dawn and new paths open up."[5]

Abhishiktananda's reflections thus confront us directly with the theological implications of understanding Jesus Christ through the Hindu category of the guru. From the journal notes, publications, and personal sources of information,[6] we can try to reconstruct Abhishiktananda's experience with Hindu gurus, to systematize his reflections on Christ as guru, and to show the connection between the two.

[5] From the as yet unpublished manuscript by James Stuart which is a biography of Abhishiktananda's life on the basis of his letters.

[6] In two trips to India, in December 1987 and January-February 1989, I met with many different people who had known Abhishiktananda personally and who elaborated upon both his experience and his thought: Bettina Bäumer (Varanasi) now president of the Abhishiktananda society; Odette Baumer-Despeigne, official trustee of the unpublished letters and manuscripts of Abhishiktananda; the Anglican Father James Stuart (Delhi) who has been working through all of Abhishiktananda's letters for the publication of a biography which is about to be published, the manuscript of which he was so kind to let me work through; the sisters of the Sacred Heart Vandana (Rishikesh) and Sara Grant (Poona) whose vision and foundation of Christian ashrams was largely inspired by Abhishiktananda; the Jesuit Father Ignatius Hirudayam (Madras) whose ashram Abhishiktananda officially opened in 1968; the Benedictrine Father Dominique (Bangalore), one of the few Christians of whom Abhishiktananda speaks with the greatest respect in his journal, Father Ishvaraprasad from the Indian Missionary Society (Varanasi) who tried to start the Pilot-seminary or ashram for seminarians which was the brain-child of Abhishiktananda; Father Nambiaparambil (secretary of the Indian Bishops Conference, Delhi); Father Francis Mahieu who lived for a year with Abhishiktananda in Saccidananda ashram, and is now guru of Kurisumala ashram in Kerala, Father Bede Griffiths who took over Saccidananda ashram after Abhishiktananda left in 1968; and the theologians Jacques Dupuis and Raimundo Panikkar.

CHAPTER ONE

Abhishiktananda and Hindu Gurus

We should simply thank God in deepest humility when we
happen to meet such a sage or saint, no matter to which
dharma he may outwardly belong, and be open to accept with
open heart his witness and message.[1]

Henri Le Saux was born in 1910 in Brittany. At the age of
nineteen, he became a Benedictine monk of the abbey of Kergo-
nan. His public life began with his arrival in India in 1948. He
joined another French priest, Jules Monchanin (1895-1957) with
whom he shared the ideal of starting a religious community which
would integrate the best of the Western monastic and the Eastern
contemplative traditions. This materialized in what they conceived of as an Indian Benedictine Ashram, called *Saccidananda
ashram*.[2] The two priests lived an ascetic life in the style of the
Hindu sannyasis, and adopted Indian names. Henri Le Saux
became *Abhishikteshvarananda*, "he whose joy is the blessing of
the Lord," and Jules Monchanin was called *Parama Arubi Ananda*, "supreme formless joy."[3]

It was not the popular sectarian traditions of Hinduism, but
the philosophical tradition of Advaita Vedanta of Shankara
which Monchanin and Abhishiktananda admired and attempted
to integrate.[4] While in India Advaita Vedanta is generally seen as

---

[1] Abhishiktananda, *Saccidananda* (Delhi: I.S.P.C.K., 1974) p. 19.

[2] The blueprint for this ashram may be found in *A Benedictine Ashram*.
(Tiruchirapalli: St. Joseph's Industrial School, 1951).

[3] Both names appear to be non-sectarian, Indian and sanscritic in the very
general sense of the term. While Le Saux from then on was generally known as
Abhishiktananda (or also Abhi, or Abhishikta) Monchanin was, and is, rarely
referred to by his Indian name.

[4] Advaita Vedanta is the Indian tradition which has become most popular

the most eminent philosophical system, it is nevertheless studied
by a small minority, and practiced in its pure form only in the
mathas, in the monasteries of the ten monastic orders allegedly
founded by Shankara. As a radically non-dualistic system, it is
philosophically most at odds with the Judeo-Christian tradition.

Monchanin and Abhishiktananda differed from one another on
the way in which the tradition of Advaita Vedanta could be
integrated within the Christian tradition.[5] Abhishiktananda was
the more radical of the two. While Monchanin held to the theory
that non-Christian religions find their fulfillment in Christianity,[6]
Abhishiktananda viewed the values and truths present in the
tradition of Advaita Vedanta not merely as partial and provisio-
nal, but as prophetic, and ready to transform Christianity.[7] He
believed that "the Pleroma of Christ will never be the fullness
that it is intended to be, either in the individual believer or in the
Church at large, so long as that experience [of advaita or non-
duality] has not been integrated by Christianity."[8] The only
access to that experience would be the Hindu guru:

> This experience of self-realization cannot be transmitted through
> words. One can only point into the direction, suggest it as do the
> Upanishads. It consists of an awakening, and only a competent
> guru is able to bring about that awakening in the disciple.[9]

among Westerners. This is mostly because of a personal and popularized version
of Advaita Vedanta, presented by many a Hindu Guru in the West starting with
Vivekananda who, at the beginning of the century, instigated the foundation of
Vedanta centers in the United States.

[5] Abhishiktananda often referred to Monchanin as his Christian guru. Cf.
Journal, introductory comments by Panikkar to the year 1957, p. 242. On the
other hand, no explicit guru-disciple relationship seems to have developed between
Monchanin and Abhishiktananda.

[6] See below, pp. 104-108.

[7] "Dieu conserve comme prophète — à côté — les non-catholiques, les non-
chrétiens, jusqu'à ce que l'Eglise soit prête à intégrer les valeurs représentées par
eux."*Journal*, 1963, p. 317.

[8] Abhishiktananda, *Saccidananda: A Christian Approach to Advaitic Experience* (Delhi: I.S.P.C.K., 1974) p. 71.

[9] H. Le Saux, *Intériorité et révélation* (Paris: Présence, 1982) p. 240.

His desire to immerse himself in the experience of non-duality thus brought Abhishiktananda in relationship with different guru-figures: the famous Hindu saint Ramana Maharshi, the holy mountain Arunachala, the living master Gnanananda, and Dr. Mehta. All of these figures revealed different aspects or modalities of the guru to him.

Ramana Maharshi

Within the first years of his stay in India, Abhisiktananda was introduced to Ramana Maharshi, the sage of the holy mountain Arunachala. By this time Ramana Maharshi had become very famous, attracting large crowds of disciples. Especially during *darshan*, which is understood as the merit-generating vision of the divine form, masses gathered in veneration or worship of the guru. Upon his first visit to the ashram of Ramana, Abhishiktananda's Christian sense revolted against the expressions of veneration and plain idolization of a human being.[10] Reflecting later upon this event, he states that he "did not know the language and in addition he had not penetrated sufficiently within to be capable of tuning in directly to the mysterious language of silence."[11]

Silence was Ramana Maharshi's distinctive way of teaching.[12] If the guru remains silent, he believed, "the seeker's mind gets purified by itself."[13] This is further illustrated by reference to the *Dakshinamurti*, the South-facing form of Shiva:

> What did he do? He sat silent. The disciples appeared before him. He maintained silence, and their doubts were dispelled, which means they lost their individual identities... The guru is quiet and peace prevails in all. His silence is vaster and more emphatic than all the scriptures put together.[14]

---

[10] *Journal*, p. 22.

[11] Abhishiktananda, *Guru and Disciple* (London: SPCK, 1974) p. 26.

[12] Ramana even became prototypical of the silence of the guru. See *Avec ou sans Maître* (Paris: Dervy, 1987) pp. 15-16.

[13] Arthur Osborne, *The Teachings of Ramana Maharshi* (London: Rider, 1962) p. 107.

[14] Quoted by A. Osborne, *The Teachings of Ramana Maharshi*, p. 102.

The silence of the guru was understood as a way for the disciples to detach themselves from the external form of the guru and discover the inner guru. Arthur Osborne points out that "Bhagavan initiated his disciples through silence, or in a dream when at a distance, or by look when they were in his bodily presence; but he did not call them disciples or give the formal initiation that postulates duality."[15] Among the few words spoken by the guru was the celebrated "who are you?" question intended to lead the disciple to self-discovery:

> There is only one thing to do: ponder into the depth of your Self. If you do it right, you will find the answer to all your questions.[16]

Ramana Maharsi thus understood the guru to be an internal reality in which there is "no difference between God, Guru and Self."[17] The awareness of the guru as an external reality is based upon the illusion of duality. "Because you identify yourself with the body, you think the Guru too is the body. You are not the body, nor is the Guru. You are the Self and so is the Guru."[18] Ramana Maharshi thus understood a guru to be:

> one who at all times abides in the profound depths of the Self. He never sees any difference between himself and others and is quite free from the idea that he is the Enlightened or the Liberated One, while those around him are in bondage or the darkness of ignorance. His self-possession can never be shaken under any circumstances and he is never perturbed.[19]

Abhishiktananda soon came to see in the person of Ramana Maharshi the essence of guruhood. Though irritated with the expressions of devotion of disciples, Abhishiktananda was immediately captivated by the smile of Ramana which he describes as "so full of goodness that one cannot forget it."[20] It was during

---

[15] A. Osborne, *The Teachings of Ramana Maharshi*, p. 101.
[16] Quoted by Paul Brunton, *L'Inde Secrète* (Paris: Payot, 1949) p. 148.
[17] A. Osborne, *The Teachings of Ramana Maharshi*, p. 99.
[18] Quoted by A. Osborne, *The Teachings of Ramana Maharshi*, p. 101.
[19] A. Osborne, *The Teachings of Ramana Maharshi*, p. 97.
[20] *Journal*, p. 22.

his second visit to Ramana that he suddenly felt a "call to the within which seemed to well up from the very depth of his consciousness, merged as it was in the primordial mystery."[21] This experience may be regarded as Abhishiktananda's initiation into the Indian tradition of Advaita Vedanta:

> Before my mind could even grasp or express it, the intimate aura of this Sage had been perceived by something in me, in the depth of my Self. Unknown harmonies awakened in my heart... In this Sage of Arunachala and of this time, it was the unique Sage of the eternal India which appeared to me; it was the unbroken lineage of sages, of renouncers, of seers; it was the very soul of India which penetrated into the depth of my own soul and entered into a mysterious communion with her. It was a call which shattered everything, which dissolved everything, which opened wide an abyss.[22]

Ramana Maharshi died very shortly after this first encounter, but Abhishiktananda continued to be drawn to the place where the presence of the Maharshi was felt. His disciples believed that "the Guru may continue to give guidance after the death of the body, when no longer in human form."[23] For many this meant continuing the *puja* of Ramana at his tomb, and meditating in the hall where he was once physically present. For Abhishiktananda, this meant going back to the source, to the origin of the very experience of Ramana, to the guru of his guru, Arunachala.

Arunachala

> There is a ruggedness about the scene. Boulders lie as though scattered by a giant hand. Dry thorn and cactus fences, sun-parched fields, small hills eroded into gaunt shapes; and yet huge shady trees along the dusty road, and here and there, near tank or well,

---

[21] Abhishiktananda, *Guru and Disciple* (London: SPCK, 1974.)

[22] Abhishiktananda, *Souvenirs d'Arunachala* (Paris: Epi, 1978) p. 27.

[23] A. Osborne, *The Teachings of Ramana Maharshi*, pp. 107-110. Osborne relates that even after Ramana's *Mahasamadhi* (leaving the body), "everywhere in the ashram his Presence is felt... As the devotees sit there in meditation it is the same as when they sat before him in the hall, the same power, the same subtlety of guidance." In *Ramana Maharshi and the Path of Self-Knowledge*, p. 190.

the vivid green of paddy fields. And rising up out of this rough beauty, the hill of Arunachala.[24]

Arunachala, the sacred "mountain of light" in the heart of Tamil-Nadu, has from ancient times been a home for many a solitary seeker, mystic or saint. It has been regarded as the very hierophany of the god Shiva. While temples are often scattered over sacred mountains, this mountain is itself regarded as a temple. The crowds do not climb the hill; they reverently walk around it from east to west. The nine mile long walk is done barefoot and at the different shrines pilgrims prostrate, hold pujas and sing hymns.

The circumambulation of Arunachala, the *pradakshina*, became one of the main devotional practices of Ramana Maharshi and his followers. It was to be done reverently and slowly, "like a pregnant queen in her ninth month." Ramana Maharshi, who is usually said to have had no guru, referred to Arunachala as his guru. He composed the *Five Hymns to Sri Arunachala* as devotional songs, reflecting the attitude of longing for union with the guru, for merging in the divine silence:

> Ocean of nectar, full of Grace, engulfing the universe in Thy Splendor, Oh Arunachala, the Supreme! Be Thou the Sun and open the lotus of my heart in Bliss.... He who turns inward with untroubled mind to search where the consciousness of "I" arises, realizes the Self and rests in Thee, Oh Arunachala! as a river when it merges in the Ocean.... He who dedicates his mind to Thee and, seeing Thee, always beholds the universe as Thy form, who at all times glorifies Thee and loves Thee as none other than the Self, he is the Master without peer, being one with Thee, Oh Arunachala! and lost in Thy Bliss.[25]

For Ramana, Arunachala represented the very principle of non-duality:

> In the recesses of the lotus-shaped heart of all, from Vishnu downwards, there shines as Absolute Consciousness the Paramat-

[24] A. Osborne, *Ramana Maharshi and the Path of Self-Knowledge* (London: Rider, 1954) p. 47.

[25] Quoted by A. Osborne, *Ramana Maharshi and the Path of Self-Knowledge*, pp. 173-174.

man (Supreme Spirit) who is the same as Arunachala or Ramana. When the mind melts with love of him and reaches the innermost recess of the heart wherein he abides as the Beloved the subtle eye of Absolute Consciousness opens and reveals himself as pure Knowledge.[26]

Abhishiktananda also felt a powerful attraction toward Arunachala. In the caves of the sacred mountain he felt a happiness and peace as never before. This he attributes to "the sages who have lived here before and who have impregnated the rocks with their inner life."[27] He later wrote to a friend: "There were times there (in the caves of Arunachala) that were so high. And this was vastly deeper than I thought at the time. Words that I wrote in those days were not fully understood until very long afterwards."[28] Abhishiktananda also composed several poems or hymns to Arunachala which he now depicts as a fire consuming him, then as a quiet ocean of peace — the two aspects of the God Shiva, dancing destroyer and quiet yogi.[29] His experience of Arunachala strengthens Abhishiktananda's understanding of the guru as an inner reality, and of the external guru as a mere projection of the inner guru:

> What do the deficiencies of the cave of Arunachala matter. It is no more than a way which the self, the deepest ground of my being, chooses to reveal itself to my present consciousness.[30]

Abhishiktananda's own experience of Arunachala drew him nearer to Ramana. It was the sacred mountain which taught him the secret of silence: "In silence, you taught me silence, o Arunachala. You who never leave your silence."[31] "Whoever immerses himself in silence will have become that very silence."[32]

---

[26] A. Osborne, *Ramana Maharshi and the Path of Self-Knowledge*, p. 50.

[27] *Journal*, 1953, p. 86.

[28] Quoted by James Stuart in "Sri Ramana Maharshi and Abhishiktananda" *Vidyajyoti* 44 (1980) p. 170.

[29] *Journal*, 1952, p. 56. The heat of asceticism, *tapas*, and the power or energy released by this, also called *tapas*, is an ageold Indian notion which is especially associated with the god Shiva.

[30] *Journal*, 1955, p. 152.

[31] *Journal*, 1952, p. 54 an 56.

[32] *Journal*, 1953, p. 108.

Arunachala and Ramana Maharshi merged in Abhishiktananda's conception of the guru. He comes to regard the holy mountain as his place of birth, his *mulagarbha*: "reborn in truth at Arunachala under the guidance of the Maharshi."[33] This experience of rebirth he understands as his true meeting with Ramana Maharshi which "took place on a plane that has nothing in common with any visual, auditory or psychic phenomena whatever — literally at the one level where Ramana can always be truly met."[34] Abhishiktananda thus comes to understand Ramana, not as the external, physical guru, but as "his own depth of being."[35]

Gnanananda

It was given to Swami Abhishiktananda (Henri Le Saux, O.S.B.), a French Benedictine monk, to lovingly make an irresistable call to the Christian to hearken to the gentle summons of the spirit mediated to him by the ancient sages of India and in recent times by Swami Gnanananda.[36]

It was by sheer chance that Abhishiktananda was introduced to Gnanananda, the sage who shortly after the death of Ramana Maharshi settled at Tirukoilur, about ten miles from Arunachala. Accompanying a friend who went to pay a visit to the sage, he was at first despondent, anticipating that "they would have to listen patiently to the exaggerated praises with which his disciples would extol him, as happens almost everywhere in the ashram world of India, and make at least a gesture of being interested in the spiritual platitudes that he would no doubt utter..."[37] He was

[33] *Journal*, 1955, p. 143.

[34] Quoted by J. Stuart, "Sri Ramana Maharshi and Abhishiktananda," *Vidyajyoti* 44 (1980) p. 171.

[35] *Journal*, 1953, p. 92.

[36] *Sadguru Gnanananda* (Bombay: Bharata Vidya Bavan, 1978) p. vii. This volume composed by disciples of Gnanananda was dedicated to Abhishiktananda, which seems to illustrate that paradoxically the disciple became the source of legitimation of the guru.

[37] Abhishiktananda, *Guru and Disciple: Gnanananda, a Sage of the East and The Mountain of the Lord* (London: S.P.C.K., 1979) p. 21. This has become one of the most popular and influential of Abhishiktananda's works, and is now in the process of being retranslated.

strongly resistant to any signs of devotion which insinuate idolatry and refused to prostrate or to touch the guru's feet,[38] while he observed that:

> Men, women, children, prostrated themselves respectfully, even affectionately. One could easily see that for them this was no empty conventional gesture or rite enjoined by good manners. Quite obviously the bodily prostration revealed the far deeper prostration happening ceaselessly in the secret place of the heart. One saw faith, love, and complete confidence in this man who had become for them nothing less than the epiphany of the invisible Presence, the outward manifestation to their human eyes of the grace and love of the Lord who dwells undivided both in the highest heavens and in the deepest depth of the heart.[39]

Gnanananda had a distinct physical appearance: short, plump, with child-like face and blissful smile. He wore his ocher robe bringing it over his head. He was a formally initiated sannyasi of one of the monastic orders established by Shankara.[40] He is reported to have travelled all over India, Nepal and Sri Lanka and to have known several Indian languages. After many years of wandering (almost a century according to his disciples) he settled at Tirukoilur and established an ashram called Sri Gnanananda Tapovanam. His life having been shrouded in mystery, miraculous accounts started to circulate amongst his disciples. His disciples believed that he "lived beyond the normal span of age—more than one and a half centuries by general estimate."[41]

While in the tradition of Shankara, Gnanananda paradoxically advocated *guru-bhakti*, or devotion to the guru as the sufficient way to liberation:

---

[38] "Europeans always feel a certain repugnance with regard to these gestures of homage which are so customary in India and just as natural as genuflecting or kissing the hand in other places." *Guru and Disciple*, p. 23.

[39] *Ibid.*, p. 26.

[40] He always introduced himself as "Paramahamsa Parivrajakacharya Varya Sri Gnanananda Giri Swami, disciple of Paramahamsa Parivrajakacharya Varya Sri Sivaratna-giri Swami, belonging to the Kashmir Mutt Peetam of the lineage of Adi Shankara Bhagavat Pada." *Sadguru Gnanananda*, p. 9.

[41] *Sadguru Gnanananda*, p. 2.

a true disciple has no sadhana to perform. He has only to surrender
himself completely to his guru.[42]

If one has guru bhakti, that alone is sufficient;
there is nothing beyond it, nothing else is required.[43]

The disciples thus came to believe that "he was God and man in
one; he was what the infinite Being and Its Power are when
manifested behind the veil of human body and feelings."[44] This
devotion was expressed through the ritual of worship of the
wooden sandals of the guru, the *Guru Paduka Puja*.[45] The
sandals represent the whole lineage of gurus and thereby symbolize the authority of the present guru:

> Through guru paduka one is not only linking oneself to a particular
> Master but to the whole parampara of spiritual masters. It has
> behind it all the sanctity and authority of long established sanc-
> tions, vast experience and a store-house of knowledge enriched by
> so many masters.[46]

While Abhisiktananda refused to engage in such explicit forms
of worship of the guru, he, almost in spite of himself, found
himself completely transformed by this first meeting. He relates
that "he realized that the allegiance which he had never freely
yielded to anyone in his life was now given automatically to
Gnanananda. He had often heard tell of gurus, of the irrational
devotion shown to them by their disciples and their total self-
abandonment to the guru. All these things seemed utterly senseless to him, a European with a classical education. Yet now at
this very moment it had happened to him, a true living experience
tearing him out of himself. This little man with his short legs and
bushy beard, scantily clad in a dhoti. . . could now ask of him
anything in the world, even to set off like Sadashiva, a dumb and

---

[42] *Sadguru Gnanananda*, p. 100.

[43] *Sadguru Gnanananda*, p. 104.

[44] *Sadguru Gnanananda*, p. 49.

[45] This consists of decorating the sandals, lighting lamps before them, carrying
them around, and paying signs of homage to them. *Paduka* (sandal) is derived
from *pad* (foot) which explains this symbol of worship.

[46] *Sadguru Gnanananda*, p. 120.

naked wanderer for ever, and he would not even think of asking him for any sort of explanation."[47] In his journal, Abhisikta- nanda writes that for the first time, he has come to understand the traditional Hindu practice of devotion to the guru, *guru- bhakti*, and the power or grace of the guru, *guru-shakti*.[48]

In Gnanananda, Abhishiktananda believed to have found the true living guru.[49] He states that nothing new had been said in his encounter with Gnanananda, but that "it had all been repea- ted in such a way that an ineffable communication had been established between the master and himself in the depths of the one as of the other."[50]

This experience becomes the basis for Abhishiktananda's most explicit reflections on the guru-disciple relationship. He comes to understand the guru as one "in whose heart the Invisible has revealed himself and through whom his light shines in perfect purity."[51] A guru is said to be:

> most certainly not some master or professor, or preacher or spiri- tual guide, or director of souls who has learned from books or from other men what he, in his turn, is passing on to others. The guru is one who has himself first attained the Real and who knows from personal experience the way that leads there; ...[52]

The main function of the guru is not that of imparting formal initiation.[53] Through the questioning and critique of false states

[47] *Guru and Disciple*, p. 27.

[48] *Journal*, 1955, p. 167.

[49] He attests having been "absolutely convinced that here indeed was the guru he had so long dreamed of, the one who would enable him to leap over the crest, if only he were to agree to abandon himself in complete trust." *Guru and Disciple*, p. 107. Monchanin and Panikkar were skeptical about the person of Gnanananda and worried about Abhishiktananda's faith in this guru. Monchanin often attempt- ed to dissuade him from going to Tapovanam, and Panikkar felt that he often projected his ideals and dreams in persons who were not what he imagined them to be.

[50] *Guru and Disciple*, p. 26.

[51] *Guru and Disciple*, p. 28.

[52] *Guru and Disciple*, p. 29.

[53] Abhishiktananda had become strongly skeptical of the practice of imparting the initiation ritual. It is often used by gurus to increase their funding or their fame. The fact that Gnanananda did not intend to initiate him increased his trust.

of identification, and with the help of mantras, myths, thought
and action, the guru guides the disciple to a different level of
consciousness.[54] The external guru is hereby understood as
nothing but the image or the instrument of the real guru who is
undivided:[55]

> The real guru is akhanda, undivided, he is advaita, non-dual. The
> Self is visible only to the self, and the true guru is no one but
> "oneself" in the depth of self.[56]

What the guru says springs from the very heart of the disciple. It is not
that another person is speaking to him.[57]

The experience of advaita or non-duality is not only the external
goal to which the guru leads the disciple. It is the very essence of
the guru-disciple relationship. Abhishiktananda states that
"advaita remains for ever incomprehensible to him who has not
first lived it in his meeting with the guru."[58]

Doctor Mehta

In the last years of his life, Abhishiktananda compares himself
with the mythical figure Dattatreya, the sage who accumulated
wisdom from all beings he encountered, and who is thus said to
have had 108 gurus.[59] For one who has the attitude of a real
disciple, anything or anyone may fulfill the role of guru. Small
events, insignificant objects, casual encounters and personal
friends may bring about a certain awareness or realization. One
of those who fulfilled this role in the spiritual growth of Abhishiktananda was his friend Doctor Mehta.

[54] *Intériorité et révélation*, p. 172.

[55] It was Gnanananda himself who introduced the distinction between the
guru-murti, "the guru in visible form, the one who can show the way" or the
karana-guru, "the instrumental guru, the one in whom the guru begins to take on a
form for the disciple as he awakens," and the *jñana-guru* or the *atma-guru* who
reveals all things.

[56] *Guru and Disciple*, p. 110.

[57] *Guru and Disciple*, p. 30.

[58] *Guru and Disciple*, p. 29.

[59] *Journal*, 1972, p. 424.

Dr. Dinshaw Mehta was a Parsi medical doctor who had been the personal physician of Mahatma Gandhi. He had founded a society which focussed on natural methods of curing and had also formed a religious association. He claimed to receive revelations, messages which he interpreted as coming from Christ, and which became the "Mehta scripts."[60] As often in India, his focus upon Christ did not imply his adherence to the church. Dr. Mehta was strongly anti-clerical and attacked both the Hindu and the Christian religious establishments. He viewed identification with any doctrine or institution as a hindrance to realization.

Dr. Mehta attempted to lead Abhishiktananda to a freedom from all religious identification. He pointed out that Abhishiktananda's fixation upon Advaita was no more than a substitution of his attachment to Christianity. He called for a total surrender:

> Surrender both of my desire to remain Christian, born from an instinctive fear, and my desire to live completely as advaitic hindu, which it often seems to me I am.[61]

This surrender is understood as a pure negation, a letting go of the attachment to all forms and institutions, and to any external guru.[62] It is the total abandonment necessary to discover the inner guide.

Abhishiktananda regarded Dr. Mehta as an instrument of the Spirit. The detachment from the external guide was facilitated by the fact that Dr. Mehta was a personal friend, whose deficiencies he knew. "These deficiencies," he states, "are themselves the proof that there is only an instrument, and that the source is

---

[60] They are recorded as "Laws" of surrender, of divine supply, etc., proclaimed by Jesus Christ in the first person. They are a mixture of Buddhist, Hindu and Christian teachings with Parsi influence coming through in a strong moral dualism.

[61] *Journal*, 1955, p. 158. It is not so much the idea of Advaita itself, as the Hindu form in which it is presented which must be surrendered: "la purification de mon advaita en la libération et le *surrender* de son support Hindu." *Journal*, 1955, p. 156.

[62] Abhishiktananda describes this state of surrender as a " nudité qui serait plus justement appelée peut-être un écorchage" and the feeling as that of being "libre et nu au sein du gouffre, suspendu." *Journal*, 1955, p. 158.

much higher."[63] This brings Abhishiktananda again to the realization that the guru is merely a projection of the inner guru, a medium of self-revelation.[64] He thus concludes that to rely upon any form of external guidance is folly:

> To expect from him a concrete directive was and is false. The practical solutions will be given in the appropriate time. And that shall occur precicely when I will have finally attained to my inner guide.[65]

Summary

> Why trouble about a guru? about Ramana? about Arunachala? *Tat tvam asi*! The guru, Ramana, Arunachala, and the rest, they are the outward projection of the Self, who hides itself in order to be found.[66]

Abishiktananda's search for the experience of advaita led him to different Hindu gurus who each revealed a different aspect of the guru-disciple relationship. Ramana Maharshi represented for Abhishiktananda the authentic sage who through his silent and timeless being brought the disciple to a search for the true Self. In compelling, through its impenetrable silence, toward an inner pondering, Abhishiktananda came to understand the sacred mountain Arunachala as a guru in the symbolic sense. Gnanananda, the sage of Tapovanam, was the only official guru with whom he had a personal relationship. In this relationship, Abhishiktananda came to discover the value of devotion to the guru and the difference between the instrumental and the real guru. The understanding of the guru as instrument was then strengthened in his rapport with his friend Dr. Mehta.

Each of these gurus led Abhishiktananda in different ways to the progressive discovery of the inner guru. He came to realize that the mystery of the guru is the mystery of the depth of the

---

[63] *Journal*, 1955, p. 147.
[64] *Journal*, 1955, p. 152.
[65] *Journal*, 1955, p. 165.
[66] *Journal*, 1964, p. 328.

heart, that the encounter with the guru is the experience of being face to face with oneself, and that what the guru appears to say in fact springs from the heart of the disciple.[67] The external person or form which presents itself to the senses as the guru is seen as the mere reflection or projection of an inner reality:

> The guru in flesh and appearance (sometimes replaced by the symbolic form of a temple or mountain as in the case of Ramana Maharshi) is as the external reflection of the unique guru present in the heart of everyone; the outward projection of the sign through which everyone is called in the Spirit to one's full truth.[68]

The role of the external guru may be seen as that of "sign and sacrament," as it points to, but also participates in, the ultimate reality which is that of the inner guru.[69] Although it is the guru "of flesh and appearance" who awakens to the reality of the guru inside, the very recognition of the external guru is dependent upon the unconscious reality and activity of the inner guru. This is expressed in the age-old Indian dictum that the guru appears when the disciple is ready.

Through his surrender to spiritual masters of a different religious tradition, Abhishiktananda comes to understand the meaning of obedience which he claims never to have understood in monastic life, namely, that "external obedience is the substitute of the surrender to the inner Spirit as long as this has not been realized."[70]

Abhishiktananda points out that the need for the guru to lead to the heart and for the disciple to listen within "applies all the more rigorously when guru and disciple do not belong to the same tradition."[71] The notion of the inner, hidden, or invisible master is often believed to refer to the same reality in the different

---

[67] *Guru and Disciple*, p. 29.

[68] *Intériorité et révélation*, p. 281.

[69] *Intériorité et révélation*, p. 281.

[70] *Journal*, 1955, p. 150.

[71] Abhishiktananda, *Saccidananda: a Christian Approach to Advaitic Experience* (Delhi: ISPCK, 1974) p. 29.

religious traditions.[72] This also seems to underly Abhishiktananda's focus upon the inner guru. However, the Hindu and the
Christian notions of the inner guru are imbedded in radically
different theological and philosophical frameworks.[73] This becomes clear in the far-reaching christological implications of Abhishiktananda's attempts to understand Jesus Christ through the
Hindu categories of guru and inner guru or *purusha*.

[72] Cf. K.G. Dürkheim, *Le maître intérieur* (Paris: Le Courrier du Livre, 1975);
A. Dauge, "Les Quatre Maîtres: Typologie du Maître spirituel" *Avec ou sans
Maître?* (Paris: Dervy-Livres, 1987.)
[73] See above pp. 177-179.

CHAPTER TWO

Abhishiktananda's Reflections on Christ as Guru

> The mystery of Christ should be studied, starting not from a
> mythos, but from an accessible reality, the jñani, the guru.[1]

Abhishiktananda's experience of the Hindu guru and of the
inner guru or *purusha* came to serve as a hermeneutical key for
understanding the mystery of Christ. The very first missionaries
had used the term guru to render the mystery of Christ in India.
While they adapted the Hindu concept to fit the established
Christian meaning, Abhishiktananda attempted to rethink the
traditional understanding of Christ through the Hindu category
of guru. His conception of the Hindu guru was, moreover, in line
with Hindu hermeneutics which bases understanding less upon
reason than on personal experience. As a Christian, however, he
did not uncritically adopt the traditional Hindu view of Christ as
just one of many gurus. It is from his struggle to understand the
figure of Christ through Hindu categories without ceasing to be
Christian that some of the crucial christological issues in the
Hindu-Christian dialogue become explicit.

Abhishiktananda's reflections were influenced by the ideas of
his friend Raimundo Panikkar whose book, *The Unknown Christ
of Hinduism*, became a milestone in the Hindu-Christian dialogue.[2] Panikkar calls for the severing of the historical Jesus from
the cosmic Christ. The expression "Jesus is the Christ," he argues,
cannot simply be reversed, "philosophically, because the *is* does

---

[1] *Journal* 1972, p. 421.

[2] This book was first published in 1964 (London: Darton, Longmann & Todd)
and appeared in a fundamentally revised and enlarged edition in 1981 (London:
Darton, Longmann & Todd.)

not need to mean *is-only* and, theologically, because in fact the risen Jesus is more (*aliud*, not *alius*) than the Jesus of Nazareth, which is only a practical identification, different from a personal identity."[3] Though it is through Jesus that Christians have come to know the Christ, he insists that "this Christ is the decisive reality," and not the monopoly of Christians.[4] In the Hindu notion of *Ishvara*, he sees the "homeomorphic equivalent" of the Christian notion of Christ.[5] The distinction between the historical Jesus resonates in Abhishiktananda's reference to Jesus as guru and the Christ as sadguru. Nonetheless, in continuity with his experience of the guru as an inner reality, Abhisiktananda mainly develops the idea of Jesus Christ as purusha. This directly confronts him with the issue of the uniqueness of Christ.

Jesus as Guru

If Christ could be presented to India in his naked beauty, free from the disguises of western organisation, western doctrines and western forms of worship, India would acknowledge Him as the Supreme Guru, and lay her richest homage at His feet.[6]

From the very beginning of the Christian mission in India, Christ has been presented as guru. Roberto de Nobili (1577-1659), one of the very first Catholic missionaries to India, spoke of Christ as *kuru* in the Tamil-speaking south of India.[7] He used

While Panikkar often points out that Abhishiktananda's vulnerable point was in the area of the logical exposition, and the theological foundation of his arguments, Abhishiktananda reproaches Panikkar for refraining from drawing the logical conclusions of his reasoning.

[3] *The Unknown Christ of Hinduism*, p. 14.

[4] *The Unknown Christ of Hinduism*, p. 29.

[5] *The Unknown Christ of Hinduism*, p. 164. The term "homeomorpic equivalent" refers to the same intentionality of the two concepts. They fulfill the same function.

[6] Quoted from the famous Indian Christian poet Narayan Vaman Tilak (1862-1919) by Jack Winslow, *Narayan Vaman Tilak: the Christian Poet of Maharashtra* (Calcutta: YMCA, 1930) p. 118.

[7] Jeyaraj argues that de Nobili's conception of Christ as divine Guru was his most important contribution to Christianity in India. See "The Contribution of

the term guru in conjunction with the concept *manusha avatar*, or human *avatar* or "descent." Since the term avatar may refer to any of the ten descents of the God Vishnu, De Nobili explicitly restricted the term to one, and used it in an exclusive sense. While the notion *manusha avatar* was used to refer to the nature of Christ, he used the term guru to refer to his function:

> That the invisible *kuru* in his divine nature,
> should become the perfect and the visible *kuru*
> for the salvation of the world through the human
> soul and body He has assumed is to be accepted.[8]

The term *kuru* came to be applied to both the Father and the Son, but also to teachers and missionaries, and to anyone past and present who participated in the function of leading the disciple towards salvation. De Nobili then used the term *carkuru* (satguru, true guru, or guru of truth) to refer to Jesus' activity during his public life: "God became human *kuru*" and "Jesus was the *carkuru* who came to teach perfectly truth to the whole world,"[9] but also with reference to a prophet, a missionary or a priest (probably to distinguish Christian from Hindu gurus). The term *tevya kuru*, or divine teacher, however, was used only with reference to Christ.[10] De Nobili emphasized the distinctiveness and the newness of Jesus Christ as *kuru*: The divine *kuru* teaches by his own actions; He exemplified not only renunciation but also service unto death; He taught not merely the way to personal

the Catholic Church in Tamilnadu in the 17-19th Centuries to an Understanding of Christ" in *The Indian Journal of Theology* 23 (1974) p. 185.

 Kuru is the Tamil word for guru.

 [8] Quoted from *Tusana Tikkaram*, p. 118 (in which de Nobili reviews critically some of the observances which are considered to be good by the Hindus) by Soosai Arokiasamy, *Dharma, Hindu and Christian According to Roberto de Nobili* (Rome, Gregoriana, 1986) p. 233.

 [9] Quoted in *Dharma, Hindu and Christian according to Roberto de Nobili*, p. 235.

 [10] To those who came before Jesus Christ, God granted grace "in view of the divine *kuru* to come." Quoted in *Dharma, Hindu and Christian according to Roberto de Nobili*, p. 234.

realization, but gave the new commandment to love one another.[11]

His attempt to establish the uniqueness of Christ by using the term *avatar* and restricting it to Christ alone has been followed by many other Christian theologians.[12] Bishop Appasamy, for example, wrote:

> We believe that Jesus was the Avatara. God lived on the earth as a man only once and that was as Jesus... It is our firm Christian belief that among all the great religious figures of the world there is no one except Jesus who could be regarded as an Incarnation of God.[13]

Against the docetic connotation of the term avatar the reality of the physical body of Christ and the historicity of the incarnation were emphasized.

The terms guru and avatara were here used mainly for proselytizing purposes. Stanley Jones, for example, relates how, after failing to gain converts through the administration of sacraments and the proclamation of the official Church teaching, he started to proclaim the living Christ as guru and hundreds of Hindus then surrendered to Jesus Christ.[14]

Around the turn of the century, new attitudes developed towards the Hindu tradition. Hinduism was no longer regarded as evil and in error, and Hindu concepts as useful only in as far as they could translate the Christian meaning. The "higher"

---

[11] Quoted in *Dharma, Hindu and Christian according to Roberto de Nobili*, p. 237.

[12] Since the term *avatara* is characteristic of the Bhakti, or devotional tradition of Hinduism, it is especially the theologians who have sought to integrate this tradition of Hinduism into Christianity who use the term. See, for example, A.J. Appasamy, *The Gospel and India's Heritage* (London: SPCK, 1942); V. Chakkarai, *Jesus the Avatar* (Madras: CLS, 1932.)

[13] A.J. Appasamy, *The Gospel and India's Heritage* (London: SPCK, 1942) p. 259. More recent works explicitly reject this transformation and emptying of Hindu concepts to fit the Christian meaning. Cf. Klaus Klostermaier, *Hindu and Christian in Vrindaban* (London: SCM, 1969) p. 115 and Geoffrey Parrinder, *Avatar and Incarnation* New York: Oxford University Press, 1982) p. 277.

[14] *The Christ of the Indian Road* (London: Hodder and Stoughton, 1925) pp. 111-115.

Hinduism was discovered and acknowledged as valid and authentic in itself but still awaiting its fulfillment in Christianity. T.E. Slater, one of the first advocates of this fulfillment theory acknowledged that "Vedantic thought is so thoroughly Indian that the Christianity of the future will of necessity take a Vedantic coloring."[15] While a more sympathetic attitude toward the Hindu tradition emerged, the superiority of Christianity, and the exclusivity of Christ remained unquestioned. Precisely with reference to the tradition of Advaita Vedanta and its gurus, Slater stated:

> The Christian Gospel thus offers all that the Vedanta offers, and infinitely more. So true is it that every previous revelation flows into the revelation we have in Christ, and loses himself in Him. Christ includes all teachers. All "other masters" are in Christ. We do not deny the truths they taught; we can delight in all. We can give heed to all the prophets; but every truth in every prophet melts into the truth we have in Christ.[16]

Among the great Hindu reformers of the nineteenth century typically Hindu views of Christ were developed. Characteristic of these views is the denial of the ontological uniqueness of Christ. Keshab Chandra Sen and Ramakrishna interpreted the union between Jesus and the Father as of a mystic rather than a hypostatic nature and Vivekananda spoke of Christ as *jivanmukta*, a term which may be applied to any realized guru in the tradition of Vedanta. Both Ram Mohan Roy and Keshab Chandra Sen emphasized the idea of universal sonhood, the former to reject the divine nature of Christ, and the latter to affirm the divinity of all. Gandhi came to regard Jesus Christ as one of the greatest moral teachers in the history of humankind.

---

[15] *The Higher Hinduism in Relation to Christianity* (London: Paternoster, 1903) p. 290. The fulfillment theory is mainly associated with J.N. Farquhar who in *The Crown of Hinduism* (Oxford: Oxford University Press, 1913) emphasizes that only Christ fulfills and brings to completion the various desires and quests revealed in Hindu history.

[16] *The Higher Hinduism in Relation to Christianity*, p. 277.

Brahmabandhab Upadhyaya, who has come to be regarded as the father of Indian Catholic Theology, was influenced (as a former Brahmin, a member and teacher of the Brahma Samaj) by the views of Hindu reformers, but he was simultaneously one of the most important exponents of the fulfillment theory of his day. He based his belief in the uniqueness of Christ (and his conversion to Christianity) on the fact that while all other saints and great religious teachers admitted to be sinners, Jesus Christ was free from sin. He is said to have "made the concept of guru applied to Christ the cornerstone of his Indian Christian Theology."[17] He used the term guru, however, not so much to compare as to contrast Jesus Christ with other gurus: "Christ fulfilled the universal desire of the Hindus who had ever been looking forward to the advent of a sinless Guru (a Sat Guru, a Nishkalanka Avatar)."[18]

Several other Indian Christian theologians developed the understanding of Christ as the fulfillment of the Hindu conception of the guru. The similarities between the Hindu figure of the guru and Jesus Christ were emphasized, only to demonstrate the superiority of the latter:

> If a guru teaches through silence, how much more is it true today for the risen Jesus? If a guru appears when the disciple is ready, what about Jesus who is pure availability? Again, if a guru is with his disciple, what about Jesus who has promised to be always with his disciples till the end of the world? He is the only guru who wants to be permanently present in the heart of his disciples.[19]

> In the Guru the shishya discovers his own individuality. Christ is the one saving Guru for all men since in his death and resurrection all can discover their own final glory and self-fulfillment. Christ is God's decisive, eschatological and soteriological presence to the individual.[20]

[17] John Chethimattam, "Theology as Human Interiority: Search for the One Teacher," *Unique and Universal, Fundamental Problems of an Indian Theology* (Bangalore: Dharmaram College, 1972) p. 186.

[18] B. Animananda *The Blade* (Calcutta: Roy, 1945) p. 35.

[19] Emmanuel Vattakuzhy, *Indian Christian Sannyasa and Swami Abhishiktananda* (Bangalore: Theological Publications in India, 1981) pp. 186-187.

[20] John Chethimattam, "Theology as Human Interiority: Search for the One

This approach does consider the typically Hindu characteristics of the guru, but only in as far as they fit the traditional Christian understanding of Christ. The superiority and unicity of Christ is presupposed and superimposed upon the definition of the guru.[21]

In the course of the past few decades, a new attitude of openness has been adopted toward other religious traditions. The Second Vatican Council emphasized the elements of truth present in other traditions, and thereby opened the way for Christianity to integrate concepts and symbols belonging to another tradition, and be itself transformed by them.

This new attitude becomes manifest in Xavier Irudayaraj's approach to Christ as guru.[22] He attempts to understand Christ through the Shaiva Siddhanta conception of the guru. According to this tradition Shiva is the only real Guru, the *Sar-Guru* or the *Jñana-Guru*. To impart grace, he manifests himself through "possessive presence," or complete union with the realized *jñani*. The one who is made into an instrument of God's grace and who prepares the soul for final realization is called *Upaya-Guru* or *Nar-Guru*. This understanding of the guru thus emphasizes the uniqueness of the guru and the importance of grace, without downplaying the role of other gurus. Applied to the figure of Christ, Irudayaraj suggests that the Shaiva Siddhanta concept of manifestations of the satguru may allow for a more dynamic view of the incarnation in terms of a progressive unfolding of its mystery.[23] Avenues are here thus opened for radical christological rethinking.

Abhishiktananda's originality lay not so much in the use of the term guru for Jesus Christ, as in his hermeneutical method.

Teacher," *Unique and Universal, Fundamental Problems of Indian Theology* (Bangalore, 1972) p. 188-189.

[21] Cf. also Prasannabhai, "Sadguru," *Vidyajyoti* 40 (1976) 315-320.

[22] Xavier Irudayaraj, "The Guru in Hinduism and Christianity," *Vidyajyoti* 39 (1975) 315-320.

[23] "The Guru in Hinduism and Christianity," pp. 347 and 351. He also points out that the Shaiva Siddhanta conception of the guru transposed upon Christ would inspire a more mystical approach to the person of Christ, based on the personal experience of his love and grace.

Rather than adapting the term guru to fit traditional christology, he attempted to understand the figure of Jesus Christ anew on the basis of his experience of the Hindu guru. Abhishiktananda believed that the paradigm of the guru provided the most generally acceptable and universally intelligible understanding of Christ:

> It is possible to refuse to believe in the divinity of Christ, and in particular, many are unable to accept it in the terms in which it was defined by the Church Councils. But the unique greatness of Christ's personality and his authority as a guru or spiritual leader of mankind can never be disputed.[24]

The understanding of Jesus Christ as guru is here based not only on functional, but also on ontological grounds. Abhishiktananda believed that it reflected Jesus' pristine experience and the nature and function of Jesus prior to his divinization in the course of the early Church Councils. He argues that it gives a plenary meaning to the term rabbi which was applied to Jesus within the Jewish context. While the term rabbi has strong scholarly connotations, the term guru emphasizes the spiritual and prophetic function of the master.[25]

Abhishiktananda's attempt to understand the figure of Jesus Christ through a new paradigm involved a reinterpretation, not only of the nature and function of the figure of Jesus Christ, but also of his experience and teaching. From within the framework of Advaita Vedanta, Abhishiktananda comes to understand the experience of Jesus as that of *saccidananda,* and the expression "I

---

[24] H. Le Saux, *Saccidananda: a Christian Approach to Advaitic Experience* (Delhi: ISPCK, 1974) p. 79.

[25] *Intériorité et révélation* (Sisteron: Présence, 1982) p. 264. It is with the Hebrew prophet that the Indian guru may more appropriately be compared according to Paul Kalluveettil. He points to the striking similarities both in form and function of prophet and guru: Prophets were "men of the spirit" who spoke the word of the only guru, God. They often gathered disciples who were called "sons of the prophet" and devoted their life to study and service of the master. Like the Hindu disciple, they held their master in great respect, and used to sit at his feet to listen to his words (2 Kings 4: 38; 6:1). See "The Guru and the Hebrew Concept of the Prophet," *Dharma* (1980) 252-261.

and the Father are one"[26] as referring to the awareness of the non-duality of atman and Brahman. The Jews, Greeks, and Romans, he argued, took from Jesus' message only that which fitted their established worldview and beliefs.[27] Had Jesus moved within the Indian context, he would have been regarded as a guru, and his message would have been understood as that of Advaita Vedanta. Abhishiktananda believed that this was closer to the real nature and teaching of Jesus.

In conceiving of Jesus as guru, Abhishiktananda came to understand the Christian tradition as the *Isha sampradaya*, the teaching tradition of which Jesus was the founding guru:

> The Lord Jesus is my guru, Isa sampradayat (of the tradition of the Lord). He is always with me, in my heart, in my thoughts, in my senses; Him only do I see, Him only do I hear, Him only do I touch.[28]

As opposed to the institutional dimension and the hierarchical structure of Church affiliation, a *sampradaya* is based upon the spiritual link of each of its members with the guru. This conception of Christ and of Christianity would then, according to Abhishiktananda, allow every Christian to feel personally connected with and immersed in Jesus Christ.

In the Hindu tradition of the guru, metaphors are provided which may be used to express this personal relationship between Jesus and every one of his believers. Abhishiktananda refers to Jesus as the *taraka*, the boatman who helps the disciple cross safely from the shore of death, darkness and non-being to that of immortality, light and being:

> Jesus effects the passing from tamas (darkness) to jyoti (light), from the asat (non-being) to sat (being), from mrityu (death) to amrita (immortality).[29]

[26] John 10:30.

[27] *Journal*, 1965, p. 187.

[28] *Journal*, 1963, p. 315.

[29] *Journal*, 1954, p. 117. He here paraphrases the famous verse from the *Brihadaranyaka Upanishad* 1.3.28.

A guru does not realize the crossing for, or instead of, the disciple. While the guru may exemplify and guide, every disciple must come to self-realization through self-effort. This brings Abhishiktananda to a reinterpretation of the traditional understanding of Jesus' suffering and death. Rather than as a vicarious offer of reconciliation, he understands Jesus' self-sacrifice in mystical terms as exemplifying the self-mortification necessary to reach salvation or liberation. It is the ultimate completion of a life which itself was pure self-surrender:

> He kept nothing for himself of all that which the Father had given him; he repeated everything, he gave everything. And finally he gave himself... For my guru is essentially a "Donation" It is in donating himself that he realized God. And the essence of his teaching is also a call to donate oneself, to love.[30]

In continuity with the Hindu understanding of the guru as one who, in emptying himself realizes himself, Abhishiktananda understands the essence and message of the life of Jesus Christ as a process of self-emptying which leads to God-realization. Although he finds this interpretation totally plausible and revealing, the radicality of it leaves him slightly uncomfortable:

> Why feel so uneasy in addressing myself to Christ as to my guru, the one who brings about the passage, the passer of the soul, the taraka? He lived in reality, he passed to the center. And in attaining the center, he made it accessible to all. And men have called him God precisely because he attained pure being.[31]

Within the Christian context, the term *sadguru*, meaning real or true guru, has often been used to establish the ontological uniqueness and exclusivity of Jesus Christ, or to distinguish Jesus Christ from other gurus. The prefix *sat*, however, is a superlative which in its original Hindu meaning does not possess exclusive connotations. The term sadguru is used by disciples to express their faith in the authenticity of their guru, their belief or experience that the guru can really lead to realization or liberation.

[30] *Journal*, 1952, p. 52 and 1956, p. 229.
[31] *Journal*, 1955, p. 163.

It is in this Hindu sense that Abhishiktananda understands the term sadguru: "the guru is the man who is able to initiate others to the knowledge-by-experience of the mystery of God which he himself has experienced — and no more, the prefix sat adds the connotation of reality, of truth, of goodness."[32] In one passage, he seems to apply the term sadguru in an exclusive sense to Jesus Christ:

> The Sadguru is the Master of Truth pre-eminently, the real and good Teacher, the "Good Master" of the Gospel (Mark 10:17). He alone introduces others to the Real, to sat; he alone communicates to his disciples his own Spirit; his words are spirit and life, and are seeds which bring forth fruit in the heart of those who receive them with faith and love (Luke 8:15). Only he can speak of Being, sat, and lead men to it, who himself dwells in the bosom of the Father, the Origin and Source of all that is.[33]

Abhishiktananda understands this exclusivity or uniqueness not in an absolute but a relative sense: Jesus Christ is unique for him. He explicitly acknowledges that the mystery which he has come to know through Christ, his sadguru, may be revealed through other symbols, other myths, other gurus:

> I acknowledge, by the way, this mystery which I have always adored in the symbol of Christ, in the myths of Narayana, Praja-pati, Shiva, Purusha, Krishna, Rama, etc. The same mystery. But for me, Jesus is the Sadguru (the real Guru). It is in him that God has appeared to me; it is in his mirror that I have found myself, in adoring him, in loving him, in consecrating myself to him... Jesus is the guru who proclaims the mystery.[34]

Christ as Purusha

In continuity with his experience of guru not so much as an external, but as an inner reality, Abhishiktananda came to focus not so much upon the historical Jesus as guru, but upon the Christ as inner guru or *purusha*. The term purusha

[32] H. Le Saux, *Saccidananda* (Delhi: ISPCK, 1974) p. 202.
[33] *Ibidem.*
[34] *Journal,* 1971, p. 406.

has been used throughout the Hindu tradition with a variety of meanings. Abhishiktananda uses the full range of meanings to render the mystery of Christ:

> The Christ is the cosmic man, the Purusha. The Christ is the embodiment of the unity of the created being. The Christ is God manifested in his totality. God is a-vyakta, non-manifested. He becomes manifest, he becomes Person in the Purusha. The Purusha is simultaneously multiple and unique. Being manifests itself in every consciousness of Being. The Purushas are not separated. No man is really man unless in the archetypal man, the Christ. Everyone is perfect, full, purna, of the sole perfection and plenitude of the adi-purusha.[35]

The term purusha here appears in its full semantic complexity. It has been used with a variety of related, yet different meanings in Sanskrit texts, and variously colored according to the philosophy of the different schools. In the *Rig-Veda*, it refers to the primordial anthropomorphic being of cosmic dimensions, the archetype through whose sacrifice the universe was created. Abhishiktananda uses this understanding of purusha in a few passages to render Christ as primordial man and as cosmic sacrifice:

> All is taken up in the liturgy of the Lamb— or, as India might call him, the sacred and immortal *purusha*—that liturgy which he inaugurated in heaven before the world began and celebrated once for all in the midst of time upon the Cross, ...[36]

> Christ is truly *the* Man who was mysteriously foreseen in the old myths—the cosmic *Purusha*, for instance, of the Rig Veda, the primordial man whose sacrifice gave birth to the whole universe and to each of its component parts.[37]

In the theistic Upanishads, the Bhagavadgita (15:17-18), and in the Samkhya Yoga tradition, the term purusha refers to the transcendent, personal God and may be identified with Ishvara.

---

[35] *Journal*, 1966, p. 344.

[36] Abhishiktananda, *Saccidananda* (Delhi: ISPCK, 1974) p. 60. In the footnotes, Abhishiktananda refers explicitly to the *Rig-Veda* 10:90, and compares it with Rev 13:8, "the Lamb slain before the foundation of the world."

[37] *Saccidananda*, p. 136.

Abhishiktananda does not explicitly use the term guru with this meaning.

Abhishiktananda most often uses the term purusha for Christ in the Upanishadic meaning of *atman,* or true Self, which is not different from Brahman.[38] Within this context, the term purusha has also been translated as "person," in an anti-individualistic sense of the term, however. Immersed in the tradition of Advaita Vedanta, Abhishiktananda exclaims "Christ is above all the *Purusha* in the depth of my Self;[39]" he is "the place of the essential Encounter," and "power of total realization."[40] This internalization of the mystery of Christ, he regards as the distinct contribution to Christianity of the Upanishadic tradition and of Advaita Vedanta.[41]

Abhishiktananda uses the superlative form of purusha, *satpurusha,* to indicate the ultimacy of the understanding of the purusha as inner Christ:

> more even than being involved in Space and Time, it is the absolutely highest level of consciousness, this last point beyond which there is only the passage to the Father.[42]

---

[38] The term purusha is within this context also often translated by the term "person," which must be understood as not only different from, but opposed to the Western individualistic conception of person. It refers not so much to that which constitutes the particularity of every individual as to that which is the most subtle, the sacred ground of existence which is universal.

[39] *Journal,* 1966, p. 345.

[40] *Journal,* p. 127, 135, 149, 195, etc. Some theologians prefer the term *antaryamin* or "indweller," "inner ruler" to the term purusha to render the notion of indwelling spirit in India. It is used especially by theologians who seek affinities between the Christian and the Bhakti traditions. It saves God's transcendence without compromising his immanence. Bishop Appasamy uses antaryamin to point to the presence of the Logos in all, to emphasize the eminent way in which the Logos was in Jesus Christ, and to explain the continued manifestation of Jesus Christ in his Church. See *Christianity as Bhakti Marga: a Study of the Johannine Doctrine of Love* (Madras: CLS, 1928) p. 43. Chakkarai also uses the term to point to the Christ dwelling within us as the Holy Spirit. See *Jesus the Avatar* (Madras: CLS, 1932) p. 116. Panikkar speaks of the antaryamin as that "which Christians call Christ." See *The Unknown Christ of Hinduism,* p. 93.)

[41] *La rencontre de l'hindouisme et du christianisme.* p. 74.

[42] *Journal,* 1955, p. 167.

This understanding of Christ as the inner purusha naturally led to a radical rethinking of traditional christology. The concept of purusha, referring to Christ as an inner reality is not equivalent to the traditional Christian understanding of the inner Christ. This becomes clear in an analysis of the notion of the inner Master in, for example, Augustine's *De Magistro*. Here, the idea of the "Inner Teacher" or "Indwelling Light" is based upon a trinitarian conception of the divine:

> Regarding all those things which we understand, it is not a speaker who utters sounds exteriorly whom we consult, but it is truth that presides within, over the mind itself; though it may have been words that prompted us to make such consultation. And he who is consulted, He who is said to dwell in the inner man, He it is who teaches —Christ— that is, the unchangeable Power of God and everlasting Wisdom.[43]

While the notion of purusha establishes the divinity of all, the Christian conception of the inner master emphasizes the transcendent source of all truth and the uniqueness of Christ.

Abhishiktananda criticizes the traditional Christian understanding of Christ as an external and transcendent reality, as Purusha in the theistic interpretation:

> Jesus has been understood by Christians only as the external guru—anyaiva, only as Purusha, Creator, Sacrificer, Saviour.[44]

He believes that Jesus fully realized the inner Christ. But the fixation upon the historical Jesus, as upon the external guru, he regards as idolatrous. It is the projection and the objectification of the absolute ground of one's own being outside oneself.

The result of this focus upon the historical Jesus is, according to Abhishiktananda, that the responsibility for salvation or liberation is projected upon the other. This is what gave birth to the

[43] *De Magistro* 11.38. *The Teacher* (Westminster: Newman, 1950) p. 177. Augustine argues that just as words have no power to make us know physical realities unless we have previous experience of those objects, so also words — and by extension all external teaching — cannot make us 'see" intelligible realities within the mind.

[44] *Journal*, 1972, p. 417.

interpretation of Jesus' death in terms of redemption and atonement. The expressions "it is to your advantage that I go away, for if I do not go away, the Counsellor will not come to you; ..." (John 16:7) and "Do not hold me ..."(John 20:17)[45] Abhishiktananda understands as admonitions to the disciples not to fixate upon his external form, but to focus within. The main theological problem with which Abhishiktananda is confronted in his attempt to integrate the tradition of Advaita Vedanta is that of the uniqueness of Christ.

The Uniqueness of Jesus Christ

> If, as non-christians maintain, Jesus is only a man, then whatever natural endowments he possesses must naturally be available to every man. And if he is the son of God, as Christians believe, then they must not forget that, according to their faith, Jesus shares with them by grace all that he possesses by right of his divine Sonship.[46]

The belief in the uniqueness of Christ has been the main stumbling block in the dialogue with non-Christian religions in general and with Hinduism in particular. Within a worldview which understands time as beginningless, endless, senseless recurrence, and which regards release from the world as the ultimate goal, the ideas of a historically decisive event and a unique saviour are meaningless. Within the Bhakti tradition, the avatars of Vishnu may be regarded as unique for a certain epoch or for a particular sect, but the term avatar does not possess exclusive connotations. Since in the tradition of Advaita Vedanta, everyone can hope one day to cite the great saying or *mahavakya* "I am Brahman," there is no ground for establishing the discontinuity of Christ.[47] In his overview of Indian Christian theology, Robin Boyd points out that the expression "I and my Father are one"

---

[45] *Intériorité et révélation*, p. 173; and *Journal*, 1956, p. 229.

[46] *Saccidananda*, p. 83.

[47] Cf. Sara Grant, "Reflections on the Mystery of Christ suggested by a Study of Sankara's Concept of Relation," *God's Word Among Men* (Delhi: Vidyajyoti, 1973) p. 110.

(John 10:30) has become the "locus classicus" of Indian Christian theology.[48]

In attempting to understand Christ as guru and as purusha, the main theological problem which faced Abhishiktananda was that of the uniqueness of Christ. His reflections on this issue went through a gradual evolution, and moved through different paradigms which are characteristic of the variety of approaches to this issue.

Fulfilling Uniqueness

> As Christians we believe that the revelation of God in Jesus is the plenitude of all revelations, and the rod with which are judged and measured all awareness of God and of the divine mystery.[49]

Abhishiktananda's early conception of the uniqueness of Christ was conditioned by the fulfillment theory of his day. This does not deny saving power to other religious figures, but emphasizes the superiority and the discontinuity with others of the life, experience and power of Jesus Christ. From this point of view, other traditions may be seen positively, and Abhishiktananda viewed Hinduism in terms of a *preparatio Christi*. A christology could be developed from the Upanishads which would necessarily be different from that which developed out of the Jewish tradition on the basis of Hellenistic philosophy.[50] While the prophets of Israel emphasized the transcendence of God which implied a more dualistic conception of reality, Abhishiktananda insists that in India, Christ should be understood as fulfilling the experience of non-duality of the Advaitic sages and gurus. He believed that "all that the Maharshi, and countless others before him, knew and handed on of the inexorable experience of non-duality, Jesus also knew himself, and that in a pre-eminent manner."[51] All that

---

[48] *An Introduction to Indian Christian Theology* (Bangalore: The Christian Literature Society, 1969) p. 29.

[49] *Intériorité et révélation*, p. 273.

[50] See *La rencontre de l'hindouisme et du christianisme*, p. 74.

[51] *Saccidananda*, p. 83. In the preface to this work, Abhishiktananda states

has been said in the Upanishads is seen to be clarified and fulfilled in the Gospel and in the experience of Jesus Christ:

> All that has been said in the Upanishads, has been said in fact about Christ. But in the clarity of the Gospel, all antinomies have been resolved.[52]
> Beyond the sages of advaita, Jesus has penetrated
> beyond is "I" to the mystery of the I of the Father,
> to the origin of his own I.[53]

The fulfillment of Christ, and of Christianity as a whole, Abhishiktananda originally understood with Monchanin as the "culmination trinitaire" of the Upanishadic experience of *saccidananda*, "being, consciousness, bliss."[54] Abhishiktananda compared the notion *cit*, which can mean intelligence, wisdom, consciousness, or knowledge, with the Christian conception of Jesus Christ to point to the superiority of the latter. It is the historicity of Christ which he understands as the ground of superiority, Christ being "not merely an aspect or mode of Brahman" but "a real procession, a real birth, first in eternity and subsequently in time."[55] He considers the relational dimension of the Christian trinity as a further development of the Advaitic conception of saccidananda, since "self-awareness only comes to be when there is a mutual giving and receiving, for the I only awakens to itself in a Thou."[56] Moreover, in the awareness of human sinfulness, and in the eternal dependency on God's grace, he found a greater depth than in the serene settlement in the state of non-duality. In

that he can no longer identify with the statements on the uniqueness of Christ and Christianity there expounded.

[52] H. Le Saux, *La rencontre de l'hindouisme et du christianisme*, p. 157. Though he usually avoids the term avatara, Abhishiktananda calls Christ once "the unique avatar," *Journal*, 1952, p. 48.

[53] *Journal*, 1954, p. 127.

[54] *La rencontre de l'hindouisme et du christianisme*, p. 74. The fulfillment of the advaitic conception of the divine as *saccidananda*, or "being, consciousness, bliss" in the Christian trinity was the underlying theme of the whole of Monchanin's theology. Cf. *Mystique de l'Inde, mystère chrétien* (Paris: Fayard, 1974) and *Ecrits spirituels* (Paris: Centurion, 1964.)

[55] *Saccidananda*, p. 179.

[56] *Saccidananda*, p. 176.

this stage, Abhishiktananda argued that there is in "the Christian's acceptance of his limitations and his involvement in time a depth of love and surrender which is beyond the understanding of the Stoic or the Vedantin." [57]

Abhishiktananda regarded the idea of the uniqueness of Christ as forstalled in the Upanishadic text:

> Nothing beyond him; nothing without him; nothing more subtle than him, nothing more ancient than him; like a tree erect in the sky, he stands alone. In this *purusha* is the Fullness, everything, *purnam sarvam*. [58]

The concept *purnam sarvam*, or complete fullness, Abhishiktananda compares with the *pan to pleroma*, the whole fullness of Col 2:9. The image of the cosmic tree reminds him "quite naturally of the Mystic Vine to which the Lord compared himself," of the "stories of Genesis and the allegories of Ezekiel," which all point to him in which all subsists. And he concludes: "In the Christ is the reality of all the images. He is the truth which all the earlier types sought obscurely to express; he is the true light, the true food, the true life, the true vine, the true *purusha*." [59] When applied to the figure of Jesus Christ, the fullness of the purusha became the uniqueness of the experience of Jesus Christ:

> Nobody has seen the Father, but he who has gone down to the bossom of the Father (John 14:6; 10:17; 1:18). No one has realized God as he did. No one has been able to possess as he did the sense of divine Consciousness. Christ is the Master Guru. [60]

Although his conception of the uniqueness of Christ becomes more and more subjective and symbolical, Abhishiktananda considers the possibility of the ontological distinction of Jesus Christ up to the very end of his life. At different times he

---

[57] *Ibid.*, p. 145.
[58] Quoted from the *Mundaka Upanishad* 1.1.6 in *Saccidananda*, p. 212.
[59] *Saccidananda*, p. 212.
[60] *Journal*, 1952, p. 51.

expresses his belief that Jesus was more pure, and more humane than all other religious figures:

> Jesus was infinitely human. He was more profoundly and fully human than was any of the great gurus, the Buddha, etc.[61]

At the very end of his life, in a letter to his disciple, he again raises the possibility of the objective superiority and the absolute uniqueness of the experience of Jesus Christ: "and we discover marvelously that Christ is simply this awakening on a degree of purity rarely *if ever* reached by man"[62]

Personal and Relational Uniqueness

> The divinity of Jesus is not separated from the "divinity" of every created being. It is its summit, its total accomplishment.[63]

As Abhishiktananda becomes more immersed in the experience and in the philosophy of Advaita Vedanta, his understanding of the uniqueness of Christ also becomes more non-dualistic and non-discontinuous. Since every person is called to realize the experience of non-duality of the Self and the absolute, the uniqueness of Christ is seen as representative of the uniqueness of every person who comes to the realization of Brahman:

> Whoever awakens to the mystery of Brahman in the name of the Father is the unique Son.[64]

Abhishiktananda argues that "in the advaitin conception of reality, one cannot conclude to either the unity or the diversity of ultimate expressions."[65] One never has any knowledge of Brah-

---

[61] *Journal,* 1972, p. 421. "Hinduism has no figure of the same purity," *Journal,* 1967, p. 357. And "no doubt no divine figure ever adored by man is of the same purity as that of Jesus Christ," *Journal,* 1971, p. 412.

[62] Letter to Marc Chaduc (February 9, 1973). My italics.

[63] *Journal,* 1954, p. 125.

[64] *Intériorité et révélation,* p. 299. Abhishiktananda believes that this is what is meant by the Christian notion that "each one of the elect is the manifestation by grace of the eternal awakening of the Father to himself in the Son." *Saccidananda,* p. 180.

[65] *Journal,* 1970, p. 380.

man outside one's own experience of the atman. Abhishiktananda then comes to understand the uniqueness of Christ as a way of expressing the uniqueness but also the unity of religious experiences:

> There is but one Presence—so say the seers, those who have contemplated the truth. It is the presence of the Self to itself which, wherever it manifests itself, is identical. For Christian faith, there is but one Son, divinely and eternally begotten. In beholding his Son, the Father sees all things; in loving him, he loves all things... Similarly every "see-er" of God beholds the Father only through the eyes of the Son.[66]

Abhishiktananda thus comes to view the uniqueness of Jesus Christ as no different from the uniqueness of every person:

> The person of Jesus is unique, just as every person is unique.[67]
> Every person is as unique for the Father as is Jesus. The distinction of Jesus with relation to other human beings is the distinction itself of every human being in relation to others.[68]

The traditional Christian understanding of the uniqueness of Christ as exclusive and discontinuous he regards as opposed to its proclamation of the value of every person.[69]

From the perspective of Advaita, Abhishiktananda then comes to view the question of the uniqueness of Christ as a "false problem,"[70] belonging to the phenomenological level, to the limited realm of duality, "where one can add, subtract, and multiply:[71]

> Why do we want to compare Jesus, make him enter into the crowd of gurus, make of him a guru apart? My guru is unique just as I am unique.[72]

---

[66] *Saccidananda*, pp. 179-180.
[67] *Intériorité et révélation*, pp. 303 and 299.
[68] *Journal*, 1971, p. 409.
[69] *Journal*, 1972, p. 419.
[70] *Journal*, 1970, p. 385; 1972, p. 442.
[71] *Journal*, 1972, p. 442.
[72] *Journal*, 1972, p. 421.

Since ultimate experiences cannot be compared within one and the same tradition, this applies even more when the masters or saviors belong to different religious traditions. Abhishiktananda then believes that to compare the manifestation of God in Jesus and in the Buddha would be nothing but a futile exercise.[73] While acknowledging other savior figures, he points out that Christ is unique "for him." It is through Christ that he has come to know God and discover himself.[74]

> The only thing important: that Christ be Everything for me. That there be nothing held back in me with regard to him. That every human being be unique, my everything to whom I give myself wholly. In this I shall have the experience of the Unique.[75]

The uniqueness of the guru is here understood not in an absolute but in a relational, relative, and even in an abstract and mystical sense. Every guru or saviour is regarded as absolute by his own disciples. In regarding every person as the manifestation of the guru, one is automatically brought to self-surrender and to the experience of the absolute.

Symbolic Uniqueness

Abhishiktananda's understanding of the uniqueness of Christ becomes more and more abstract. At a certain point, he comes to analyze the idea of uniqueness in purely philosophical terms. Using structuralist categories, he sees the uniqueness of Christ as essentially related to the larger symbolic whole of the Christian religion in which every symbol fulfills a unique and irreplacable semantic function:

> Christianity is a symbol... Within the symbolic system of Christianity, the elements of the symbol cannot but be unique. The uniqueness of the Incarnation is part of the Christian symbol.[76]

---

[73] *Journal*, 1970, p. 385.
[74] *Journal*, 1972, p. 423.
[75] *Journal*, 1973, p. 455.
[76] *Journal*, 1970, p. 384.

Uniqueness may also be seen, according to Abhishiktananda, as the way in which, from an epistemological point of view, the absolute is necessarily grasped: "this uniqueness is precisely the way in which consciousness integrates the absolute nature of the mystery." The uniqueness of Christ is then understood as the way in which Christians grasp the unicity of the absolute. From this point of view, the avatars of Vishnu, the Buddha, and Christ are not two, or three, or many. They are different unique symbolic experiences and expressions of the absolute in different contexts:

> As truly as the unicity of God, the unicity of the symbol of Christ is of a transcendental order and cannot be compared or opposed to any other symbol, equally transcendent in as far as it also attempts to express the totality of Being.[77]

Conclusion

Abhishiktananda's attempt to understand Christ on the basis of the categories guru and purusha may be seen as a lived exercise in cross-cultural or dialogical hermeneutics. This has been defined as "an attempt to interpret through categories belonging to one cultural and religious tradition, what has been captured and formulated within a different philosophical and symbolical context."[78] It consists not merely of contact or confrontation, but of mutual penetration of different categories, so that hidden, yet inherent meanings may be revealed.[79] Abhishiktananda attempted to interpret the figure of Jesus Christ through the

[77] *Intériorité et révélation*, p. 202.

[78] Felix Wilfred, "Inculturation as a Hermeneutical Question" *Vidyajyoti* 52 (1988) p. 425. He explains the specificity of cross-cultural hermeneutics in contrast with the traditional Western understanding of hermeneutics: "While the West has thus a historically and existentially oriented hermeneutics, the hermeneutics we are concerned about in inculturation is not only a matter of bridging the gulf between the past and the present. Our need is to understand from our cultural situation, tradition, and experience, what has been shaped and formulated in a different cultural setting."

[79] Cf. Michael von Brück, *Einheit der Wirklichkeit. Gott, Gotteserfahrung und Meditation im hinduistisch-christlichen Dialog* (München: Chr. Kaiser, 1988) p. 20.

Hindu categories of guru and purusha which he had come to understand through personal experience. From this, a radically new understanding of the nature, the function and the traditional understanding of the uniqueness of Jesus Christ emerged.

Abhishiktananda's experience with Hindu gurus led him to the conception of the guru as ultimately an inner reality. His attempt to conceive of Jesus as guru then logically led to the understanding of Christ as an inner reality. In continuity with the Hindu relativizing of history and individuality, he came to regard the historical Jesus as "passed and surpassed."[80] The fixation on the historical Jesus, he sees as idolatry, as the objectivation of the mystery of Christ which is in essence a transcendent and internal reality. Jesus' suffering and death are then also understood in symbolical or mystical terms as the self-mortification needed to come to that internalization.[81]

The main theological question which Abhishiktananda is then brought to confront is that of the uniqueness of Christ. He moves from the missionary theory of his day which understood Jesus Christ as the fulfillment of all other saviors to a conception of uniqueness as purely personal and relational. Jesus Christ is for him unique, just as any guru is unique for his disciples, and just as every person is unique in the eyes of God. This implies that the traditional Christian view of the discontinuity of Jesus Christ is dissolved. It opens the way for religious leaders and masters of other traditions to be regarded as the full manifestation of the divine and for any person to have access to the ultimate religious experience and divine status. Abhishiktananda may thus be regarded as a pluralist theologian *avant la lettre*.

In comparing the term purusha with the word "theandric"

---

[80] *Journal*, 1960, p. 279.

[81] This tendency to de-emphasize the historical Jesus has been criticized by other Christian theologians such as M.M. Thomas who regard the historical anchorage of the Christian faith as Christianity's particular contribution to India. See *The Hindu Response to the Unbound Christ* (Madras: Christian Literature Society, 1974) p. 150.

(both divine and human), of Christian Patristics,[82] Raimundo Panikkar also tends to minimalize the discontinuity of Christ: "It would destroy the whole mystery to envisage in separation from one another — even more so live — ... the homogeneity to man of the personal mystery of Christ."[83]

While acknowledging the possibility of the manifestation of the divine in other religious figures, Abhishiktananda remained attached to the figure of Jesus Christ. He admonishes his disciple not to change religious affiliation because: "It is under the sign of Jesus Christ that we have awakened to Brahman (God) even if it required the Veda to make us fully aware of him."[84] Jesus was for Abhishiktananda the full manifestation of Christ, and the one through whom Christians have come to believe in the reality they call Christ. Panikkar also pointed out that one cannot merely change the symbol of Christ for another religious symbol such as, for example, Rama. Symbols are not created or changed at will.[85]

In severing the historical Jesus from the inner Christ and in holding on to Christ as the symbol of the ultimate reality, Abhishiktananda comes to recognize his Hindu guru as Christ. Understood as the possibility of self-realization present in all, he sees Christ as realized in the authentic Hindu guru:

> The Christ whom I have first known and loved in his historical life in Jesus and later in his epiphany in the Church, has appeared to me at the end of time (of my time) in Bhagavan Sri Ramana.[86]

> Why would I oppose Christ and my guru? Isn't my guru the very form through which Christ becomes present to my senses, my sight, my hearing, my prostrating, so as to allow me to attain to him in

---

[82] *The Unknown Christ of Hinduism*, note 128, p. 91. Panikkar defines the term theandric as "the classical and traditional term for that intimate and complete unity which is realized paradigmatically in Christ between the divine and the human and which is the goal towards which everything here below tends—in Christ and the Spirit." *The Trinity and the Religious Experience of Man* (London: Darton, Longman & Todd, 1973) p. 71.

[83] *The Unknown Christ of Hinduism*, p. 72.

[84] Letter to Marc Chaduc (June 25, 1972).

[85] *The Unknown Christ of Hinduism*, pp. 26-29.

[86] *Journal*, 1955, p. 164.

the depth of my soul, where he is and who he is in reality. The Christ is more really close to me in my guru than in the memory which I may have of his apparition on earth. The encounter with the guru is really an epiphany.[87]

Abhishiktananda's understanding of the guru as epiphany of Christ may be seen as a (daring) concretization of Panikkar's expression of the continuation of the incarnation in the notion of *Christophany*, which he defines as the essence of every theandric being.[88] Panikkar holds that Christ fulfills his incarnation in anyone who is "completely empty of himself, is in a state of kenosis, of renunciation and annihilation."[89] Abhishiktananda states that "Jesus is every man upon whom the Spirit rests" and since the guru is one who is "heavy" or "weighty" with the Spirit, "Jesus manifests himself in every actual guru."[90] Against a too easy identification of any guru with Christ, Panikkar, nonetheless, warns: "Christians should recall that the Spirit makes all things new, and that in Christ we are a new creation, and that this does not happen once and for all, for we die every day. Also Hindus should recall that only at the end of many transformations does true realization come."[91]

---

[87] *Journal*, 1956, p. 177.

[88] *The Trinity and the Religious Experience of Man*, pp. 54 and 68. This concept has only been alluded to in a few of Panikkar's words and awaits its full development.

[89] *The Unknown Christ of Hinduism*, p. 61.

[90] *Journal*, 1968, p. 365.

[91] *The Unknown Christ of Hinduism*, p. 93.

III

The Guru in Catholic Ashrams:
A State of Affairs

> How can we not remind ourselves here of what is at times
> said by Hindus, that if the Christian preachers were really
> Gurus of that kind in India, people could not but flock to
> them.[1]

Abhishiktananda attributed the failure of the Christian mission
in India, not to a lack of efforts or means on the part of
Christianity, but to a surplus of resources within Hinduism, to
the central role which the guru plays in the Hindu tradition:

> It is because India has not only its scriptures which it believes to be
> sacred and revealed, but it has its "saints" and "sages" who
> continuously show the way and who save it from the surrounding
> materialism and from the latent secularism, who recall it, uplift it,
> and who render to the best the sense of the *neti*, who have them
> follow in their steps, adorning incessantly the skies of India with
> new spiritual constellations.[2]

Spoiled by this rich tradition of saints and mystics, the Indian
soul had become receptive only to those who speak from their
own experience and who are able to guide others to the same.
Abhishiktananda felt that Western Christianity had mostly delivered preachers and *pujaris*, ritual performers. What India awaited
were Christian sages, men and women who through their life and
teaching were able to testify to their personal experience of
Christ:

---

[1] Abhishiktananda, "An Approach to Hindu Spirituality" *Clergy Review* 54
(1969) p. 171.

[2] Jules Monchanin and Henri Le Saux, *Ermites du Saccidananda* (Tournai:
Casterman, 1956) p. 48.

India will set out in the following of Christ, only if, in the wake of Christ, she will have recognized great souls who, iluminated by His light, strong of His Spirit, will have realized in themselves the spiritual ideal for which she yearns.[3]

Within the Hindu tradition, such a spiritual master most often lives together with disciples in what is called an "ashram." This term may refer to the four major periods or stages into which the lifespan of a Hindu is traditionally subdivided, and which must be successively passed through. It is used here with the meaning of "house of peace," or "abode of tranquility" to refer to the place where seekers exert themselves (*shram*) to reach liberation.

It was in this sense that Monchanin and Abhishiktananda called the religious community which they envisioned "an Indian Benedictine Ashram" or "Saccidananda Ashram." The ashram, they believed, would be the ideal context to form and give birth to Christian rishis, Christian sages and gurus.[4]

When Monchanin died and the attempt to found a Catholic ashram seemed to have failed, Abhishiktananda retired into the Himalayas where he was visited by many a seeker and became the guru of a few Hindus and of the French seminarian Marc Chaduc. In the last five years of his life, he thus came to experience the other side of the master-disciple relationship. The journal notes relating to this period are incomplete, but letters written to family and friends reveal Abhishiktananda's self-understanding as a Catholic guru.

Catholic ashrams sprung up in the footsteps of Abhishikta-nanda. Although the Saccidananda ashram did not ultimately prove to be successful, he continued to believe in the ideal, which finally broke through at the "All-India Seminar on the Church in India Today" in 1969.[5] The final document of the workshop on

---

[3] J. Monchanin, and H. Le Saux, *Ermites du Saccidananda* (Tournai: Casterman, 1956) p. 48. "If someone would manifest through his life, and in a way which is valid for India, that he lives really within, there where the Father generates his Son in the unity of the Spirit, then he would be heard, he would be believed, even if he witnesses to the Lord Jesus and to his unique work on earth." *Ibid.*, p. 51.

[4] J. Monchanin, and H. Le Saux, *Ermites du Saccidananda*, p. 52.

[5] This conference was held in Bangalore from May 15 to 25, 1969. It proved to

spirituality, in which Abhishiktananda played an important role,[6] strongly insisted on the integration of Indian values and gifts which were recognized as being from the Spirit: "deep personal prayer, meditation, meditative silence, a sense of adoration, the yoga technique, the spirit of penance, and the sannyasi type of life."[7] Therefore, it was suggested that "priests, religious and lay people with a charisma for initiating others into truly interior prayer should at all costs be set aside for this work which should be recognized as absolute priority,"[8] and that "charismatic persons who may show signs of a special vocation to an ashram type of life, should be given all encouragement to do so, even if they are already living a priestly or religious life."[9] The need to stimulate the contemplative dimension of the Church in India by providing the appropriate context and guidance was reiterated at the Nagpur International Theological Conference in 1971 and at the Patna National Pastoral Consultation in 1973.

Large numbers of Catholic ashrams then suddenly came into existence. Regular cloisters, spirituality centers, retreat houses, and centers for dialogue started to call themselves ashrams. In many cases the term was used merely to translate the Western notion of religious community or because the Indian lifestyle and some customs had been adopted. Bishops in some cases "appointed" priests to "found" ashrams. This is against the ashram spirit.[10] Since the term ashram is vague and fluid, the number of

---

be one of the most important events in the recent history of the Church in India. Its suggestions, which were published in the *All India Seminar on the Church in India Today* (New Delhi: C.B.C.I. Centre, 1970), were taken into serious consideration in all segments of the Church.

[6] In a personal letter to Raymondo Panikkar he writes: "I got very large majorities for two amendments, one calling for ashrams of pure prayer and silence, and the other for a Liturgical renewal in depth, drawing on the values of Indian interiority" (June 25, 1969).

[7] *All-India Seminar on the Church in India Today*, p. 318. This was based on the belief that "these values belong to Christ and are a positive help to an authentic Christian life," and that they would help to "enter whole-heartedly into the response that India must make to the Divine Call of Redemption"(p. 561).

[8] *All-India Seminar on the Church in India Today*, p. 314.

[9] *All-India Seminar on the Church in India Today*, p. 319.

[10] As a reaction against this indiscriminate use of the term ashram, the term

Catholic ashrams quoted in different sources varies from eight to one hundred and eight.[11]

About a decade after the All-India Seminar, the "All-India Consultation on Ashrams" was held so as "to have a correct understanding of what an Ashram is, and to share it among the Christians of India."[12] A Catholic ashram was described as:

> A place of an intense and sustained spiritual quest, centered around a Guru, man or woman (usually one—sometimes more such persons) recognized by others as a person of deep spiritual experience. In an ashram primacy is given to this relentless quest through "sadhanas" or specifically Indian spiritual practices. It is a place where above all, people can experience God, and live in an ever-deepening awareness of His Presence. This is fostered by renunciation and detachment and an atmosphere of silence, peace and joy.[13]

The description further states that an ashram must be open to all who are in search of peace and enlightenment, that the lifestyle is simple in the Indian tradition and the food vegetarian, and that the essential work is *sadhana* or spiritual exercise through any of the three classical Indian *margas* or ways. The specificity of a Christian ashram is said to lie in the centrality of the bible and the experience of God in Christ. Characteristic of an ashram is, however, also the importance which is given to the reading from scriptures from other religious traditions, especially the Indian.

has recently been avoided. In Kalady, the birthplace of Shankara in the north of Kerala, the Jesuit Sebastian Painadath started in 1986 a center in a similarly quiet and beautiful natural environment like that in which ashrams usually emerge. Focussing on spirituality and inter-religious dialogue, it was intended to lead those who come to a deepening of their experience of the divine. Rather than being called an ashram, it was deliberately called a "spirituality center," *Sameeksha.*

[11] While the secretariat of the Indian Bishops Conference lists eight Catholic Ashrams, in his critique of Catholic ashrams and gurus, Sita Ram Goel counts one hundred and eight Catholic Ashrams. See *Catholic Ashrams* (New Delhi: Voice of India, 1988.) In her sociological study of Christian ashrams, Helen Ralston reports that she visited fourteen Catholic ashrams. See *Christian Ashrams. A New Religious Movement in Contemporary India.* (Lewiston: Edwin Mellen, 1988.)

[12] D.S. Amalorpavadass, "Ashram Aikiya: Whence and Whither," *Word and Worship* 17 (1984) p. 307.

[13] *Statement of the All-India Consultation on Ashrams*, point 3.

As in the traditional Hindu ashrams, a guru-figure is thus regarded as the constitutive cause, the *raison d'être* of a Catholic ashram. The sociologist Helen Ralston points out that, in this, Catholic ashrams differ from the Protestant ones which took after the Gandhian model of an ashram.[14] In Gandhi's Satyagraha ashram, the emphasis was upon political and social action, and only God was seen as Guru:

> The guru in whom Brahma, Vishnu and Shiva merge and who is the Supreme Brahman Himself cannot be an embodied man with his humors and diseases.[15]

Catholic ashrams would be "more inclined to regard a human guru as essential and to accept that authority rests in the guru." This distinguishes a Catholic from a Protestant ashram.[16] Abhishiktananda emphasized that "the real foundations of any worthwhile ashram are to be found not so much in the soil where the huts are as in the heart of the guru who lives there and in his personal contact in depth with the inner indweller."[17] Another pioneer of Catholic ashrams, Sister Vandana, states: "whether she/he is called guru, acharya, mataji or behnji is not too important, but her/his role is indispensable."[18]

Catholic ashrams are led by strong charismatic figures. Nonetheless, the term "Catholic guru" has not been unequivocally applied to the leaders of these ashrams. In a study of Christian ashrams, the sociologist Richard Taylor writes: "I know of no actual Christian ashrams that are led by gurus."[19] While some leaders hesitantly allow themselves to be called guru, others radically reject, or modify the title. The status, function and

---

[14] Helen Ralston, *Christian Ashrams: A New Religious Movement in Contemporary India* (New York: Edwin Mellen, 1987.)

[15] *The Collected Works of Mahatma Gandhi*, vol. XXXVI (1928), nr. 486, p. 387.

[16] H. Ralston, *Christian Ashrams*, p. 112.

[17] *Toward the Renewal of the Indian Church* (Ernakalum: KCM, 1970) p. 74.

[18] *Social Justice and Ashrams* (Bangalore: Asian Trading Corporation, 1982) p. 3.

[19] R. Taylor, "Christian Ashrams as a Style of Mission in India" *International Review of Mission* 68 (1979) p. 290.

authority accorded to the guru within the Hindu tradition are concentrated in the figure of Jesus Christ within Christianity.[20] Abhishiktananda's reflections on Jesus Christ as guru illustrate the radical implications of applying the term guru even to Christ.[21]

While the title of guru may generally be rejected, certain aspects of the Hindu institution of the guru may be integrated within Catholic ashrams. This becomes clear only through an analysis of the role of the charismatic leader in the origin and development of Catholic ashrams, in the relationship of Catholic ashrams with the Church, and in the ritual and social life in Catholic ashrams.

In *Ashrams, Past and Present*, the very first elaborate study on Christian ashrams, the question of the status and the role of the Christian guru is not discussed because the authors felt that "the details must emerge from experiments, and practical exigencies for which no rules can be previously laid down."[22] The practice and experience of several decades now provides ample food for reflection.

In the course of visits, during January and February, 1989, I studied the historical, institutional, theological, ritual and social dimensions of those Catholic ashrams which measure up to the standards cited by the Ashram Aikiya: Jeevan Dhara ashram in Jaharikal (in Rishikesh during the winter), Matri Dham ashram in Varanasi, Anjali ashram in Mysore, Aikiya Alayam ashram in Madras, Saccidananda ashram in Kulithalai, Kurisumala ashram in Vagamon, Tirumalai ashram in Nagercoil, and Christa Prema Seva ashram in Poona.[23] I also passed by religious communities which call themselves ashrams, but which do not answer to those

---

[20] See above, pp. 78-79.

[21] See above pp. 127-130.

[22] The ashram of the famous artist Jyoti Sahi in Bangalore could certainly be added to the list, but because of its selective audience (it is particularly for artists who seek to integrate art and spirituality) it has not been the object of my research.

[23] This Ashram Aikiya, or "Communion of Ashrams" also has a permanent channel of dialogue in the biannual *Ashram Aikiya Newsletter*.

standards: Jesu ashram and Maria Mai ashram in Varanasi. And the two Hindu ashrams which have exercised the strongest influence upon Catholic ashrams (Shivananda ashram in Rishikesh and Ramanashram in Tiruvannamalai) were also visited.

In each of these places, I stayed from one to eight days, participated in the daily life and the religious rituals of the ashram, interviewed the visitors, disciples, and leaders of the respective ashrams, inquired into some of the external responses (from both the Hindu and the Catholic communities), and reflected upon formal and informal statements made by the leaders of Catholic ashrams in books, articles, and in the reports of their gathering every two or three years in the "Ashram Aikiya."[24]

[24] P. Chenchiah, V. Chakkarai, *et al. Ashrams, Past and Present* (Madras: Indian Christian Book Club, 1941) pp. 267, 273.

CHAPTER ONE

The Origins and Development of Catholic Ashrams

Christian ashrams are a twentieth century phenomenon in India. While most Catholic ashrams have emerged since the Second Vatican Council and the All-India Seminar on the Church in India Today, the earliest Protestant ashrams date back to the beginning of the century. According to Helen Ralston, the leaders of Protestant ashrams "drew their inspiration from the Neo-Hindu reformers who founded ashrams for the collective reshaping of Indian society."[1] In recovering the pristine religious, social and educational structure of the past, they sought to restore India to its own creative source. Just as in the past, social, political, and ideological renewal had originated in ashrams, so they believed that the reform called for in modern times would arise from ashram communities. The Hindu ashrams from which the early Protestant ashrams drew their inspiration were the Aurobindo Ashram in Pondicherry, Tagore's Shantiniketan, and especially the Satyagraha ashram of Gandhi. The first Protestant ashrams, the Christakula, founded in 1921 by E. Forrester Paton and S. Jesudason, and the Christa Seva Sanga, started by J.C. Winslow in 1927, were associated with Gandhi.

Rather than with Protestant ashrams and the Neo-Hindu movement, it is with the more purely contemplative branch of the Hindu ashram tradition that Catholic ashrams may be associated. Saccidananda ashram, the first Catholic ashram had strong connections with the famous Hindu saint, Ramana Maharshi, whose ashram was located at the foot of the sacred hill Aruna-

---

[1] H. Ralston, *Christian Ashrams. A New Religious Movement in Contemporary India* (New York: Edwin Mellen, 1987) p. 113.

chala in Tiruvannamalai. Unlike Gandhi and Tagore, he did not engage in the active struggle for social justice or the cultural uplift of the Indian people. He represented the end of all struggle, inner peace, equanimity, and detachment from the world. The profound impact of Ramana Maharshi upon Abhishiktananda has already been demonstrated.[2] Many contemporary Catholic ashram leaders continue to draw inspiration from the example of Ramana Maharshi and undertake pilgrimages to Arunachala. Another more direct and concrete influence on Catholic ashrams has been the Sivananda ashram and its gurus in Rishikesh. Between Abhishiktananda and Swami Chidananda, a very close relationship developed. Several of the gurus of Catholic ashrams stayed for more or less extended periods at the Sivananda ashram and its influence is apparent in both ideas and practices.

Catholic ashrams follow a timetable based upon that of contemplative Hindu ashrams:

    4:30 Rising (bath, personal prayer, yoga)
    5:30 Pratah (morning) Samdhya
          Arati (waving of lights welcoming the day)
    6:30 Eucharist (Bharata puja or Indian celebration)
    7:30 Breakfast
    8:30 Ashram seva (service in the kitchen or on the grounds)
   10:15 Coffee
   10:30 Upadesha or Spiritual Discourse (not always organized)
   12:00 Madhya (midday) Samdhya
   12:30 Lunch
          Rest or study. In silence
   15:30 Tea
   16:00 Ashram seva
   16:30 Upadesha
   18:30 Sayan (evening) Samdhya
          Arati and Bhajans
   19:30 Dinner
   20:00 Satsang (gathering to share experiences of the day)

---

[2] See above, pp. 85-88.

While Hindu ashrams are implanted within a long tradition with specific conventions in matters of succession, continuity and development, Catholic ashrams are a new reality. From their relatively early history, the way in which each ashram emerged, developed and envisions the future, the particularity of a Christian ashram becomes manifest.

The Origins of Ashrams in Hinduism

Ashrams emerged in the Upanishadic period as a reaction against or an alternative to the official or institutional Brahmanical religion. The exaggerated ritualism and materialism of the Vedic sacrifice drove men of more contemplative nature into the forest to seek liberation in quiet and solitude. They internalized the sacrifice and practiced asceticism and contemplation. Soon, people in a state of spiritual unrest went in search of a sage in the forest and often settled nearby. Small communities then emerged of people exerting themselves to reach spiritual realization or liberation under the guidance of a spiritual master or guru. This is how the early ashrams came into existence.

When the laws of Manu codified life in four successive stages, the ashram style of life came to fit with the state of the *vanaprastha*, when the householder has seen the face of his grandson and retires, often with his wife, to the forest for a life of contemplation. The sannyasa state of life was understood as a life of homelessness and wandering and thus not associated with the sedentary life of an ashram. Later, different kinds of sannyasis were distinguished, some of which could live in ashrams.

From the more poetic parts of the Indian epics and from the play *Shakuntala* of Kalidasa a picture of these early ashrams may be drawn:

> That hoary hermit, world-renowned
> For holy deeds, within this ground
> Has set his pure and blessed home,
> Where gentle silvan creatures roam.[3]

[3] *Ramayana.* Book III, Canto XI (Griffith, trans.)

Roam Dandak wood observing well
The pleasant homes where hermits dwell,
Pure saints whose ordered souls adhere
To penance rites and vows austere.
There plenteous roots and berries grow,
The noble trees their blossoms show,
And gentle deer and birds of air
In peaceful troops are gathered there.[4]

The king who visits the ashram in *Shakuntala* takes off his jewels and puts away his bow before entering and describes the ambiance in the ashram:

I look with amazement both at their simplicity
and at what they might enjoy.
Their appetites are fed with air
Where grows whatever is most fair:
They bathe religiously in pools
Which golden lily-pollen cools:
They pray within a jewelled home
Are chaste where nymphs of heaven roam:
They mortify their desire and sin
With things that others fast to win.[5]

The ashram tradition receded in the intermediary period but came again into vogue with the Hindu reform movement. Although the aims were different and the form was slightly adapted to modern times, the basic structure of the ashram, centered upon a guru, remained. In his comparison of ancient and modern Hindu ashrams, Jesudason states that "all modern Hindu ashrams, like the ancient ones have some outstanding features. First of all there is a central personality, the founder or inspirer of the whole institution, the object of reverential love and devotion and filial love for all the inmates of the ashram, the one who corresponds to the Maha Rishi of ancient ashrams."[6]

---

[4] *Ramayana.* Book III, Canto VIII.

[5] *Sakuntala,* act VII: description of the ashram of Kasyapa. Quoted from P. Chenchiah, V. Chakkarai, and A.N. Sudarisanam, *Ashrams, Past and Present* (Madras: Indian Christian Book Club, 1941) p. 22.

[6] S. Jesudason, *Ashrams, ancient and modern* (Vellore: Sri Ramachandra, 1937) p. 10.

Though the vision — whether social, educational, political or spiritual — often became predominant, it remained inseparably related to the visionary: Aurobindo, Gandhi, Tagore, Sivananda, Ramdas, or Ramana Maharshi.

Early Catholic Gurus

Roberto de Nobili

That nothing less than a real spiritual master would be able to seduce Indians to Christianity, the very first Western missionaries to India knew. At his Madurai mission, Roberto de Nobili (1577-1656) wore the orange cloth of the Hindu sage and had his head shaven except for a tuft of hair at the back. In order to appeal to the Brahmin caste, he presented himself as a Brahmin from Italy, wore the sacred thread of the twice-born, and kept strictly to the caste prescriptions and to the purity rules. He studied Tamil and Sanskrit and read the Veda. He entered into philosophical debates with Pandits, and soon became fully integrated within the Brahmin community of Madurai. He was regarded as a guru with his own particular teaching and gathered many disciples around him. The affiliation of these Brahmin disciples, was, however, not so much with the Church as with the person of de Nobili. As a result, very few remained Christian after his death.

Although de Nobili exposed a very advanced degree of empathy with the Hindu religious tradition, his attitude towards Hindu beliefs and the Hindu philosophical system was demeaning. His appearance as guru was more of a ruse to convert Hindus, rather than evidence of a belief in the values and truth of the Hindu tradition. It arose suspicion within the church, and he encountered much opposition.

Brahmabandhab Upadhyaya

When, three centuries later (in 1894), Brahmabandhab Upadhyaya donned the ocher robe of the sannyasi, a whole different attitude towards the Indian religious tradition lay at its basis.

Around the turn of the century, a radical change of attitude towards Hinduism occurred. Max Müller's translation of the sacred scriptures of the East had given access to the wealth and depth of insight imbedded in the ancient Indian scriptures. The fulfillment theory of non-christian religions came into vogue and enhanced the interest in India's religious tradition (if only as a *praeparatio evangelica*.) The independence movement swept all along in a feeling of national and cultural pride. Like de Nobili, Upadhyaya believed that "it is the *Sannyasi* (monk) alone who is capable of presenting to our countrymen the mysteries of the Catholic Faith."[7] But unlike de Nobili, the sannyasi he envisioned would be profoundly immersed in the Hindu religious tradition. A convert from Hinduism, Brahmabandhab knew and continued to respect the religion of his ancestors. Although the Christianization of India remained the ultimate end, the Indianization of Christianity was no longer regarded as merely a means. Brahmabandhab believed that Christianity itself could be enriched by dropping its Western gown and adopting an Indian one. More than on the conversion of Hindus, he concentrated on the transformation of the Church.

Realizing that "this transformation can be effected only by the hands of Indian missionaries preaching the Holy Faith in the Vedantic language, holding devotional meetings in the Hindu way and practicing the virtue of poverty conformably to Hindu asceticism,"[8] Brahmabandhab saw the urgent need for the formation of an Indian type of Christian monk, of Christian sannyasis. Near the marble rocks of Jubbulpore he retired with two disciples to start a Catholic *math*, a monastery along Indian lines where he hoped that "in the midst of solitude and silence will be reared up true Yogis to whom the contemplation of the Triune Saccidanandam will be food and drink."[9] In calling the Kasthalik a math

---

[7] B. Animananda, *The Blade: Life and Work of Brahmabandhab Upadhyaya* (Calcutta: Roy & Roy, 1945) p. 70.

[8] B. Animananda, *The Blade*, p. 75.

[9] *The Blade*, p. 78.

rather than an ashram, he remained closer to the Western conception of monastic life as a permanent commitment.

At first Brahmabandhab received the support from the bishop of Nagpur, but his initiative was rejected by the papal delegate and he was forced to abandon the Kasthalik. From Jubbulpore, he moved to Calcutta and for a time worked closely with Rabindranath Tagore in developing the ashram at Shantiniketan. Increasing Church opposition, however, baffled every attempt at dialogue and inculturation. Soon even his journals *Sophia* and *The Twentieth Century* were banned.

Brahmabandhab Upadhyaya (which literally means "the teacher") had one true disciple, called Animananda or Rewachand, who joined in the Kasthalik experiment. In *The Blade*, the famous biography Animananda wrote about Brahmabandhab, their relationship is not explicitly discussed. The careful way in which every event and reflection of his master is recorded attests to a deep devotion. Nonetheless, Animananda himself had some misgivings about the orthodoxy of his master's practices, as is reflected in the remark: "Krishna worship and the Sarasvati festival had shaken my belief in the guru."[10] Even though he followed Brahmabandhab through trials and tribulations and was profoundly submerged in his thought, he still maintained a critical distance and his Christian faith remained predominant over his devotion to the guru.[11] While Brahmabandhab failed to gather a following during his life, his role as pioneer and guru became manifest only after his death. Monchanin came to refer to him as his guru:

> I have towards him a filial feeling, as if in some distant way, he was somehow my guru.[12]

---

[10] *The Blade*, p. 188.

[11] Animananda himself later had an ashram called Rewachand in Ranchi but does not seem to have gathered disciples.

[12] Jules Monchanin, *Mystique de L'Inde, mystère chrétien* (Paris: Fayard, 1974) p. 154.

Saccidananda Ashram

An Indian Benedictine Ashram

It took half a century before the tradition initiated by Brahma-bandhab Upadhyaya was picked up again and new attempts were made to integrate the Hindu spiritual tradition within Christianity. In 1939, the French priest, Jules Monchanin arrived in India, and worked for ten years as a priest in various parishes in the area of Tiruchirapalli.[13] Ten years later, he was joined by Henri Le Saux. Together they retired from the world in the way of the Hindu sannyasin, and settled in huts on the banks of the river Kaveri in Tamil Nadu. Their goal was "to realise in India an attempt of monastic life which, while being solidly based upon the foundations of Christian monasticism, would manifest itself clearly as a natural product of the spiritual climate of India and of its aspirations, as the authentic fruit of the Indian soul of all times.[14] The ashram was called "Saccidananda ashram," reflecting the attempt to integrate the experience of the divine as a state of Being, Consciousness and Bliss with the Christian Trinity. The blueprint for the ashram was laid down in *An Indian Benedictine Ashram*, published in 1951.[15] The purpose of the ashram was to give birth to Christian sannyasis who would be less Christian monks become sannyasi, than sannyasis become Christian.[16]

The original Saccidananda ashram never really took hold.[17] The reason, according to Richard Taylor, was that "they were too Benedictine" and that "the rules of Western Monasticism and the style of an Indian ashram just cannot mix."[18] The starting

[13] In Panneipatti, he called the hut which he had built "Bhakti-Ashram."

[14] J. Monchanin and H. Le Saux, *Ermites du Saccidananda* (Tournai: Casterman, 1956) p. 55.

[15] The title was later changed to *A Benedictine Ashram* (because it was felt that an "Indian ashram" was a tautology) and the content was further developed in *Ermites du Saccidananda*.

[16] *Ermites du Saccidananda*, p. 57.

[17] When Monchanin died in 1957, not one person had permanently joined the ashram and Abhishiktananda felt more and more called to the Himalayas.

[18] R. Taylor, "Christian Ashrams as a Style of Mission in India," *International Review of Mission* 68 (1979) p. 286.

point and fundamental inspiration of the ashram remained the Benedictine Rule. There were attempts to correct or complement the traditional understanding of the role of the abbot with that of the guru:

> His main role is not to administrate, nor merely to have the Rule obeyed and to decide upon precise applications of the Rule. He is first of all a spiritual master, the father and guru of every monk who has been entrusted upon him by the Lord. He carries for God the responsibility of conducting everyone toward the divine path according to the way which is best adapted to the personal temperament and the spiritual gifts of each. He must help the disciple attain to the state of perfection, of love and wisdom to which God has predestined him.[19]

The Hindu notion of the guru thus could be a reminder to the abbot of the primacy of his spiritual role. Yet while the guru in Hinduism is autonomous, the spiritual master or the abbot in the Christian tradition is ultimately subject to a higher authority or Rule. This makes the Christian monastic tradition hard to reconcile with the Hindu structure of the ashram.[20]

It was only after Abhishiktananda retired to live as a real sannyasi in the Himalayas that his fame as guru began to spread. He had become spiritual director in several convents and the guru of the Carmelite sister Thérèse. People went to visit him in his hut in Gyansu, seminarians stayed with him during the holidays, and two Hindus, Ramesh and Lalit, lived with him as disciples for extended periods of time. More and more people sought his counsel and direction and in several letters he mentions the "request, coming to me both from young Europeans who come to India and from young Indian priests, to be more accessible."[21] He accepted to stay in a place in Lucknow where he stayed while

---

[19] *Ermites du Saccidananda*, p. 99.

[20] Other reasons for the apparent failure of Saccidananda ashram may be extrinsic: the experiment may have been merely premature, the average Christian uninformed, and the church unprepared to promote the ashram life in the church before it proved its validity. Every new venture must pass through trial and error and the so-called failures may be indispensible steps which only later on reveal their relevance.

[21] Letter to Raimundo Panikkar (December 8, 1970).

he was in the plains, but declined the offer of the bishop of Benares to start an ashram in his diocese.

One of the many Europeans who wrote to Abhishiktananda expressing the desire to travel to India and to meet him was Marc Chaduc, a French seminarian from Bourg. They started an intensive correspondence, and in October 1971, Marc arrived in India. In him Abhishiktananda found the perfect disciple, someone to whom he could pass on everything he had experienced and realized. This allowed him to personally experience the meaning of the term Upanishad as a "secret teaching which can only be transmitted in the communication from the guru to the disciple."[22] While many saw Abhishiktananda as their guru, he himself felt that he only had one disciple. Just before his death, he wrote to Marc Chaduc:

> I think you are the only one to whom I have been able to say and transmit everything, through words and beyond words... You have accepted the "tabula rasa" and from this tabula rasa, sparks have come forth.[23]

Abhishiktananda felt that his disciple had actually gone beyond himself, that Marc Chaduc actually lived and experienced everything that he had merely written about. The direct lineage descending from Abhishiktananda was, however, broken. Shortly after Abhishiktananda's death on December 7, 1973, Marc Chaduc disappeared in the Himalayas never to return.[24]

A Camaldolese Ashram

When in 1968 Abhishiktananda left Saccidananda ashram, Bede Griffiths, an English Benedictine monk who had arrived in India in 1955 and had been the co-founder of another Catholic ashram, took over. The first permanent members, Amaldass and Christadass, joined in 1971 and, four years later, two Tamil

---

[22] Letter to Odette Baumer (May 22, 1972).
[23] Letter to Marc Chaduc (November 23, 1973.)
[24] The door of his hut was found open and his glasses shattered on the ground.

brothers were added to the core group. For many years therafter, no more permanent members joined. The bishop of Tiruchirapalli dissented and some conservative Christians became actively opposed. Against this opposition, Griffiths searched for an institutional status to gain general recognition and to ensure the continuity of the ashram. In 1982, Saccidananda ashram affiliated with the Italian order of Camaldoli which provided the necessary institutional support without interfering with the freedom of the ashram. The permanent members of the ashram then simultaneously became professed monks of the order of Camaldoli. Among the core members of the ashram, there are now four solemnly professed, four simply professed, and two oblates.

It is not so much from the core community, as from the number of temporary members, short term visitors and sympathizers who flock to the ashram that the success of Saccidananda ashram, or rather its guru, may be measured. With the many books and articles he wrote, Bede Griffiths has become one of the most popular Catholic gurus for Westerners in India.[25] People from all over the world flock to Saccidananda ashram to stay for a few days, weeks or months.[26]

From Saccidananda ashram, several offshoots led by disciples of Bede Griffiths have emerged both in India and abroad. The famous Indian Catholic artist Jyoti Sahi who was a disciple of Bede Griffiths, started an artist's ashram in Bangalore. Like Da Fonseca before him who lived in the Christa Prema Seva ashram in Poona, he felt that the ashram provided the Indian contemplative context needed for the development of real Indian Christian art.[27] Another disciple of Bede Griffiths, Amaldass, took over the

[25] Inspired by the spirituality of the guru and of Saccidananda ashram, several attempts have been made to start similar contemplative communities in the West: in the United States, in Germany, and recently the proposal circulated to start a Saccidananda ashram in Belgium.

[26] Since there was a shortage of room and manpower, a female community under the leadership of Sister Marie Louise has settled near the ashram to help Griffiths run the ashram and to accommodate visitors.

[27] In most other ashrams, and in many a church and seminary, Jyoti Sahi's work has pride of place.

leadership of an ashram in Madhya Pradesh. He has gained some fame as a Yoga teacher. In the United States and in Europe, religious communities have emerged modelled after Saccidananda ashram. Disciples abroad stay in contact with their guru through letters, regular visits and mutual support.

Kurisumala Ashram

Prior to taking over the Saccidananda ashram, Bede Griffiths had been involved in the foundation of another ashram in the Kottayam district of Kerala. In 1955, the Belgian Cistercian monk Francis Mahieu had left for India to join Monchanin and Abhishiktananda. Soon, however, he was invited by the Syro-Malankara bishop of Kerala to start an ashram on the top of the rugged mountain, called *Kurisumala*, "mountain of the cross," in Vagamon. With Bede Griffiths, he thus laid the foundations for the ashram which kept the name Kurisumala.

Since Kurisumala ashram began under the auspices of the Syro-Malankara Church in India, attempts at inculturation had to take account not only of the Western and Indian traditions, but also of the Syrian tradition. Kurisumala thus tried to combine the Cistercian way of life with the Syrian liturgy and the Indian ashram tradition. The Cistercian lifestyle manifests itself in the attempt to establish a balance and harmony between physical and spiritual labor. In keeping with the self-reliance characteristic of Western monasticism, a dairy farm was started. This has become one of the most important milk supplies of Kerala. All monks are involved in farming activities. Their physical labor is interrupted by long periods of meditation and elaborate liturgy, in which the Syrian character of the ashram becomes manifest. The Syrian Qurbana has also been translated in four volumes entitled *Prayer with the Harp of the Spirit*.

As ashram, Kurisumala is an open community which welcomes visitors for more or less extensive periods of time. It has also introduced the Hindu monastic stages or states of *sadhaka*, *brahmacharya* and *sannyasa*. While it is the Rule which governs the life of the community, the Rule is strongly connected to the leader of the ashram, who has called himself *acharya*, or teacher, and has generally come to be known as Francisacharya.

The membership of Kurisumala is less permanent than that of traditional monasteries, but more so than in other ashrams, both Catholic and Hindu. The core members of the ashram have, for more than three decades, numbered about twenty. Although the rule has become more flexible over the years, life is still more severe, rituals more elaborate and the discipline more strict than in other ashrams.

Kurisumala ashram has given birth to several offshoots. The most successful of these is Saccidananda ashram which Bede Griffiths took over after having been the co-founder and joint leader of Kurisumala ashram. Several other sannyasis from Kurisumala have attempted to start their own ashram, mostly without success. One of these is, however, of particular interest because of its peculiar development.[28]

At the invitation of the bishop of Kottar, Mariadass, one of the first disciples of Francisacharya settled in 1972 in the impoverished area of Nagercoil near Cape Comorin. At the foot of a hill, he, along with a few other sannyasis, started the Tirumalai ashram, or the ashram of the transfiguration. The miserable condition of the people living in the neighborhood immediately called for social action. Houses were built for the poor potters who lived around and elementary medical care was provided. The workers were organized and informed about their rights. Gradually, social work came to dominate life in the ashram. This was the work of the more active members of the ashram. Fr. Mariadass retired to a more quiet place behind the mountain. This caused a split between the purely contemplative ashram and what came to be known as the Tirumalai ashram social center, coordinated by Father James and Sister Lieve, who had both been socially active in that area. While community health-care re-

---

[28] Two other ashrams were started in Kerala as offshoots of Kurisumala, the Chayalpadi ashram and the Dhyana ashram, neither of which has been successful.

mained the main focus of concern, a great many other activities and services have emerged from the ashram: women's organizations, child-care training, potters' cooperatives, basic communities uniting the fishermen, dialogue groups and so forth. The activities of the Tirumalai ashram social center have had an effect upon about 35,000 families in 126 villages. Three hundred local people are involved in the coordination of the different groups and are trained for this by thirty staff members. The more or less permanent members of the Tirumalai ashram social center, however, do not number more than six. Except for occasional visitors and groups for retreats, Mariadass has remained alone.

Christa Prema Seva Ashram

Originally called Christa Seva Sangha, this ashram was one of the earliest Christian ashrams in India. It started in 1927 with a small group of Indian and English Christians who sought to live the gospel in a thoroughly Indian way. The founder of the community, the Anglican missionary Jack Winslow wrote in the constitution:

> The Sangha seeks to develop its whole life and work in India in relation to Indian conditions, and not to reproduce there all characteristics of any existing community or any particular religious system of the West.[29]

The use of the term Sangha, rather than ashram, seems to insinuate that the community saw itself in continuity with the Buddhist rather than the Hindu monastic tradition. Buddhist monasticism generally emphasizes the equality of all monks rather than the preeminence of the guru. It is the community, rather than the guru-chela relationship, which is at the basis of the formation of Buddhist monasteries. This suits the Protestant emphasis upon community rather than hierarchy.

There was pluralism in the structure of the ashram which consisted of a first order of celibate men, a corresponding second

---

[29] Quoted by S. Grant, *Lord of the Dance* (Bangalore: Asian Trading Corporation, 1978) p. 108.

order of women, and a third order of married couples and lay people.[30] The Sangha ended, partly because of internal disagreements on the admission of married members in the core group and partly because the successor of Father Winslow, Father Bill Lash, was appointed Bishop of Bombay. The property then came under the Bombay Diocesan Board of Trustees of the Church of North India.

In the late sixties, the Anglican bishop of Bombay, Christopher Robinson, tried to start the ashram again as an ecumenical experiment. The sisters of the society of the Sacred Heart then joined with the Anglican community of St. Mary the Virgin to form an ecumenical ashram. The leadership of the Christa Prema Seva ashram has been moderated by the use of the term acharya rather than guru, and by shared leadership.[31] This leadership is now shared by Sister Sara Grant, R.S.C.J., and the Anglican Sister Brigitta.

From the beginning, the ecumenical dimension of the ashram has been extended to non-Christian religions, as well as to lay and married people. Though their motives for living in the ashram were secondary, students of yoga and Indian dance were welcomed in the ashram. There is always an occupancy of about twenty to thirty people. The core group presently consists of four religious, two priests and four lay people.

Jeevan Dhara Ashram

Before Sisters Sara and Brigitta, Christa Prema Seva ashram had been led for a few years by Sister Vandana, R.S.C.J. In 1976, she left the Christian ashram to immerse herself completely in the

---

[30] C.F. Andrews was for some time a member of the Sangha and Gandhi was a friend of Winslow and a regular visitor. Angelo da Fonseca, one of the first to develop authentic Indian Christian art, lived in the ashram.

[31] It was not immediately clear what the status and the role of the head of the ashram would be. During the first month, an orientation program had people with ashram experience such as Abhishiktananda and Dadasaheb Pandit. The people interested shared their experience and expectations. The status and role of the head of the ashram was discussed but as Sara Grant pointed out "not fully solved."

Hindu ashram life. She visited a variety of Hindu ashrams and stayed for a year in the Shivananda ashram in Rishikesh. With another sister and two novices, she then settled in a few *kuttirs* or small abodes in the North. More and more people gradually came to stay with them and the need was felt for a larger place. In 1981, a piece of land in the Himalayas was donated by the Bishop Mundadan and an ashram called Jeevan Dhara, or "living waters," was constructed to house about twenty to thirty people.

In Jeevan Dhara ashram, spiritual authority is shared by Vandana and Ishapriya, an English Sister of the Sacred Heart of Jesus, who was already involved in the Christa Prema Seva Ashram. They are addressed as *mataji*, a term used to address older women or female gurus. The ashram closes during the coldest months of the year and the four or five permanent members of the ashram then move to the kuttirs in Rishikesh or travel to give seminars or retreats in different places all over the world. Both Vandana and Ishapriya have gathered a large number of followers who periodically stay with them in the Jeevan Dhara ashram. During the warmer season of the year, the ashram is thus usually full.

Seminary Ashrams

The Seminary-cum-Ashram

Even though Abhishiktananda's own experience as guru did not generate a lineage, his ideas on the need for Christian gurus gradually spread. When in the late sixties, the need for the inculturation of seminary life was felt, Abhishiktananda was consulted. When he was asked for "formulas," Abhishiktananda answered:

> What you need is a guru, you need men who are interiorly open, who have the sense of the Presence. Automatically they will find ways to communicate their experience to those disciples who are aware of the Presence.[32]

[32] Quoted in a letter to Odette Baumer (November 9, 1969.)

For Abhishiktananda, this project was an incentive to think about the basis and structure of a seminary adapted to the Indian lifestyle and needs, of a seminary which would be an ashram. In an unpublished article entitled "An Ashram-Seminary," he pointed out that the aim of the ashram cum seminary or seminary cum ashram would be the preparation of "monk-priests" or "sannyasi-priests," who would function not only as administrators of the rituals, but as real gurus:

> in one word we need people who, as Christians, insert themselves in the age-long tradition of *gurus* and lead their brothers, wherever they may still be in their path towards Christ, to deepen in the centre of their heart their experience of the indwelling spirit.[33]

The program would emphasize ascetic and contemplative formation, the study of Sanskrit and the reading of Hindu scriptures. Initiation into both Christian and Hindu scriptures was intended to lead the seminarian to the experience rather than to feed his mind with what Abhishiktananda regarded as irrelevant data.

The experiment of what came to be known as the "Pilot Seminary" failed. Rather than a full seminary program, the idea was presented as an opportunity for priests to have a year's ashram experience. The first experiment took place in the Christ Panthi Ashram in Varanasi under the leadership of Father Isvaraprasad and Father Bhatt, both priests of the Indian Missionary society. The first year eight volunteers participated and the first evaluation (after ten months) was unanimously positive. A year later, however, only six showed interest in the project and, the year after, so few volunteered that the venture was stopped. The idea of a "Guru-Shishya Model of Formation"[34] nevertheless remains present and most seminaries implement in their curriculum an extensive study of the Hindu religious tradition.

---

[33] "An Ashram-Seminary", unpublished article, pp. 2 and 6.

[34] This is the title of an article by Antonio Rodrigues in *Indian Theological Studies* 20 (1983) 308-326.

Matri Dham Ashram

In several religious orders or congregations, attempts have been made to integrate an ashram experience into the seminary formation so as to awaken and cultivate the contemplative dimension and the sensitivity for the Indian culture. The Indian Missionary Society has been a pioneer in this area. In 1954 already, Monsignor Joseph Fernandez, who was the superior of the Indian Missionary Society, bought a plot of land next to the seminary, planted trees and built huts with the idea of having seminarians spend a few years of their training in solitude and contemplation. The project, however, was not successful and the huts were left in ruins. Father Isvaraprasad, who had been involved in the "Pilot Seminary," revived the initiative. He built new huts and a new chapel, cleaned the forest and planted vegetables so that from the ruins of the old a new ashram emerged in 1982.

Ishvaraprasad then became the acharya of the Matri Dham ashram. Every year, four or five seminarians have the opportunity to fully immerse themselves in Indian Christian spirituality and contemplative life. The ashram, however, also welcomes individuals and groups for retreats. The property, the acharya and the ashramites remain, however, all under the auspices of the Indian Missionary Society.

Aikiya Alayam

The Jesuit Father Ignatius Hirudayam also hoped to integrate seminary and ashram life in building an ashram large enough to house about forty theologate students and ashramites. While ashrams are usually located in idyllic places in the countryside, Father Ignatius consciously chose an urban setting to start his ashram called Aikiya Alayam. Besides the normal functions of an ashram, his purpose was to provide a place for inter-religious dialogue within the city and to promote the study of the Shaiva Siddhanta school of Hinduism, and Tamil arts.

The Aikiya Alayam ashram was inaugurated in 1968 in a house made available by the bishop.[35] Four years later, the Jesuit province provided the means to build a new ashram, which in 1979 also provided residence for Jesuit theology students. The emphasis in Jesuit theological education was then, however, less upon spirituality and the values which the ashram represents than upon liberation theology and grass-roots apostolate. As a result, two separate communities came to live side by side in mutual aggravation. The core membership of the Aikiya Alayam ashram consists of a few faithful disciples and a few temporary members who stay in the ashram while pursuing their university education in Tamil arts or literature. The tension which exists in the ashram illustrates the difficulty of establishing an ashram within an existing institutional setting. Father Ignatius remains in the first place loyal and obedient to the Jesuit order.

Anjali Ashram

It was in order to balance a merely intellectual understanding of Christianity with a more experiential one and to experiment with the possibilities of inculturation that the Anjali ashram emerged. Father D.S. Amalorpavadass started the ashram in 1979, a week after he had been appointed to the Chair of Christianity at the university of Mysore. He believed that theoretical study "ought to be coupled with and supported by a genuine Christian community life, lived in an Indian tradition, context and atmosphere, following an Indian life-style."[36] The name "Anjali" ashram was adopted to illustrate the hospitality and love with which everyone was received in the ashram.[37]

Anjali ashram was first located near the university, but it was moved a few years later to large and quiet grounds outside the city, just under the famous Chamundi Hill. It became the most

[35] It was Abhishiktananda who gave the inaugural speech.
[36] In the brochure of Anjali ashram.
[37] "Anjali" is the closed handpalm gesture with which Hindus greet each other in respect.

organized and organizing of all Catholic ashrams. While other ashrams accommodate themselves to the needs of the visitors, Anjali ashram itself designs programs and courses which volunteers can attend on fixed dates. For example, the first week of every month, the ashram offers a week-long introduction to Indian Christian spirituality called *Atma Purna Anubhava*. Twice or three times a year a follow-up course called *Brahma Saksatkara Anubhava* is organized. Each month at least a hundred people, mostly Indian religious, priests, novices and seminarians, but including some Westerners, participate.[38]

Apart from these courses, Anjali Ashram differs little from other ashrams, structurally as well as numerically. There are about seven core members, and in times when there are no courses, there is an average of about twenty visitors.

Summary

While Catholic ashrams may appear to be very similar to the Hindu prototype, certain aspects of their origins and development reveal the radically different religious context within which they are imbedded and the *tour de force* needed to introduce a religious structure within a different religious tradition. Within the Hindu tradition, ashrams emerge spontaneously around a spiritual master or guru. They are self-sufficient, self-reliant, and completely autonomous. Catholic ashrams, however, were often "founded," or started through the initiative or the support of a particular bishop or congregation. The zeal for inculturation often led to the planning, building and inaugurating of Catholic ashrams before there were any disciples. Except for Abhishiktananda, none of the Catholic gurus became guru in the ordinary Hindu way, this is, after having gone through discipleship and after having been recognized as guru by another guru.

[38] According to the ashram statistics, in 1988, eleven sessions of *Atma Purna Anubhava* were organized in which 1072 seekers participated. There was one session of *Brahma Satsatkara Anubhava* with 46 participants. In the whole, 1160 people stayed for a week in the ashram, 119 for two or three weeks, 30 for one to six months, and 20 for one year or more.

This often unnatural foundation of Catholic ashrams has, however, been remedied by history itself. Only those ashrams have survived and flourished where the charisma of the spiritual master proved strong enough to attract disciples. The element of spontaneity was thus again introduced. The different Catholic ashrams gradually took the identity of their respective head who may be a woman or a man, young or old, religious or lay. Some ashrams remained closely connected to a particular religious order or to a monastic community while others attempted to assume as much freedom as possible; some integrated intellectual study or social action, while others remained purely experiential; some held to a severe discipline while others became more flexible. As in the Hindu tradition, every Catholic ashram may then be seen as a separate and unique reality, dependent upon the particular spiritual leader. Nevertheless, the absolute autonomy which is characteristic of a Hindu ashram can never be assumed in Christianity.

Numerically speaking, Catholic ashrams may appear to be an insignificant phenomenon. Although on the whole, two to three thousand people may yearly visit Catholic ashrams and stay from a few days to several months, the number of core members in each ashram does not number more than twenty. The total amount of people fully involved in Catholic ashrams is thus no more than a few hundred, which, considering the fact that there are about fourteen million Catholics in India,[39] may seem negligable. Yet it is in the Catholic ashrams that the pioneering efforts toward inculturation on all levels have taken place. Angelo da Fonseca and Jyoti Sahi, the two most famous Indian Christian artists, lived in Christian ashrams. Some of the chapels of Christian ashrams have come to stand as exemples of the inculturation of Christian architecture. The Indian liturgy, often called the Christian Bharata puja, has been developed in Christian ashrams. Finally, the model of spiritual authority which is present in Catholic ashrams may become a challenge to the whole Church.

---

[39] This is less than two percent of the whole population.

CHAPTER TWO

Catholic Ashrams and the Church in India

Within the Hindu tradition, ashrams and gurus are completely autonomous and self-sufficient. The attempts at inculturation through Catholic ashrams thus naturally raises questions concerning the relationship between these ashrams, and their leaders, and the institutional Church. While the institution may have supported and sometimes even established a Catholic ashram, the success or failure of an ashram is dependent solely upon the charismatic authority of the leader. This authority is not invested by the Church hierarchy, but results from the personal qualities of the master, and the surrender of disciples. Helen Ralston points out that: "Ashram literature and ideology, particularly in the Catholic ashram movement, tend to neglect that the sufficient condition for the creation and continuing existence of the community is the ongoing relationship between guru and disciples."[1]

This puts Catholic ashrams and their leaders in an ambiguous situation with regard to the institution. As ashrams, they are supposed to be completely autonomous and self-sufficient. But the epithet "Catholic" involves a certain degree of submission to the authority of office. It may thus be seen as a manifestation of the age-old and essential tension which exists between charismatic and authority within the Church.

Charisma as the Mainspring of Hinduism

The Hindu tradition knows of no central authoritative body, of no overarching institution which would control matters of faith

---

[1] H. Ralston, *Christian Ashrams*, p. 51.

and order. There are various philosophical schools and sects which submit to a particular worldview and certain beliefs, and there are authoritative *pandits*, Sanskrit teachers who transmit the sacred Vedas, who may be consulted on issues of grammar, ritual correctness, and right pronunciation and who may be called in as jury in philosophical debates. Yet this in no way affects the authority of one who is regarded as realized. The guru is seen as being beyond all limited worldviews and norms, beyond the normal standards of moral judgment. The authority of the guru is absolute. It needs no external legitimation, and is therefore not dependent upon external control. The lineage of gurus, the *guru-parampara*, may guarantee the authenticity of the living guru, but every single guru in the lineage incarnates the full authority of the traditions. When a disciple reaches the level of spiritual realization of the guru, he is recognized as an equal and thereby, in turn, assumes total freedom.

While the ordinary way of becoming a guru is through the recognition by another guru and the surrender of disciples, the latter is sufficient for someone to become installed as guru. An individual who belongs to no particular lineage or teaching tradition may be regarded by disciples as a guru. This is how new teaching traditions or lineages are born.[2] The authority of the guru is thus finally self-legitimizing. Since there is no central institution, there is no tension between the authority of office and charismatic authority.

Charismatic Authority in the Church

The situation within the Catholic tradition is very different. The existence of a centralized and hierarchical body of institutional authority places every authority which is not derived from the institution in a position of potential threat. Within the Catholic tradition, charismatic authority has been kept in a dialectical tension with the authority of office. While the authority of office

---

[2] In some cases, institutionalization may try to substitute for the relative lack of charismatic authority in successors. This only works, however, when the charisma of the founder is still strongly alive, as in the case of the Ramanashram.

is represented by the hierarchical ministry which is conferred sacramentally and constituted juridically, charisma may be defined as the "non-hierarchic and non-sacramental special gifts of the Holy Spirit which summon and enable a Christian to minister in a more extraordinary way in the Church and in the world."[3] While office secures stability and continuity, charisma stands for renewal, reform, development, and growth. The relationship between office and charisma is thus a delicate but a vital one. Without charismatic input, the authority of office risks becoming a dry and static bureaucracy. Unchanneled charisma, on the other hand, may end up in complete dispersion and splintering. Without centralized authority, every charismatic leader may start his or her own new religion.

Charismatic authority always represents the risk of heresy and schism within the Church. It emerges within the margins and in spite of the authority of office. It is self-sufficient, self-legitimizing, non-structural, non-hierarchic, and non-sacramental. Charisma is incorporated in the Church only by way of deliberate surrender to the authority of office. This willingness to surrender to the official authority in the Church is, in turn, often regarded as a guarantee of authentic charisma.

Throughout the centuries, the Indian Church has settled into a rigid and formal authority structure. It is the glaring discrepancy between this highly institutionalized Church structure on the one hand and the Hindu propensity toward spirituality on the other which led to the critique of Abhishiktananda and Monchanin. They called upon the Church authorities to turn from administrative to more spiritual matters and to become real spiritual masters:

> And the Hindu will come to the leaders of the Holy Church to ask for the nourishment of his soul, only when he recognizes in them real gurus, true spiritual masters.[4]

---

[3] A. Bruggeman, "Charisma and Office: The Dialectic of Ministry," in D.S. Amalorpavadass, ed., *Ministries in the Church in India* (Delhi: C.B.C.I. Center, 1976) p. 21.

[4] J. Monchanin and H. Le Saux, *Ermites du Saccidananda* (Tournai: Casterman, 1956) p. 44.

They thus came to understand inculturation as the presence of spiritual or charismatic authority, not alongside of, but within the official Church authority. Abhishiktananda never tired of calling upon the Indian Church "to answer to the challenge of interiority and spiritual depth put to her by Hinduism — by the Spirit, as we would confidently affirm, through Hinduism."[5] The All-India Seminar on the Church in India Today encouraged priests, religious and lay people with a charisma for initiating others into truly interior prayer to be set aside for this work, and promoted the ashram lifestyle. Yet it is almost by definition that charismatic authority has emerged at the margins of the official institutional structure within the Indian Church.

Catholic Ashrams and the Church

The call for more charismatic authority in India has been answered in the form of Catholic ashrams. This, however, raises questions concerning the relationship between Catholic ashrams and the church, and the juridical status of an ashram. The very idea of the institutional identity of an ashram is a contradiction in terms. In one of the very first studies of Christian (Protestant) ashrams, it was argued that ashrams should not submit to the authority of office:

> we cannot commend nor envisage the subordination of asramas, to be founded by christians in India, whatever their character, to the regular Church and its chiefs. Hence, the inclination to bring the existing asramas under the oversight of ecclesiastical heads should be resisted.[6]

Yet in remaining within the Catholic Church, the Catholic ashrams automatically acquired a juridical position.

Almost all Catholic ashrams in India came under the jurisdiction of a bishop. The sympathy and support of the Church hierarchy was, initially at least, indispensible for the foundation

---

[5] *Towards the Renewal of the Indian Church* (Ernakulam: KCM, 1970) p. 11.
[6] P. Chenchiah, V.Chakkarai, *et al.*, *Ashrams, Past and Present* (Madras: Indian Book Club, 1941) p. 262.

of a Catholic ashram. Bishops often donated land and funded the building of a Catholic ashram. Ultimately, however, it was only the charisma of the spiritual leader which accounted for the success of an ashram. Once established, the Catholic identity of the ashram thus came to depend upon whether or not the spiritual master freely submitted to the authority of office.

The personal prudence of the various official authorities has also come to determine the nature of the relationship with the charismatic authority figures in the ashrams. While most ashrams have been given the freedom to experiment with inculturation, the opposition of some bishops has led to tension.

In the Christa Prema Seva ashram, obedience to institutional authority is built into the very principles of experimentation. Although, as an ecumenical community, it functions under the authority of three bishops, there is a commitment "to keep the ground-rules of our Churches and do nothing we are not prepared to tell our bishops about if asked."[7] Some of the members of the ashram, who are also religious sisters, continue to belong to the jurisdiction of their respective congregations. Sister Sara Grant relates that a perfectly harmonious relationship exists with the superiors of the different congregations which are represented in the ashram:

> They are most understanding of our unique situation, and while they are always ready to listen to us and give us their opinion, and decisions when necessary, they give full weight to the fact that it is difficult to judge our situation from the outside, and this gives us great liberty of spirit. They know that we are all very much at peace with the ashram life as an expression of the charisma of our religious congregations, and we take full part in the life of our own provinces, so they have no anxiety about our religious vocations.[8]

Most, but not all speak about such supportive and encouraging relationships with their respective bishops and superiors. It has been reported that some bishops have strongly discouraged their

[7] S. Grant, *Lord of the Dance* (Bangalore: Asian Trading Corporation, 1987) p. 160.

[8] *Lord of the Dance*, p. 161.

flock from participating in or joining an ashram. Certain religious orders which do not regard the ashram lifestyle as reconcilable with the charisma of their congregation have their members who decide to live in an ashram exclaustrated.[9] The opposition of a bishop may even force the ashram into searching for other institutional protection, as was the case with Saccidananda ashram.

Nonetheless, the general tendency is one of benevolence, both ways. Despite the difficulties which have occurred with the bishop, Bede Griffiths still feels that institutional control is necessary. This is partly because of practical reasons — the centrality of the eucharist in Christian ashrams requires a priest to be always present — but, principally, because too much freedom may run out of hand. Between belonging to the jurisdiction of the bishop or to that of a religious order, he believes that the latter is more congenial with the ashram spirit because there is less chance that other ecclesiastical functions will be bestowed upon the member of the ashram:

> If the ashram is under the jurisdiction of a bishop, this means that the priest is ordained for the diocese and this may mean that he will be required for service outside the ashram. On the other hand, if an ashram belongs to a religious order, it can expect to have its ideals respected and not subjected to change.[10]

One of the issues at stake in the institutional affiliation of an ashram is the question of continuity. Now that some of the pioneers of Catholic ashrams are growing old, this is becoming an important issue. To secure continuity, there may be a tendency to compromise.[11] However, insecurity and complete reliance on divine providence are essential features of an authentic ashram.

---

[9] The I.C.M. sisters apply the *exclaustratio qualificata* which allows a probation period for Sisters who feel they have a charisma for the ashram life.

[10] *Ashram Aikiya Newsletter*, May 1983, p. 3.

[11] It was to avoid this that Saccidananda ashram affiliated with the order of Camaldoli. Within a few years, the ashram will have become an independent branch of Camaldoli which implies that the guru, and not the order, will have the right to appoint a successor.

The continuity of an ashram depends upon the continuity of charismatic authority. If there is no one to succeed the previous guru, the ashram is supposed to dissolve. Richard Taylor points out that, since an ashram is leader-centered rather than institution-centered, "it is going to be an unusual ashram that has a thriving second generation."[12]

While the Catholic ashrams up to the present voluntarily belong to one or the other institutional jurisdiction, there is a search for a particular status which would be more in accord with the essential nature of an ashram. The general hope is that "in the course of time an ashram will come to be recognized as a distinct way of life in the Church."[13] Amalorpavadass therefore argues that Catholic ashrams should become *sui juris*. Besides being in accord with the nature, identity and uniqueness of an ashram as an Indian reality or experience, this would solve the problem of the double juridical status of priests and religious. The original juridical Church status could be maintained and would then not come to clash with membership in an ashram. More recently, Amalorpavadass has been pleading for an institutional status of "personal prelature," independent from the local hierarchy. No official intervention has as yet settled the issue.

Summary

The notion "Catholic ashram" seems to be, institutionally speaking, a contradiction in terms. While an ashram is essentially autonomous, the epithet "Catholic" implies that it submits to institutional prescriptions and control. And while the guru is in the ashram regarded as the highest, and absolute authority, the Catholic spiritual master remains answerable to his or her respective bishop or superior. In her sociological study of ashrams, Helen Ralston argues that "in a sense, they are considered as

---

[12] Richard Taylor, "Christian Ashrams as a Style of Mission in India" *International Review of Mission* 68 (1979) p. 285.

[13] From the contribution of Bede Griffiths in *Ashram Aikiya Newsletter*, February 1986, p. 3.

communities 'outside the organization' of the Roman Catholic Church; as such the locus of authority is within the ashram itself for the purpose of experimentation in indigenous liturgical rituals and life-styles, and the development of indigenous Christian theology and spirituality."[14]

The precarious balance which exists between the Catholic ashrams and the official church authorities in India is merely a manifestation of the dynamic tension which always exists between charismatic authority and the authority of office. In remaining within the Church, Catholic ashrams may then fulfill the creative and reinvigorating function which charisma has always played in the Church. On the other hand, it is possible that charismatic and official authorities come to clash, that disciples are confronted with divided loyalties, and that the ashram finds itself outside the body of the church. Or the ashram may drift almost unconsciously and unnoticed outside the church.

[14] H. Ralston, *Christian Ashrams. A New Religious Movement in Contemporary India*, p. 103.

CHAPTER THREE

The Guru in Catholic Ashrams: Internal Reflections

Catholic ashrams, just as their Hindu prototype, are led by strong charismatic figures, the kind of person Hindus call "guru." Since they, moreover, dress, live, meditate, and often speak like Hindu gurus, the term guru has spontaneously been applied to the leaders of Catholic ashrams. There is, nonetheless, a certain reservation and ambiguity about the use of the term guru within Christianity, especially when applied to the head of a Catholic ashram. Although the use of the term guru within the Christian context has not been the object of systematic theological study, this ambiguity surfaces in casual and implicit reflections and reactions, as well as in the alternative titles which have come to be used for the head of a Catholic ashram.

Abhishiktananda's experience as guru in the Hindu sense of the term illustrates the difficulties involved in introducing it into Christianity. It was only during the last years of his life that he came to ponder the depths of guruship. To a friend, he wrote that one can only understand guruhood and the relationship with the disciple through experience: "It is really the chela who makes the guru, and you have to have lived it in order to grasp this relationship 'beyond words.' Frightening, and what a responsibility."[1] He believes that it is an experience which goes beyond the Western understanding of spiritual direction and beyond spiritual, and even natural fatherhood. It is mainly in the letters to his disciples that Abhishiktananda's self-understanding as guru is manifest.

---

[1] Letter to Odette Baumer (January 7, 1972).

The experience of advaita which he pursued throughout his life, he came to experience more than ever as guru. He writes to his disciple: "I am following you, or better I am you here, and you are I there."[2] In giving himself to his disciples, Abhishiktananda feels that he empties himself of the last residues of the ego, and thus comes to realize himself. In the intimacy of the guru-disciple relationship, he comes to realize non-duality.

Abhishiktananda has become deeply convinced that, in experiencing this non-duality, he recapitulates the experience of oneness with the Father of Jesus Christ.[3] He interprets this experience as a "sense of Christ beyond all forms."[4] Abhishiktananda is clearly aware of the theological difficulties inherent in these statements. In a letter he wrote:

> I believe that in order to understand it, you have to try to work your way back to the very mystery of the Father and the Son. Yet another case in which all our ideas — western and (exported) Mediterranean Christian — are passed beyond. But then what that implies and foreshadows is such a total upheaval that one takes fright and prefers to curl up and remain silent.[5]

In applying the term guru in the Hindu sense to the Christian spiritual master, the difference between Jesus Christ and the human master, or the discontinuity of Christ, dissolves. Hence Abhishiktananda's fear to pursue this thought.

In the official description of a Catholic ashram, the head of the ashram is described as "a Guru, man or woman (usually one — sometimes more such persons) recognized by others as a person of deep spiritual experience."[6] The term guru is here used in the most general sense of the term. Further in the same document, a distinction is made between Jesus Christ as the Sadguru and the leader of the Catholic ashram as *acharya* or teacher:

---

[2] Letter to Marc Chaduc (December 6, 1971.)
[3] Cf. Letter to Marc Chaduc (November 23, 1973.)
[4] Letter to Odette Baumer (November 3, 1971.)
[5] Letter to Père Lemarié (January 5, 1972.)
[6] *Statement of the All-India Consultation on Ashrams* (Bangalore: NBCLC, 1978) point 3.

The members of the ashram are formed into a fellowship led by the Spirit of Christ, the "Sadguru", under the guidance of a Guru or Acharya.[7]

Christ as Sadguru

All Catholic ashrams have come to refer to Christ as Sadguru. The term has been used within Christian circles prior to the establishment of Christian ashrams. While it was once used as a translation of Western christological titles, it is introduced within Christian ashrams as a way to establish a more personal relationship with Christ. In his journal entitled *Guru Jesus*, Robert Van de Weyer relates that while traditional christological expressions had "cluttered my conception of him, and made it impossible for me to conceive of having a direct relationship with him,"[8] the experience of living in a Christian ashram helped him to discover Christ anew as his personal guru:[9]

> I recognized him as a supremely wise and happy man, and, in the Hindu tradition, gave him my complete and unquestioning obedience so that he could show me the way to wisdom and happiness. It was only after making Jesus my Guru, and after clumsily trying to follow his instructions on prayer that I gradually came to believe in a supernatural God.[10]

The understanding of Christ as guru thus seems to provide a helpful alternative to ancient and foreign models which had lost, or in India never had, evocative power.[11] While some ashrams only verbally refer to Christ as guru in prayers and songs, others dress the blessed sacrament in orange, place it on a leopard skin, and hang a *mala* (Indian prayer beads) and a garland of flowers around it while chanting the words:

---

[7] *Statement of the All-India Consultation on Ashrams*, point 7.

[8] R. Van de Weyer, *Guru Jesus* (London: S.P.C.K., 1975) p. 116.

[9] He lived for several months in the Christa Sishya ashram founded by the Anglican bishop Walsh.

[10] R. Van de Weyer, *Guru Jesus*, p. ix.

[11] Cf. also X. Irudayaraj, "The Guru in Hinduism and Christianity," *Vidyajyoti* 39 (1975) pp. 315-320.

> Om Guru Hail, have mercy on us, world Guru, highest Guru, true
> Guru, protect us; the first Guru, the one-only Guru, bliss Guru,
> have mercy on us; great guru, Lord Master, Om Guru, protect
> us.[12]

While the pastoral benefit of approaching Jesus Christ as guru
has thus been generally acknowledged and cultivated in Christian
ashrams, its theological implications have not been systematically
studied. Abhishiktananda's attempt to understand Christ as guru
and purusha remains the most explicit and elaborate reflections
on the topic.

The term Sadguru may also be used in Christian ashrams to
establish the uniqueness of Christ with reference to other gurus of
Hindu ashrams and to the human leader of a Catholic ashram.
Vandana uses the term both to compare and contrast Jesus Christ
with Hindu gurus. She points out that "the most striking difference in Jesus the *Satguru* is that he comes as one who serves,"
and that he called his disciples friends.[13] In the Christa Prema
Seva ashram in Poona, the belief that Christ is the only guru in
the ashram is printed, as a label, on a poster at the threshold of
the ashram:

> The Guru of this Ashram is the Risen Christ, present among us by
> His Spirit, and by his Word and Sacrament. A central concern of
> the community is to reflect on and enter more deeply into the
> mystery of the relation of Christ to the Selfcommunication of God
> in and through the other great spiritual traditions of the world.

---

[12] Cf. in the Christa Prema Seva ashram in Poona, and the Jeevan Dhara
ashram in Jahairikhal. An often sung bhajan in Anjali Ashram is:
The basis of my meditation is the form of my Guru,
The basis of my worship is the feet of my Guru,
The basis of my mantra is the word of my Guru,
The basis of my salvation is the grace of my Guru.
[13] In "The Guru as Present Reality" *Vidyajyoti* 39 (1975) p. 353. In describing
the other characteristics of the guru, however, Vandana alludes to the similarities
rather than the differences between the Hindu understanding of the guru and
Christian notions of Christ. In describing Swami Chidananda, she explicitly points
to the similarities with Christ: "In the few months I sat daily at the feet of Swami
Chidananda for instance, I found no Ahamkar in him. In his gracious courtesy,
gentle humility and unfailing thoughtfulness, he reminded me of Jesus" (p. 129).

> High points in this endeavour are the daily Eucharist and Medita-
> tion, Arati times and the Satsang.[14]

The emphasis is here on the risen Christ as living guru. This is also illustrated in Sara Grant's words: "we feel that the Lord takes very seriously his role as Guru, as very often we are quite unaware of what has been happening in the way of inner transformation, though at times it is quite clear."[15] With this conception of the Christ as the living guru, the need for a human guru becomes superfluous, as expressed on a second poster at the entry of the Christa Prema Seva ashram: "we cannot waste time and energy pining for guidance which will relieve us of all risks and secure us against mistakes."[16]

The belief in Jesus Christ as Sadguru has also found its expression in art. Almost every ashram has a painting or statue of Christ seated in the lotus-position in which gurus are traditionally depicted. Many of these paintings are the work of Jyoti Sahi who has become one of the most prominent promoters of Indian Christian art. He lives in a Christian ashram for artists in Bangalore. Sahi points out that Indian artists have always spontaneously portrayed Jesus Christ as guru. Having lived several years in Kurisumala ashram, he began painting Jesus Christ as a Guru walking along the Indian countryside "in the same manner as monastic artists in the Middle East and later Europe had imagined Christ as living and moving with them near their own monastic settlements."[17] He was more and more led to see Christ as the indwelling Lord. His art is the expression of this inner guru which may lead others to surrender to Christ.[18]

---

[14] The original statement seems to have been "The Fellowship has no Guru or Head but Jesus Christ, our ever-present Master." Cf. R. Taylor, "From Khadi to Kavi: Toward a Typology of Christian Ashrams," *Religion and Society* 24 (1977) p. 26.

[15] S. Grant, *Lord of the Dance* (Bangalore: Asian Trading Corporation, 1987) p. 162.

[16] Words of Rev. M. Allyne, C.S.M.V.

[17] J. Sahi, *Stepping Stones: Reflections on the Theology of Indian Christian Culture* (Bangalore: Asian Trading Corporation, 1986) p. 64.

[18] *Stepping Stones*, p. 69.

The portrayal of Christ as guru was thus more than the clothing of Jesus in an Indian monastic garb. It was the expression of Sahi's personal devotion to the indwelling Lord.

The Koinonia as Catholic Guru

At a certain stage in his reflection on the guru in Christianity, Abhishiktananda emphasized that the Christian equivalent of the Hindu guru is the Christian koinonia, the Church. He points out that "the Christian does not derive instructions from any human being however eminent, who may have become personally realized, but from the Spirit which lives and reveals itself in the community of the Called."[19] Rather than to an individual, it is to the Church that Christ transmitted his authority. From this perspective, Abhishiktananda emphasizes that "the individual announces Christ only in the name of the koinonia. It is the Church (the koinonia) which generates the Christ in me."[20]

The communal conception of authority is also based upon the communal understanding of salvation in Christianity.[21] As opposed to the Hindu tradition, no single individual is saved, liberated or realized before all are saved. Hence, no single individual can claim absolute spiritual authority.[22]

In Protestant circles, the Christian ashram has come to be understood as an eschatological community, harbinger of the Kingdom of God, and the guru as the community itself.[23] Helen Ralston pointed out that in Protestant ashrams, "the community

[19] *Journal*, 1961, p. 290.

[20] *Journal*, 1961, p. 290. The pleroma of Christ, Abhishiktananda emphasizes, is realized in the eschatological church (and not in the actual manifestation of the church in India, which he did not stop criticizing.)

[21] *Journal*, 1955, p. 136.

[22] Abhishiktananda, however acknowledges that the pleroma of Christ may also be manifested in the mystic: "The Christ is simultaneously in the pleroma attained in the eschatological Church, and in the profound consciousness which the mystic attains in himself." *Journal*, 1955, p. 137.

[23] Cf. P. Chenchiah, V. Chakkarai, *et al., Ashrams, Past and Present* (Madras: Indian Christian Book Club, 1941) p. 275-288.

is the locus of authority and decision-making is by community consensus."[24]

Sara Grant emphasizes that Christ is present, not only or even mainly in one individual, but in every person as the *antaryamin* or indweller.[25] Since Christ works in and through every individual, his will reveals itself through attention and listening to all.[26] More than in the other ashrams, then, in the Christa Prema Seva ashram, importance is given to the evening *satsang*, or "gathering of saints," which is the time of sharing experiences.[27] From the insights and resolutions which emerge from the community, the will of God is discerned.

While Bede Griffiths defines the ashram as centered around the guru, he equally emphasizes that the individual is not the sole repository of truth in Christian ashrams, but that the graces of God are showered over all and that all partake in the responsibility to sustain and guide the other's search. He views this as one of the essential elements which distinguishes a Christian from a Hindu ashram:

> In a Hindu ashram, each sadhaka is related directly to the Guru, and has no essential relation with the other members of the ashram, whereas in a Christian ashram the essential relation of each member is with the other members of the community through whom and with whom he comes to God.[28]

The authority in Catholic ashrams is thus ideally diffused and based upon the mutual support and guidance among ashramites.

---

[24] H. Ralston, *Christian Ashrams*, p. 113.

[25] S. Grant, "Growth in Community: A Theological Perspective," *The Way. Supplement* 62 (1988) p. 33.

[26] *Lord of the Dance*, p. 119.

[27] "Saints" may here be understood in the Pauline meaning of those gathered in a holy community.

[28] *Ashram Aikya Newsletter*, Christmas, 1984, p. 3. However, in his study of the life and thought of Bede Griffiths, Jesu Rajan emphasizes that in practice, the spiritual relationship of the ashramites is to Bede Griffiths, and not to each other. J. Rajan, *Christian Interpretation of Indian Sannnyasa. Study Based on the Vision and Experience of Swami Bede Griffiths* (Rome: Pont. Universitas S. Thomae, 1988) p. 257.

The Christian monastic understanding of "divine koinonia" predominates in Francisacharya's understanding of the community:

> A divine koinonia is experienced in the very sharing of our common life, in the life of the community of men dedicated to God, in the intensified exchange and reciprocity between Him and us, as well as among ourselves. And all this has its root in the initial working of the Divine Spirit.[29]

The understanding of the koinonia as guru is expressed in the belief that "it is not so much the individual but the institution which carries enlightenment."[30] He regards Kurisumala ashram not so much as a community which has gathered around one enlightened individual, but as a coming together of individuals who have heard the same call to the great renunciation. In practice, however, it is to Francisacharya that the other members of the ashram refer as their "master and guru."[31]

The Acharya

Even in the ashrams where the community dimension is emphasized, there is still a figure around whom the ashram revolves, at least practically. Some leaders of Catholic ashrams have radically rejected the title of guru and explicitly adopted the term *acharya*, which means teacher or master. The designation generally conotes an educational function. This lies behind Francis Mahieu's adoption of the name Francisacharya.

In describing the general features of ashrams, one among which is the central role of the guru, Sara Grant points out that "not all ashrams have such spiritual leaders or gurus, either because the original ones have died and it seemed unnecessary to

[29] *Kurisumala: A Symposium on Ashram Life* (Vagamon: Kurisumala Ashram, 1974) p. 123.

[30] *Kurisumala: A Symposium on Ashram Life*, p. 128.

[31] In the dedication of the book celebrating the silver anniversary of Kurisumala, the disciples wrote: "Here, you are our Satguru, father and mother, sister and brother, our all in all." *Kurisumala: A Symposium on Ashram Life*, p. 7.

replace them, or because it had always been so strongly felt that God is the only Guru that there was no need to have a human one."[32] She is called acharya and sees her role as "one who is recognized as the visible facilitator for the invisible Indweller in the hearts of all, who leads the community in discerning the promptings of the Spirit."[33] In using the term acharya, Sara Grant thus expresses the secondary and subservient, rather than constitutive, function of the head of the ashram:

> her chief task must be to be as transparent as possible to the light of God, not imposing her own ideas but being open to his initiatives from whatever quarter they come. She must also be willing to help any member of the community in their own personal quest.[34]

Sara Grant explicitly states: "we do not feel any inclination to call this leader our guru."

The term acharya is the safer one, the one least laden with controversial meaning. It is therefore often added to the title guru ("acharya-guru") to soften its absolute meaning.[35]

The Upaguru

While all Catholic ashrams refer to Christ as Sadguru, this, according to most, is not irreconcilable with the idea of a human guru in the ashram. Usually, derived terms are then used to refer to the human guru. Vandana, in following Abhishiktananda,[36] uses the terms *karana* or instrumental guru who may be seen as the image or *murti* of the Satguru,[37] while Isvaraprasad speaks of the *upa-guru* or the guru who is near, but under, the real guru who is Christ. Vandana points out that her views on the possibility of a guru in Christian ashrams had changed: "Until recently I tended to agree that in a Christian Ashram the only guru should

---

[32] "Growth in Community: A Theological Perspective," *The Way. Supplement* 62 (1988) p. 35.

[33] "Growth in Community: A Theological Perspective," p. 35.

[34] S. Grant, *Lord of the Dance*, p. 119.

[35] See the reference to D.S. Amalorpavadass in the letters from Anjali ashram.

[36] *Guru and Disciple* (London: S.P.C.K., 1974) p. 110.

[37] "The Guru as a Present Reality," *Vidyajyoti* 38 (1975) p. 356.

or could be the risen Christ alone. Of late, after close observation, study and prayerful pondering, I have come to see that here is a value of Indian spirituality that we can explore, very usefully."[38] She feels that the divinization of the guru is justified in as far as "surrender to the guru means surrender not to the mere man but to God who, for me, can act through him."[39]

While the functional similarities between the Hindu and the Christian guru are clear, the difference in the conception of the nature and the status of the guru are also emphasized. While the Hindu guru is often characterized in absolute terms as "God-realized," the Christian guru is said to have merely "a certain depth of religious experience." While the Hindu guru refers to his own experience, the Christian guru refers to the experience of Christ.[40] And while the Hindu guru is believed to be "established" in a state of realization, the Christian conception of the human guru is more dynamic: the guru is moving with the disciples toward the ever-receding end. Amalorpavadass defines an ashram not as a place, but a state of "relentless quest for the absolute," embodied in a living person who "is called in India a *guru.*"[41] He explains the essence and role of the guru in Christianity through a word-play on the term *guru-anubhava*:

> He is the one who had a guha experience and a rupa experience: one who has an experience of God in the depth of his being, in the core of his heart (gu-ha) and who is capable of giving expression to it (ru-pa) by sharing it with others and leading them to it.[42]

While the guru may have had "an experience of God in the depth of his being," Amalorpavadass insists that the quest is a relentless one, in which the guru, rather than being "on the other shore," moves along, ahead of, but still with the disciples. Amalorpava-dass defines a Christian guru as one who is a true disciple of Christ, who possesses the spirit of service and self-giving love of

---

[38] "The Guru as Present Reality," *Vidyajyoti* 38 (1974) p. 352.
[39] "The Guru as Present Reality" *Vidyajyoti* 38 (1974) p. 355.
[40] "The Guru as Present Reality" *Vidyajyoti* 38 (1974) p. 353.
[41] In the brochure of Anjali Ashram, p. 4.
[42] In the brochure of Anjali Ashram, p. 6.

Christ, and who lives according to the values of Christ. In this sense all Christians are called to become a guru.

The purely instrumental function of the visible guru comes through strongly in Jyoti Sahi's understanding of the guru-disciple relationship as manifested in the way Hindus relate to art, to images:

> Hindu esthetics has been permeated by the GuruSishya relationship. Entering the temple, the great forum of the Hindu arts, the worshipper approaches the image as the disciple approaches the teacher.[43]

The artistic creation which emerges from contemplation is the expression of the inner guru of the artist. As visible guru, it is meant to lead the one who contemplates the image to his or her own inner guru. Sahi points out that "the image as an exterior object, like the Guru as an exterior man, is unimportant. Or at least it must never hinder the search for the inner truth."[44]

Summary

While the spiritual leaders of Catholic ashrams have often spontaneously been called guru, the use of this term within a Christian context has very radical theological implications. The status and authority attributed to the guru in Hinduism is, in Christianity, reserved for the figure of Jesus Christ. Abhishikta-nanda's attempt to understand Jesus Christ as guru led to a radically new interpretation of Christ in which the traditional understanding of the redemptive function and the discontinuity of Christ are dissolved. When explicitly confronted with the issue, the leaders of Catholic ashrams demonstrate real prudence.

Christ is generally referred to as the Sadguru to distinguish him both from Hindu gurus and from the spiritual master in Catholic ashrams. For some, this excludes any living master from assuming the title guru. At best, the status and authority of Christ as

[43] *Stepping Stones*, p. 92.
[44] *Stepping Stones*, p. 92.

Sadguru may be seen as continued in the koinonia, which is the church. Several leaders of Catholic ashrams then insist on being called acharya, rather than guru. For others, the term guru in a qualified sense may enlarge the traditional Christian notion of the spiritual master and be used beneficially. They insist, however, on the functional or instrumental aspect of the term guru and point to the ontological differences between a Hindu and a Christian guru. The understanding of the head of the Catholic ashram as guru thus differs little from the traditional understanding of the spiritual father in Christianity as representative of Christ and instrument of the Spirit. Theoretically, no radical steps have thus been taken within Catholic ashrams to rethink the nature and function of the spiritual master. The practice, however, has moved far ahead.

The Role of the Catholic Guru in Rituals and Sadhana

In the daily life of the ashram, everything is permeated with religious meaning. Every aspect of ashram life, from the position of the huts to the way in which food is served may then reveal elements of functional or religious differentiation. It is from the structural whole that meaning emerges. The guru may be served first or last, but either way a special status is implied. Whether located in the center or on the outskirts of the ashram, the room or hut of the guru occupies a strategic place. It is, however, in the religious practice proper, in ritual and *sadhana*, that the role and status of the spiritual master in Catholic ashrams explicitly appears.

Sadhana is the general Indian term used for religious practice or spiritual discipline. It refers to the whole complex of prescriptions which the religious seeker, or *Sadhaka*, must follow to reach a certain spiritual goal. In India, it is traditionally the guru who assigns a certain spiritual path to the individual disciple and who follows the progression. The disciple is to blindly and religiously follow every instruction. While this is the essence of a Hindu ashram, the religious practice in Catholic ashrams follows in addition the ritual life of the Church. The roles of spiritual master and priest may coincide, but when the head of a Catholic ashram is a woman or a lay person, the distinction and often the discrepancy between charismatic and official authority is strongly felt.

Catholic ashrams have been given considerable liberty to experiment with the inculturation of the liturgy and other rituals and to adopt Hindu practices which are not in contradiction with Christian faith. Besides individual spiritual direction, the ritual life in Hindu ashrams evolves around the three (or four) *samdhyas* or gathering times for prayer and meditation. One or different forms of yoga represent the essence of religious practice in Hindu ashrams. Various initiation rites, for example that of studenthood, *brahmacharya*, or that of the great renunciation, *sannyasa*, may also be performed. Hindu ashrams are characterized by a ritualized form of worship of the guru, the *guru-puja*. It is from the way in which these rituals and religious practices are adopted and the degree to which they are modified that the specificity of Catholic ashrams and of the status and role of the spiritual leader in Catholic ashrams may emerge.

The Three Samdhyas

The peak moments of the day are traditionally the time just before sunrise, when the sun is at its zenith, as the sun sets, and at midnight. In the Indian contemplative tradition these are times of gathering to celebrate and meditate, to establish a harmony with nature and with the divine. These meeting moments or *samdhyas* also mark the day in Catholic ashrams. There are special prayers and hymns for each time of the day. The readings are from either or both Hindu and Christian scriptures. At the end of the samdhya, the *arati*, or waving of lamps in front of the holy sepulchre and other venerated objects or people is performed.[1] The flame is then passed for all in the community to touch as a gesture of purification, bringing the hands to the forehead.

The samdhyas are traditionally understood as a gathering around the guru or as meditation in the presence of the guru. In Christian ashrams, the community gathers around Christ. Nonetheless, the human guru may still fulfill an important, if not constitutive, role in these Christian samdhyas. The depth of experience of the spiritual master is regarded not only as a model,

---

[1] While in most Catholic ashrams, this is only done in front of the holy sepulchre and then passed around in the group, in Jeevan Dhara ashram, the lamps are also waved in front of the Bible, an image of our Lady, and the pictures of Abhishiktananda and Chidananda, gurus revered in the ashram.

but also as effecting a deepening of the religious experience of the disciple. In some Catholic ashrams, the quality and intensity of a samdhya without the spiritual leader is reported to be markedly different from when he or she is present. The role of the human guru in these gatherings may thus be seen as sacramental.

The Liturgy

The central role of the eucharist is one of the distinctive characteristics of Catholic ashrams. It is understood as the sacramental gathering around the Sadguru Christ and is celebrated daily, usually after the morning samdhya. Christian ashrams have made an important contribution to the inculturation of the liturgy in India. While the Church was struggling with controversies which arose around often minor points of inculturation, the ashrams experimented freely with the use of Indian symbols and ways of worship.[2] Indian prayers and hymns or *bhajans* were composed in ashrams and Indian musical instruments used to accompany them. A typically Indian eucharistic liturgy, often called *Bharata Puja*, came to be fully developed and daily celebrated in Catholic ashrams.[3] The ritual may slightly differ from one ashram to the next. The religious diversity and symbolic richness of the Hindu tradition allow for the use of a wide variety of symbols, texts, ideas and gestures in the inculturation of the liturgy. The form which the Bharata Puja has taken in a particular ashram often reflects the identity and the sensitivies of its spiritual leader. In some, the process of inculturation has enhanced the participation of the community in the eucharist, while in

---

[2] On the official reception of the inculturation of the liturgy between 1963 and 1984, see Julian Saldanha, *Inculturation* (Bombay: St Paul Publications, 1987) pp. 47-61.

[3] In addition to the Bharata puja, the Syrian Qurbana is celebrated in Kurisumala ashram. It is a very elaborate liturgy with intricate ritual and a strong sense of the divine presence in the eucharist. The attraction of the Syrian liturgy is for Francisacharya its "vivid sense of the Resurrection always united with the cross, a lively awareness of the communion of Saints in the act of contemplation and an existential understanding of Christ's incarnation." See *Kurisumala. A Symposium on Ashram Life* (Vagamon: Kurisumala Ashram, 1974) p. 118.

others the central role and status of the officiating priest has been emphasized.[4] When the priest is also the spiritual master, he may give an individual rather than a collective blessing at the end of the eucharistic celebration.[5] In ashrams where the spiritual leader is not a priest, and no ordained minister is present, a para-liturgy may be held.[6]

Since non-Catholics, both Protestants and non-Christians, are often present in Catholic ashrams, the issue of intercommunion and the participation of the non-baptized in the eucharist and in the communion has become a crucial one. This has led to much reflection and discussion. Sara Grant relates that the separation between the Anglican and the Catholic communities in the ashram is most strongly felt in the eucharist. While Anglicans and Catholics share the same eucharistic faith, the intercommunion is only half-way:

> All communicate when the celebrant is a Roman Catholic priest, but at the weekly celebration according to the rite of the Church of North India, the Catholic members communicate from the Reserve.[7]

Those who are not baptized usually receive a flower from the tray on which the communion is passed. Sara Grant, however, points out that this leaves Hindus, who do not have a juridical sense of religious belonging, unsatisfied. They fail to understand why they are excluded and cannot participate in the communion of the

---

[4] In the Anjali ashram, which has experimented the most with the inculturation of the liturgy, gestures and symbols were introduced which emphasize the sacrality of the priest, who is most often the guru. In the beginning of the liturgy, the arati is performed to him, and during the sermon, the priest-guru holds his hands in the hand gesture used in Buddhist art to express the teaching authority of the Buddha.

[5] This may be done, as in Anjali ashram, by individuals who advance to touch the feet of the guru.

[6] This situation has, strangely enough, not led the female heads of Catholic ashrams to argue for the ordination of women or to take explicit feminist stances. Vandana has not touched upon this subject and Sara Grant takes a rather conservative position on "Women in the Church." *Lord of the Dance* (Bangalore: Asian Trading Corporation, 1987) pp. 165-172.

[7] S. Grant, "The Bread of Life" *The Tablet* 242 (January 7, 1989) p. 9.

Christ they profess and regard as their guru.[8] She then argues for "a revised form of a pedagogy to Christ, where the Lord's Supper would be the initial stage of incorporation into the community of his followers and baptism be reserved for a later stage."[9] Despite the difficulties, Sara Grant states that the centrality of the eucharist in the life of a Christian has never been questioned:

> We have lived together through times of great anguish over this, but there has never been the slightest doubt about the Eucharist being our life-spring and the bond of our unity and peace.[10]

Bede Griffiths, on the other hand, argues that the belief that "the eucharist is the source of the life of the Church and the summit of its activity is a specifically Roman way of understanding the Church,"[11] and pleads for a more pneumatological ecclesiology:

> The Eucharist is essentially a sacrament and a sacrament belongs to the world of signs... But surely the source of the life of the Church, though it is manifested in the liturgy and the Eucharist, is the Holy Spirit. It is the presence of the Holy Spirit which is received in baptism, established in confirmation and renewed continually in the Eucharist, which is the real source and summit of the activity of the church.[12]

---

[8] She usually refers here to a young Hindu couple who had been fully participant members of the ashram and worshippers of Christ, and who had come to feel very strongly the dissonance with their being excluded from full sacramental participation. See "Towards a Practical Indian Ecclesiology" *Vidyajyoti* 44 (1985) pp. 30-31.

[9] "Towards a Practical Indian Ecclesiology," pp. 31-32. She is supported in this suggestion by Jyoti Sahi. Though the issue is a general theological or ecclesiastical one, it is particularly manifest in India where the Christian missionary practice of the past has made the step toward baptism a very difficult one for Hindus to take. It meant a radical break with the traditional social environment and customs and the alienation from all that had been previously treasured.

[10] "Growth in Community: A Theological Perspective" *The Way. Supplement* 62 (1988) p. 37.

[11] In *Garland of Letters*, p. 7. Griffiths sees the liturgy as flowing from and reaffirming the supremacy and authority of the Pope and Bishops, and as a means to make the spiritual life of the Christian subject to the institutional church.

[12] *A Garland of Letters*, p. 7.

Catholic ashrams should represent, according to Griffiths, an image of the Church as the dwelling place of the Spirit. From this perspective, rather than the liturgy, "it is contemplative prayer when the Holy Spirit is experienced in its immediate presence and not through outward signs that becomes the center of the life of a monk."[13] It is in this context that Bede Griffiths also touches upon the uniqueness of the ashram and the role of the guru:

> An ashram is not primarily a community life like a monastery. It is a group of disciples gathered around a Master, or Guru, who come to share the prayer life, the experience of God, of the Guru. The life, therefore, centres not on the common prayer of the liturgy but on the personal prayer of each member. It is the hour of meditation at dawn and sunset, the traditional time of meditation in India, which forms the basis of the life, the silent communion with God, and the common prayer of the community is, as it were, an overflow from this.[14]

A Christian sannyasi, Bede Griffiths believes, is one who has passed beyond the need for symbols and rituals. His model is Serafim of Sarov who, once he took the grey dress, was no longer bound by sacraments, not even by that of the eucharist. In Saccidananda ashram, however, the eucharist is celebrated every morning.

Yoga

While the basic doctrines and techniques of Yoga have been systematized in the *Yoga-sutra* of Patañjali, many variations upon this basic structure have been developed. Common to all forms of yoga, however, is the indispensability of the guru.[15]

Numerous books have been written on the integration of yoga in Christianity, on the use of yogic techniques in Christian prayer and meditation. In Christian ashrams, as in Hindu ones, yoga has

---

[13] *A Garland of Letters*, p. 7.

[14] B. Griffiths, *The Marriage of East and West* (Illinois: Templegate, 1982) p. 24.

[15] Mircea Eliade, *Yoga, Immortality and Freedom* (Princeton: Princeton University Press, 1969) pp. 5-6.

become the main form of religious discipline. Courses in the various branches of yoga, both Hindu and Buddhist, are provided, and yogic postures are used for prayer and meditation.[16] Yoga has come to be seen as no longer belonging to a particular religious tradition, but as a universal "art of harmonizing the body and the mind so that they become responsive to the movement of the spirit."[17] Bede Griffiths understands the integration which is reached through yoga in Christianity as "the experience of God in Christ through the presence of the Spirit."[18]

One of the traditional functions of the guru in yoga is the giving of the mantra. The essence and realization of the guru is believed to be condensed in the mantra. By whispering the mantra in the ear of the disciple, the guru is then believed to transmit his sacred power. While mantras are also used in the yoga practice in Catholic ashrams, the belief in the sacred power of the guru, and thus the esoteric and magical aspect of the transmission of the mantra are obliterated. Mantras are mainly used as prayers or as preparation for meditation. At best they refer to Christ or the Spirit. The root-mantra *Om* is chanted in Christian as well as in Hindu ashrams. Specifically Christian mantras such as "om Jesu" have also been introduced. In Kurisumala ashram, Francisacharya uses the ancient hesichast Jesus-prayer "Jesus, son of the living God, have mercy on me" or the Sanskrit "Om shri Jesu Bhagavate namaha" as mantras.

Sannyasa

With Abhishiktananda and Monchanin, the purpose of Catholic ashrams has been seen as that of giving birth to Christian

---

[16] Catholic ashrams are eclectic and few gurus have developed their own technique. Amaldass, one of the first disciples of Bede Griffiths, the head of an ashram in Madhya Pradesh, is a specialist in Yoga and has written several works on Christian yoga.

[17] B. Griffiths, *Garland of Letters*, p. 7. He sees it as a way of discovering the "underlying unity of religion" or "the point of the Spirit where all those different traditions meet."

[18] *Garland of Letters*, p. 7.

sannyasis. While from the beginning of the mission in India Christians had dressed as sannyasis as a means of gaining respect, authority and Hindu converts, Abhishiktananda emphasized that the taking of sannyasa was not merely a means, but a goal in itself:

> We must remain clearly aware of the fact that sannyasa is not a way or a means for other things, ... and it is precisely that which differentiates the sannyasa as taken by Roberto de Nobili from the traditional sannyasa we are speaking of now.[19]

Although the gurus and members of all Catholic ashrams dress and live as sannyasis, in utmost poverty and total dedication to the pursuit of the absolute, the actual initiation ritual has been adopted only by Abhishiktananda, Francisacharya, and Bede Griffiths.

In preparing for the initiation of his disciple Marc Chaduc, Abhishiktananda reflected elaborately upon the Hindu tradition of sannyasa, and he distinguished two forms. One is the realization of the state of sannyasa in which the desire to leave the world overcomes a person naturally and without formal initiation. The initiation ritual is here "simply the public acknowledgment of the inner freedom which [the sannyasi] has already himself realized at the very source of his being."[20] The function of the guru is here limited to acknowledging the state of realization reached by the sannyasi. For the second kind of sannyasa, the initiation ritual is held, not as an expression of, but as a step towards the ultimate state of realization. Here, the role of the guru as one "who has not merely heard or read about the path to salvation (*moksha*), but who has himself reached the goal, and is

---

[19] *Towards a Renewal of the Indian Church*, p. 75. There are still some missionaries who adopt the lifestyle of the sannyasi in an attempt to convert Hindus to Christianity. There is a Jesuit in Nasik who calls himself Shilananda, dresses in orange and sings Hindu bhajans, who plainly admits doing this in order to gain converts. That he is to be seen as an exception, however, is evidenced by the fact that his views on sannyasa and Catholic ashrams have elicited strong reactions from the other members of the *Ashram Aikiya*. See the discussion between Shilananda and Sara Grant in the *Ashram Aikiya Newsletter*, 1986.

[20] "Sannyasa," *The Further Shore* (Delhi: ISPCK, 1975) p. 22.

therefore able to guide others from his own experience" becomes much more important.[21] It is the guru who guides the disciple step by step, who imparts knowledge, and who fosters discrimination and renunciation. Absolute trust in the divine nature of the guru is here required of the disciple.

Abhishiktananda originally did not believe in the value of an initiation ritual for his disciple. In answer to Marc Chaduc's request, he wrote:

> I do not believe that this diksa would have any power in itself to liberate you from all rites. This freedom exists or it does not exist.[22]

Nonetheless, he designed a Hindu-Christian initiation ritual to sannyasa which was administered in conjunction with Chidananda, the guru of Shivananda ashram in Rishikesh. In this ritual, the guru meditates and prays with the disciple, dresses the disciple with the orange garb of the sannyasi, affirms the disciple's vows, and sends him along. Abhishiktananda, however, emphasizes that the external guru is the manifestation of the unique and eternal Guru who is within:

> Here indeed it is not only one man who gives the initiation. For the disciple in whom the inner light has shone, this man is only the manifestation at this moment of the unique Guru who manifests himself at every place and time, whenever the heart is opened from within.[23]

Francisacharya's initiative to introduce the Hindu form of initiation to sannyasa was based on the instruction on the Renewal of Religious Formation promulgated on the feast of the Epi-

---

[21] "Sannyasa" *The Further Shore*, p. 12.

[22] Letter to Marc Chaduc (April 24, 1973.) However, in participating in the ritual, Abhishiktananda came to understand its sacramental power. After the initiation he wrote to Marc Chaduc (July 5, 1973):
In reclothing you (in Kavi)
in contemplating you recovered
I discovered
that the kavi is not only a sign
but a mystery (...)
[23] "Sannyasa" *The Further Shore*, p. 53.

phany, 1969, which stipulated that "All religious institutes —superiors general or general chapters—are invested with the power of determining themselves the various stages of progress in the religious life leading to the final commitment."[24] According to Francisacharya this implies that religious communities may also integrate the ascetic and contemplative traditions whose seeds were sometimes already planted by God in ancient cultures prior to the preaching of the gospel. Francisacharya saw in the stages from *sadhaka* through *brahmacharya* to *sannyasa* a model of religious formation which may be fruitfully applied in Christianity.

The appeal of the ancient Indian structure of religious formation was for Francisacharya its contrast with the legalistic understanding of vows in the West. The initiation to monastic life in the East is seen as a real consecration or dedication to the sacred. The one who desires to embark upon the religious life is first admitted as aspirant or sadhaka. This is a probation and preparation period of about two years. Then follows the stage of brahmacharya. As opposed to the Hindu, but like the Buddhist tradition, Francisacharya views brahmacharya as a preparation for sannyasa. It involves "austerity of life, abstinence, self-control, chastity and sanctity in a life of service of the guru, including the humble tasks of housework, together with the performance of sacred rituals."[25] After a period of brahmacharya which may last from six to about twelve years, the disciple may be found ripe for the final initiation to sannyasa.[26]

Both the initiation to brahmacharya and to sannyasa in Kuri-

---

[24] Quoted in the manual — which he typed himself — which explains the theological ground and the concrete procedure of the ritual as performed in Kurisumala ashram. It is used in the ashram and has undergone some changes throughout the years.

[25] In the personal manual of Francisacharya.

[26] Most sannyasis remain in Kurisumala after their initiation and there is thus a basic continuity between the states of brahmacharya and sannyasa. Francisacharya sees brahmacharya not as temporary vows but as a "commitment for life but without the solemn character of sannyasa which remains the crown of the monastic experience in India."

sumala follows six steps starting with the signation of the sadhaka with the sign of the cross. The rites of renunciation which consist of the tonsure and the stripping of garments follow. The clothing with the new habit (white for the brahmachari and ocher for the sannyasi) symbolize the rite of dedication. The three following steps are the washing of the feet, the reception into the community, the imposition of the cross on the shoulder and the exchange of the kiss of peace.[27]

Bede Griffiths sees Catholic ashrams as "cradles in which Indo-Christian sannyasa should be born and grown. They should be centres of hybridization."[28] He follows Abhishiktananda's conception of sannyasa, both in theory and in practice. The main functions of the guru in the ritual are to pray, chant and meditate with the disciple, to immerse the disciple in the sacred river, to dress with the kavi, and finally to send forth. About seventy Westerners have thus received sannyasa from Bede Griffiths.[29] The concrete form which this renunciation takes in the West differs from one person to the next.[30] The Christian sannyasi needs to keep to the three observances of obedience, poverty and chastity. The vow of obedience is understood as to the Father, the *Paramguru*, through Christ, the Sadguru, represented by the human guru of the Catholic ashram. Within this context, the human guru is described as:

[27] Francisacharya points out that the structure of Antiochean clothing of the monk and the Hindu Brahmacarya and Sannyasa diksha have much in common. The symbol of the cross is of course unique, but the elements of shaving, bathing and clothing are present in both.

[28] J. Rajan, *Christian Interpretation of Hindu Sannyasa. A Study Based on the Vision and Experience of Swami Bede Griffiths.* (Rome: Pont. Universitas S. Thomae, 1988) p. 255.

[29] Sannyasa is given to disciples who have been sadhakas for some time, and usually upon their own request.

[30] The first to take sannyas from Griffiths in 1976 was the fully professed Camaldoli monk Bernaldino, who felt that sannyas would take him beyond the community rule into complete freedom, total reliance on God's providence and unconditional openness towards others. Since then, a few other members of Western monastic orders have received sannyas from Bede Griffiths.

a person who has experienced God and is able to lead others to that experience. He is the Mediator between God and man, and should be of spotless character. He is the representative of God and the disciple is expected to respect the Guru and see God in him.[31]

Rather than as a period of studentship or preparation for sannyasa — usually associated with celibacy — Bede Griffiths understands brahmacharya as the general attitude or state of "walking with or moving toward Brahman." He has thus taken the liberty to give brahmacarya not only to disciples who prepare for the final vows of sannyasa, but also to married people who have no intention of becoming renunciates.[32]

The initiation of Christians to sannyasa has been strongly criticized in certain Hindu circles. They argue that sannyasa is a typically Hindu religious institution which cannot be taken over by other religions. In the Laws of Manu, sannyasa is presented as a fourth stage, or *ashrama*, in life, which presupposes the three previous stages of student, householder, and forest hermit, and thus the Hindu identity:[33]

A twice-born man who seeks final liberation without having studied the Vedas, without having begotten sons, and without having offered sacrifices, sinks downward.[34]

But all (or) even (any of) these orders, assumed successively in accordance with the institutes (of the sacred law), lead the Brahmana who acts by the preceding (rules) to the highest state.[35]

---

[31] J. Rajan, *Christian Interpretation of Indian Sannyasa*, p. 238.

[32] Bede Griffiths has been much criticized for this, both by Hindus and Christians, and even by his closest friends and admirers. The practice of giving brahmacharya to married couples is the main criticism of Jesu Rajan in *Christian Interpretation of Indian Sannyasa*, his dissertation on Bede Griffiths. The vagueness on the identity and way of life of Western sannyasis also raises mistrust and elements of criticsm, not only among conservative Hindus and Christians, but also among more liberal thinkers in both communities.

[33] In the Dharmasutras, however, the four stages in life are regarded as different alternative lifestyles which a person may choose: "Some declare that he who has studied the Veda may make his choice which among the orders he is going to enter." *Gautama Dharmaśāstra* 3.1.

[34] *Laws of Manu*, 6.37.

[35] *Laws of Manu*, 6.88.

It is also argued that the initiation to sannyasa is replete with typically Hindu symbols and references, and can thus not be copied by other religious traditions.[36]

Against these arguments, Abhishiktananda contested that sannyasa originally meant "merely leaving one's home and village and departing into the forest or taking to the roads" and that the conception of sannyasa as the fourth *ashrama* was "the attempt of Hindu society to win back and, at least to some extent, to reintegrate within itself those who had renounced everything."[37] He sees sannyasa rather as an *atyashrama*, a state beyond every stage in life, radically transcending all religious systems.[38] Since the fourth stage implies the renunciation of the three others, there is essentially no continuity between the first three and the fourth stage in life. The sannyasi represents absolute freedom, the transcendence of all signs and symbols, of all rules, all karma, all dharma.[39]

Guru Puja

While the guru is the principle subject in the ritual life of an ashram, he or she also becomes the object of veneration on the day of the guru, generally celebrated on Thursdays in Hindu ashrams. On this occasion, the divinization of the guru is expressed in the *guru puja* or worship of the guru. The praise of the guru is then recited in mantras, sung in bhajans (the *guru-gita*, or song of the guru) and expressed through the offering of flowers. The main ceremony is the *Guru-pad-puja* or the veneration of the feet of the guru through washing, anointing, and the offering of flowers at the feet of the guru, or, when he is no longer alive, to the *padukas*, or wooden sandals of the guru.

---

[36] Sita Ram Goel, *Catholic Ashrams* (New Delhi: Voice of India, 1988.)

[37] "Sannyasa" *The Further Shore*, pp. 4, 17. Historical and scriptural evidence indeed seems to sustain his argument.

[38] "Sannyasa" *The Further Shore*, p. 17.

[39] Abhishiktananda points out that this is the main point of the medieval Sannyasa Upanishads which are a restatement of the early tradition where there is no mention of "orders." "Sannyasa" *The Further Shore*, p. 28.

Among the Catholic ashrams, it is only in Jeevan Dhara ashram that the guru puja has been introduced. At this time, the holy sepulchre and a picture of the shroud are garlanded. Rather than having her own feet washed, Vandana washes the feet of all those present emphasizing that "Jesus, the Satguru, instead of having his feet washed, as would be expected, himself washed the feet of his disciples, and told them to do as he had done, — a symbolic gesture showing his willingness to serve and love, which means his willingness to die."[40] Vandana thus emphasizes the difference between the average Hindu guru and Jesus Christ and the merely representational function of the human guru in Catholic ashrams.

Though not cultivated and sometimes even strongly discouraged, traditional Hindu expressions of veneration of the guru such as garlanding, touching the feet and service are nevertheless practiced in Catholic ashrams. Touching the feet of the guru is an Indian custom which may be done towards any superior and towards parents. It may be seen as an expression of respect which does not differ essentially from the genuflection which used to be habitual in Western culture. Some Catholic gurus then at times allow this expression of respect from disciples, and view it as a sign of inculturation. The explicit forms of veneration of the guru, as represented by the guru-puja, however, have not found entry into Catholic ashrams.

Summary

In the adoption of Hindu rituals in Catholic ashrams, the role of the head of the Catholic ashram seems to have moved ahead of theoretical reflection. Any absolute understanding of the status and the authority of the acharya or upaguru in Catholic ashrams is theoretically denied, but in practice, rituals are adopted which in the Hindu tradition presuppose belief in the absolute nature of the guru. The Samdhyas are traditionally gatherings around a

---

[40] Vandana, *Waters of Fire* (Madras: The Diocesan Press, 1981) p. 99.

realized being. The receiving of the mantra in the initiation to yoga is based on the belief in the extraordinary power of the guru, condensed in the mantra. Sannyasa is believed to be a state beyond all rituals and symbols, including the symbol of Christ. The one who initiates the disciple to sannyasa is supposed to have already reached this state. The expressions of veneration of the guru, however minor, are based upon the faith in the divinity of the guru. In introducing these rituals within Catholic ashrams, a certain confusion may thus arise concerning the status of the human guru. While Christ is referred to as the only guru in Catholic ashrams, the head of the Catholic ashram fulfills exactly the same ritual function as the guru in Hindu ashrams. The emphasis in Catholic ashrams is then always upon the representational role of the human guru. Nonetheless, ambiguity remains. The distinction or gap between the functional and the ontological status of the guru does not exist in the Hindu tradition.

Catholic Ashrams and Social Action

The tension which exists between action and contemplation has been resolved in a variety of ways in different religions, in different groups within one religion and in different periods in the history of a single religion. It has been generally seen as a basic difference between Eastern and Western religions. Hinduism and Buddhism are then seen as religions which view the material world as suffering and evil and social action as irrelevant to final liberation, while the Semitic religions regard the world as a divine creation and active involvement in the world as an essential dimension in the economy of salvation.

The struggle against the massive poverty and human misery has often been felt to be a particular responsibility of Christianity in India. A disproportionately large percentage of Indian schools and hospitals are run by Christians. Christian missions have often been a refuge for the hungry and the dying. Ashrams, on the other hand, are often associated with "escapism" and elitism, with the search for personal salvation without care for others, and with detachment from and indifference toward the world and social issues. From this perspective, the attempts at inculturation through Catholic ashrams may be seen as a betrayal of the particularity of the Christian mission or as an unhelpful homeopatic therapy. At the conference of the East-Asian Third World Theologians (EATWOT) in 1981, Christian ashrams were severely criticized:

> The ashramic movement of the 1960s was a reaction to the development theology of the West. Both recognized the poverty in Asia. Development theology saw the cause as lack of economic growth; the ashramic movement discerned the enemy as greed. The

movement was unable, however, to move from the microethical level to the macro-structural, because it failed to see the structural greed of systems and institutions. Lacking the full perspective, the people of the ashramic movement remained in passive solidarity with Asia's poor and oppressed without actually participating in the struggle.[1]

In his typology of Christian ashrams, "From Khadi to Kavi," Richard Taylor argues that Protestant ashrams were more involved in the social struggle than were the Catholic ones. The Protestant ashrams followed the Gandhian model of ashrams where *khadi*, the homespun cloth which served as the symbol of the nationalist movement, was worn, while Catholic ashrams were more in continuity with the traditional Hindu ashrams where the total renunciation of the world was expressed in the wearing of the ocher robe, or *kavi*. Catholic ashrams have thus been criticized for uncritically adopting the ancient Hindu ashram tradition which both in theory and practice has been reserved for the elite. The tradition of Vedanta, which was the philosophical basis of many ashrams, was handed down in sanskrit only to twice-born Brahmins, to those who could afford the leisure to retreat to the secluded atmosphere of the ashram. The ancient Hindu ashrams were regarded as a radical break with the world and with social entanglements in the pursuit of final liberation. Suffering was seen to be illusion, unrelated to the ultimate reality which was pursued. Social action in the ashram has thus traditionally been limited to the sharing of food and accommodation in a spirit of detachment.

The early ashram tradition may, however, also be seen as a radical break with the existing social structure. Contemplatives retired into the forest in reaction against the monopoly of the Brahmin caste. Ashrams were based upon revolutionary principles of the equality of classes and sexes. Brahmans were, sometimes disciples of the warrior class, and women could be initiated into the highest knowledge.

---

[1] *Statement of the EATWOT Conference* (East-Asian Third World Theologians), section 58. See *Vidyajyoti* (1982) p. 92.

Although an ashram essentially emphasizes contemplation, it may also become a nucleus of social reform, first of all represented in the lifestyle within the ashram, but also in the social action which is generated, either directly or indirectly, from the ashram. Sara Grant acknowledges that "those of us in ashrams need to be alert to the danger of developing ways of worship and spirituality that may be deeply rooted in the Brahminical tradition of the past, and for that very reason alien to the 'poor and oppressed.'" She points out, however, that the escapist and the elitist tendency is not essential to the ancient ashram tradition and feels that it is unnecessary to relinquish "all that is good and of permanent value in the ancient traditions."[2]

Challenged to demonstrate the social relevance of Catholic ashrams, the essential complementarity of action and contemplation has been emphasized:

> The Christian contemplative can never ignore the reality of the society and the need to transform it if he is true to his calling to participate in the Incarnation. On the other hand, there is no true, liberating action which is not inspired by an inner vision and orientation to deep communion with God. In other words, there is no true action without contemplation.[3]

Michael Amaladoss sees the specific role of Catholic ashrams as threefold: exemplary, formational and promotional.[4]

The Catholic Ashram as Basic Christian Community

Catholic ashrams have been understood as basic Christian communities understood as "communities of faith, prayer, service, mission, and worship through the celebration of the Eucharist and the Word of God, where there is mutual acceptance, interpersonal relationship and fraternal love."[5] The difference

---

[2] "The Ashram Movement and Social Justice," *Vidyajyoti* 46 (1982) p. 461.

[3] Jyoti Sahi in *Ashram Aikiya Newsletter*, 1983, p. 22.

[4] "Ashrams and Social Justice," *Word and Worship* 15 (1982) p. 206.

[5] Joseph Prasad Pinto, *Inculturation through Basic Communities* (Bangalore: Asian Trading Corporation, 1985) pp. 229-230.

between an ashram and a basic religious community is that "an ashram is centred around a guru, whose personality and religious experience have deep influence on the ashram life; whereas in a basic Christian community, usually there is an animator, whose role is only to facilitate the members to participate actively and creatively in a community setting."[6] Vandana similarly describes Catholic ashrams as:

> basic Christian communities, which follow the Indian spiritual tradition from which they draw their daily sustenance—in their way of prayer, meditation, worship, simple lifestyle, etc., and have a God-experienced person at its head.[7]

Since Catholic ashrams gather around a god-experienced person, rather than around social issues, the degree of social action in the ashram will depend upon the degree of social involvement of the spiritual leader.

Liberation, moreover, means something very different within the context of Latin American liberation theology, which is the original context of basic Christian communities, than in the Indian religious tradition in which Christian ashrams were inculturated. Liberation is understood in Latin America as deliverance from oppressive social structures. In India it is understood as release from the human condition. In Catholic ashrams it is interpreted not so much as an individual release from the world of suffering and death, but as the all-round liberation which considers the exigencies of the practice of social justice as "an indispensable and inseparable condition for the attainment of moksha."[8] The specificity of Catholic ashrams is, according to Amaladoss, that it does not focus one-sidedly on economic and political analysis and problems, but that its approach is integral, that it also takes account of the psychological, cultural, and

---

[6] *Inculturation through Basic Communities*, p. 230.

[7] Vandana, *Social Justice and Ashrams* (Bangalore: Asian Trading Corporation, 1982) p. 27.

[8] "Spirituality for Social Action or Liberative Spirituality" *Brochure Anjali Ashram.*

religious dimensions of the situation.[9] Catholic ashrams attempt to keep a balance between the fixation on contemplation alone, typical of ancient Hindu ashrams, and the purely active orientation of many basic Christian communities.

The Catholic Ashram as Model of Social Justice

In the description of Catholic ashrams, the All-India Consultation on Ashrams insisted upon the importance of material poverty in ashram life:

> The ashram life-style is necessarily simple in the Indian tradition and context; a genuine expression of a life of contemplation.[10]

The emphasis upon simplicity and the satisfaction of no more than the elementary material needs is based not only on the detachment necessary for spiritual growth, but also on solidarity with the poor. It is to the living-standards of the poorest of their neighbors that Catholic ashrams in India adapt their lifestyle. The ashram, its land, cattle, huts, and books are common goods and shared with all. There is little or no furniture in the ashram, and the sleeping facilities are limited to a wooden board, a mat, a blanket, and, where indispensible, a mosquito net. Food is very simple and vegetarian.

Amaladoss feels that ashrams may represent a "model of the community that every movement for social justice wants to create through its struggle."[11] The ashram exemplifies the ideals of freedom, equality, and justice which are pursued in the social struggle. Catholic ashrams are egalitarian communities open to people of any race, sex, religion, age, or class. All caste distinctions — which are at the basis of much social evil in India and which have contaminated even Christian communities — are abolished in Catholic ashrams. Women, who are still strongly

---

[9] "Ashrams and Social Justice," *Word and Worship* 15 (1982) p. 212.

[10] *Statement of The All-India Consultation on Ashrams* (Bangalore: NBCLC, 1978) point 5.

[11] "Ashrams and Social Justice," *Word and Worship* 15 (1982) p. 211.

subjugated in India, are often the guru and thus regarded as the highest authority in the ashram.

The lifestyle of the ashrams is also meant to be a challenge to the church which in terms of possession and wealth sides with the rich in India. Catholic gurus have taken very provocative stances in this area. This illustrates their critical and independent attitude toward the official institution.

The Catholic Ashram as Oasis of Recollection

Another area in which Amaladoss sees the social function of a Catholic ashram is that of being "a place of training where people who wish to engage in service can be trained in ideals, motivation, and method."[12] It may also be a place of retreat and recollection for those already fully engaged in social action. For those who are not involved in social action, the atmosphere and ideals of the ashram may fulfill a conscientizing function. Those who come to the ashram to flee from the world and to cultivate a privatized form of spirituality may be awakened to social consciousness and to the need to participate in the social struggle.

As opposed to the EATWOT criticism which claimed that Christian ashrams lacked a full perspective, most gurus of Catholic ashrams are clearly aware of the structural causes of oppression and poverty and do not fail to address this issue when possible.[13] The integral approach as advocated by Amaladoss includes:

> an integral view of human development and fulfillment both personally and socially, an integral analysis of the situation and appropriate methods of promoting this in the context of a given situation.[14]

The focus on inculturation in Catholic ashrams may bring social workers to an awareness of the specificity of every situation and

---

[12] "Ashrams and Social Justice," *Word and Worship* 15 (1982) p. 211.

[13] The structural analysis of the causes of oppression in India forms an integral part of the Indian Christian spirituality courses in Anjali ashram.

[14] M.Amaladoss, "Ashrams and Social Justice," p. 212.

to the realization that, in order not to loose their authenticity, it is the community itself which must provide the dynamism for social change.

Catholic ashrams understand their role in the social struggle as based upon a necessary balance between action and contemplation, upon the conviction that authentic action comes from contemplation and leads back to it, and that justice derives from inner peace. Vandana emphasizes that any real change in social structures will derive from a changed being and that "the ashram's primary role of service is to change man's inner structure."[15] Sara Grant sees an ashram as a place "to which those in the field can go to recover their perspective, to take the time and the leisure for a depth of prayer that will sustain them in the often exhausting, frustrating, and only too easily embittering labor of their daily living."[16] In response to the EATWOT criticism, she comments on the role of the guru or acharya in the social struggle:

> Personally, I do not see that those who give their whole lives to providing such resource-centres for fellow-men in need, living as simply as possible, welcoming all comers without distinction of caste, creed, community, race, or class, and themselves remaining so far as they can at the Source of existence that alone gives ultimate meaning even to the struggle for justice are in mere "passive solidarity" with those involved in the laborious task to develop a more just society.[17]

Observing that more and more people engaged in active life and in the search for social justice visit the ashram, Bede Griffiths remarks that "they are more and more finding that any worthwhile exterior activity needs to be supported by a correspondingly deeper prayer." He suggests that it is one of the functions of an ashram to "provide an environment in which the two dimensions of Christian life, the search for God in prayer and meditation,

---

[15] Vandana, *Social Justice and Ashrams*, p. 12.
[16] "The Ashram Movement and Social Justice," *Vidyajyoti* 46 (1982) 462.
[17] S. Grant, "The Ashram Movement and Social Justice," p. 462.

and the demands of social justice can be reconciled."[18] In some ashrams, there are retreats organized especially for people involved in the social struggle. These focus upon their particular needs and problems.

Social Action in the Catholic Ashrams

The leaders of Catholic ashrams all seem to agree that a Christian spirituality properly understood and lived corresponds to a spirituality of social action. Concern for the suffering of others is not merely a possible outcome of a life dedicated to spirituality; it is the very sign and standard of spiritual development. Amaladoss sees a third[19] possibility for participation in the social struggle in India in the actual involvement in social action. He warns, however, that "such involvement should not be detrimental to the first two roles of such ashrams that we have outlined. They are more basic, in a sense, and very necessary."[20] In one of the earliest works on Christian ashrams, it was also emphasized that while social involvement is necessary,

> Christian asramas should, however, fully realize that social work, however important, is only an auxiliary activity to tapas and yoga. Spiritual exertion must have primacy in the asrama.[21]

In Kurisumala ashram, it is the combination of a spirituality of intense labor and sober lifestyle which has led to a surplus of means and goods. The traditional monastic ideal of self-sufficiency prompted Francisacharya to start a dairy farm importing new breeds of cattle and new kinds of grasses which would be better suited for the high ranges of the Kottayam district in Kerala. Soon the milk production grew beyond the immediate needs of the community and the profits could be shared with poor neighbors. The farm provided work for many young men in the area and after having been trained at Kurisumala, many

---

[18] *Ashram Aikiya Newsletter* 1984, p. 3.
[19] See above p. 201.
[20] *Ibid.*, p. 212.
[21] P. Chenchiah, V. Chakkarai, *et al.*, *Asramas, Past and Present*, p. 272.

started their own family-size farms and have been organized into a cooperative farmers society. Here, the social dimension is indirect and fortuitous rather than intentional.

In Tirumalai ashram, the intense involvement in social action of some members led to a split within the ashram between the "Tirumalai ashram social center" located near the village and the Tirumalai ashram proper which moved to a quiet place on the mountain. This split between the two ashrams illustrates the difficulty of combining contemplation and full-time social action in one and the same ashram. By symbolically maintaining the same name, however, they illustrate the essential complementarity of action and contemplation. Each ashram now attracts people with inclinations and needs of either sort. The presence of one beside the other provides a continuous reminder of the other and a corrective to a one-sided approach to religious life.

In most other Catholic ashrams, some form of social service has been developed. In the Matri Dham ashram in Varanasi, Isvaraprasad, who had worked as a missionary in social development, organized a small rickshaw-service, which allows the poor of the neighborhood to rent a rickshaw for a nominal fee and thus make a basic living. Anjali ashram is located next to a poor community with which it shares its water and other facilities. Aikiya Alayam ashram is engaged mostly in the promotion of Tamil arts and houses students who study classical Tamil music at the University of Madras. Saccidananda ashram has been working closely with activities of the Sarvodaya movement in the area. It has built houses and started a sewing center for poor girls who can thus earn their dowry and gain some independence.

Summary

Catholic ashrams have, on the one hand, been considered to be purely contemplative groups with little or no social outreach. On the other hand, they have been identified with basic Christian communities, whose very essence lies in social development. Neither of these extremes corresponds to the reality. While the main orientation of an ashram is toward prayer and contemplation, Catholic ashrams have attempted to maintain the precarious and difficult balance between action and contemplation. Much has depended upon the personality, the personal interests and inclinations of the spiritual leader of a particular ashram. Generally, Catholic ashrams have fulfilled an exemplary and an educational role and they have come to be seen as an oasis of rest and recollection for those engaged in the social struggle. Some form of active social service has, moreover, been integrated in all Catholic ashrams.

SUMMARY REFLECTION

Though a fairly recent and relatively small and marginal phenomenon, Catholic ashrams have been the object of considerable interest and also controversy in India. They have been understood as a New Religious Movement,[1] a new style of mission in India,[2] a reaction to the development theology of the West,[3] an Indian version of basic Christian communities,[4] eschatological communities,[5] contemplative hermitages that revolve around both Christian and Hindu ideals, or as "institutions to brainwash and convert India's unwary masses."[6] While there has been much sympathy and support from both the Hindu and the Christian communities in India, Catholic ashrams have also confronted opposition. In *Catholic Ashrams*, Sita Ram Goel, a member of a fundamentalist movement within Hinduism which seeks a return to the pure Vedic religion, severely attacks and ridicules the phenomenon of Catholic ashrams.[7] It is suspected of merely being the latest missionary strategy, ultimately intent upon destroying Hinduism. The author argues that Catholic ashrams do

[1] H. Ralston, *Christian Ashrams: A New Religious Movement in Contemporary India* (New York: Edwin Mellen, 1987.)

[2] R. Taylor, "Christian Ashrams as a Style of Mission in India" *International Review of Mission* 68 (1979) 281-293.

[3] *Statement of the EATWOT Conference*, 1981.

[4] J.P. Pinto, *Inculturation through Basic Communities* (Bangalore: Asian Trading Corporation, 1985) pp. 229-230.

[5] P. Chenchiah, V. Chakkarai, *et al.*, *Asramas, Past and Present* (Madras: Indian Christian Book Club, 1941) pp. 275-279.

[6] S.R. Goel, *Catholic Ashrams* (New Delhi: Voice of India, 1988) p. 3.

[7] This book is a reproduction of a series of articles which appeared in *Hinduism Today,* Nov.-Dec., 1986. The proverbial tolerance and indifference of Hinduism toward other religions does not seem to apply to all segments of society, at least not when another religion strikes too close to home. This book has received a positive response from Christian apostates to Hinduism who are often among the strongest opponents of Catholic ashrams and gurus. They have acquired a new identity which, just as the previous one, needs to be established in opposition with the other. Catholic ashrams and gurus may then be felt as a threat to their identity.

no more than "ape" the Hindu tradition without undergoing a real transformation. He states that "Hindus are seriously questioning whether yoga, puja, and sannyas, which are so deeply rooted in particular Hindu theological concepts, can ethically be adopted by Christianity," that is, if Christianity does not question its own fundamental beliefs and theological presuppositions.[8] As long as Christians are not prepared to question their own fundamentals of faith, more precisely the belief in the uniqueness of Christ, Hindus, according to Goel, will remain suspicious of Catholic motives for starting ashrams.[9]

Precisely the opposite fear and suspicion lives in certain circles of conservative Christians in India. They regard the wearing of the robe of the sannyasi and the adoption of the Hindu lifestyle and Hindu rituals as the implicit acceptance of the entire gamut of Hindu world views and beliefs and as a betrayal of the Christian faith. As a minority religion, Christianity has throughout its history in India attempted to preserve its identity by emphasizing its distinctiveness and expressing it in language, dress and institutions. Once these are no longer upheld, the Christian identity is threatened, they feel.

Concern for the preservation of the distinctive role of the church in India comes not only from conservative, but also from social movements. Those especially sensitive to the function of the church as critical catalyst fear that the Christian version of ashram life may become as individualistic and escapist as traditional Hindu ashrams have often been. The Sanskrit language often used in Christian ashrams is the language of the elite, the highest caste which used that language precisely to establish and preserve their exclusivity.

The same fundamental question thus lies at the basis of both the Hindu and the Christian criticisms. It concerns the relationship between form and content, between the adoption of symbols and rituals and theological inculturation and transformation.

---

[8] *Catholic Ashrams*, p. 17.
[9] *Catholic Ashrams*, pp. xlix, 1, 14, 19-22.

While Hindus accuse Catholic ashrams of not confronting the theological challenge, Christians are afraid that the traditional belief system may be challenged too much, that Christian ashrams may sink too deep into the Hindu world view and belief system and ultimately be absorbed in the Hindu fold.

Both criticisms ultimately relate to the figure of the guru as the constitutive element of not only Hindu but also Catholic ashrams. The historical development of Catholic ashrams illustrates that, even though the church may have instigated the foundation of Catholic ashrams, it has been the ability of the particular spiritual leader to attract disciples and inspire surrender which accounted for the success or failure of the particular ashrams. The ritual life of Catholic ashrams has also evolved around the figure of the spiritual master. It is he or she who assigns a certain spiritual discipline to the disciple. In the particular Hindu rituals which have been adopted such as the three samdhyas, the yogic practices and the initiation to brahmacharya and sannyasa, the guru traditionally plays a constitutive role. The degree and form of involvement of the ashram in social action, which is usually seen as distinctive of Catholic ashrams, is also dependent upon the particular head of the ashram.

Catholic ashrams may thus be seen as *sui generis*. They emerge from the spontaneous surrender of disciples to the charismatic authority of a master and can strictly speaking not be "founded" or "instituted" from above. They operate within the margins of the Roman Catholic Church, from where they may become both a blessing or a threat. Christian ashrams may fulfill a complementary and reinvigorating role in the Church, as Chenchiah and Chakkarai envisioned:

> For experimentation, meditation, and for all deeper religious search, the asrama is more suited than the Church bound by tradition, compelled by ritual, controlled by priesthood, all meant for the weak and timid and those in search for safety and security.[10]

[10] *Asramas, Past and Present*, p. 288.

They may, however, also manifest their essential independence from the authority of office, and may, at any given moment, break with the Church and become a separate sampradaya, or an independent teaching tradition.

Although the head of the Catholic ashram fulfills the same central and constitutive function as the Hindu guru, the term guru is generally avoided, at least in theory. The radically different worldview in which this term is imbedded makes its application in Christianity problematic, or at least theologically challenging. The status and authority which the guru assumes in Hinduism is, in the Christian tradition, concentrated in the figure of Christ. Abhishiktananda's reflections illustrate the radical Christological implications of understanding Christ through the category of guru: the traditional grounds for the historical decisiveness and the uniqueness of Christ become dissolved. The superlative term "Sadguru" is then most often used for Christ and the qualified "upaguru" or the less loaded term acharya is used to refer to the head of the ashram.

Some leaders of Christian ashrams see themselves as in continuity with the Desert Fathers of the early Christian tradition and with the *startsy* or elders of the Eastern Orthodox tradition. In all three cases, the authority of the master is purely charismatic, constituted by the spiritual qualities of the master and the surrender of disciples. The master need not be ordained and may thus be a woman or layman. Like the Desert Fathers and the Russian startsy, the Catholic guru may be seen as one who retires from society and from the established church stuctures to lead a life of poverty and contemplation. Disciples spontaneously gathered around them for practical counsel and spiritual guidance. Thus religious communities came to be formed. While not dependent upon the institution, both the Desert Fathers and the startsy remained within the Church through their free submission to the authority of office.

Although all Catholic ashrams and gurus ultimately submit to the authority of office, some emphasize the Catholic identity of the ashram by keeping strictly to the doctrinal and ritual prescriptions of the church, while others are less concerned with the distinctive characteristics of Catholic ashrams. Inculturation in the Hindu spiritual tradition and the dialogue between religions has often become an absolute priority. Exclusive beliefs are ignored or reinterpreted and rituals are adapted to allow non-Christians to participate. Some gurus explicitly minimalize the difference between Hindu and Christian ashrams and have come to see the ashram as a trans-religious community. Amalorpavadass argues that "we need to transcend this distinction of Christian mysticism and Hindu mysticism, Christian ashrams and Hindu ashrams, Christian spirituality and Hindu spirituality" because "religious experience, including contemplation or mysticism, or God-experience, wherever it is found, is genuine, the work of the spirit and the manifestation of his grace."[11] Bede Griffiths sees an ashram as "not an exclusive Christian community, but a centre of universal love, a place where people of any religion or of none can come and learn to find themselves, that is, find the real meaning and purpose of their lives."[12] Rather than being seen as an exponent of one particular tradition, the guru is then regarded as a channel of dialogue and encounter between different religions. There has been little or no inclination to expect or direct towards formal conversion in Catholic ashrams.

As both the result and the agent of inculturation in India, each Catholic guru may be seen to be on the verge of, on the one hand, being coopted by the Catholic institution and, on the other hand, becoming lost in the embrace of Hinduism. It is precisely this tension which has been a source of great creativity.

[11] "Ashram Aikiya, Whence and Whither," *Word and Worship* 17 (1984) p. 307.
[12] *Garland of Letters*, p. 9.

CONCLUSION

The encounter between the Catholic and the Hindu tradition in India has given birth to the Catholic equivalent of the Hindu guru. Around these Catholic "gurus" Indian-style religious communities called ashrams have emerged. The notions "guru" and "ashram" are, however, foreign to traditional Catholicism. They are imbedded in a radically different world view, philosophical tradition and belief system, and they cannot be incorporated into Christianity without representing a fundamental challenge, both theologically and institutionally. Catholic ashrams and their gurus thus find themselves in a position of ambiguity which, however, may reveal itself as a healthy challenge and an opportunity for the church. Since the figure of the guru is the constitutive element, the *raison d'être*, of an ashram, it is around the notion of the guru within Christianity that the discussion evolves.

The term guru is generally avoided when referring to the head of a Catholic ashram. Its absolutist connotations are seen to be irreconcilable with the Christian conception of the spiritual master as representative of Christ and instrument of the Spirit. The head of the Catholic ashram, moreover, is not autonomous as is the Hindu guru, but remains answerable to the authority of office represented by a bishop or superior. The absolute status and authority which the guru may assume in the Hindu tradition is concentrated in the figure of Jesus Christ and in the church as the continuation of Christ in the world. Abhishiktananda's reflections on Jesus Christ as guru, however, illustrate that the application of the Hindu category of guru to Jesus Christ would shake the very foundations of traditional christology. It would dissolve the traditional understanding of the historical decisiveness and the uniqueness of Jesus Christ. The term guru can thus not be introduced into Christianity without radical theological implications.

The institutional status of a Catholic ashram is equally ambiguous. Within the Hindu tradition, every ashram is a self-sufficient and independent religious community, which exists and persists solely on the basis of the charismatic authority of the guru and the surrender of disciples. To remain within the church, a Catholic ashram must submit to the doctrinal and disciplinary decrees of the official authority and allow institutional control. The institution may in turn guarantee the continuity of the ashram. This, however, is opposed to the original ashram spirit. From the institutional point of view, the notion "Catholic ashram" may thus be seen as a contradiction in terms.

Inculturation has come to be understood as a process of mutual fecundation in the course of which both traditions involved are enriched and transformed. Catholic "gurus" and ashrams are not only the outcome, but also the agents of inculturation. At the junction between the Christian and the Hindu conception of the spiritual master, they may become a channel of dialogue and fulfill the function of mutually critical catalyst.

The guru-disciple relationship which is meant to lead to the highest good may easily succumb to the worst perversion. The risk of manipulation and abuse is inherent in the unconditional surrender which is expected of the disciple. The Hindu tradition contains no defence against this danger. There is no higher authority than that of the one who has come to self-realization. The guru is often considered to be beyond morality and normal human rationality. Although in theory moral impeccability is presupposed, the surrender of disciples — which in practice makes the guru — does not necessarily guarantee the fulfillment of this condition. Hindu gurus do not go uncriticized in the Hindu community as a whole. There was and is considerable reaction against such figures as Rajneesh and Sai Baba. Yet, within the circle of disciples, the authority and power of the guru are limitless. What may appear to be against the laws of morality and rationality may be justified in terms of the mysterious ways in which the guru works. The more mysterious the guru's ways, the stronger the faith of the disciple. A vicious circle is thus created which cannot be broken by an external agency of control or appeal.

In the Catholic tradition, the possibility of abuse inherent in the master-disciple relationship is precluded — theologically by the emphasis upon the uniqueness of Christ, institutionally through the possibility of appeal to the authority of office. While dialogue with non-Christian religions has often led to the minimalization of the traditional belief in the uniqueness of Christ, it may also lead to a re-valuation, although from a less substantivist perspective. The belief in the uniqueness of Christ and in basic human sinfulness, as expressed in the Christian principle of the eschatological proviso, denies every human claim to perfection and absoluteness. Though the unconditional obedience which is exacted from the disciple may raise the Catholic spiritual master to a functional position of absolute authority, he is never regarded as ontologically absolute or infallible. There always remains the possibility of appeal to and control by the church which is considered to be the ultimate depository of authority in the Catholic tradition. The church hierarchy may interfere when a spiritual master-disciple relationship becomes distorted.

In view of the possibility of abuse, the absolute status and immune position of the Hindu guru may thus be reconsidered in dialogue with the Christian concept of the spiritual master. This is reflected in Amalorpavadass' more dynamic understanding of a Catholic ashram, not as a static place constructed around a realized guru, but as a journey of relentless quest for the absolute in which disciples participate not in contrast with, but along with the guru.

The Hindu tradition of the guru may, however, also represent a valuable challenge, both theologically and institutionally, to the traditional Christian notion of the spiritual master. The Christian belief in the uniqueness of Jesus Christ has often led to an objectivation of the figure and the soteriological function of Jesus Christ and to a fixation on the historical Jesus. Dialogue with the Hindu understanding of Jesus Christ as guru may lead to a more internal and personal understanding of Christ, without necessarily neglecting its inseparable connection with the historical Jesus. The traditional understanding of the radical discontinuity of Jesus Christ may be reconsidered and the Catholic guru understood in terms of the continuation of the incarnation. From this perspective, every Christian is called to participate in the mystery of Christ, and to become "guru," spiritually weighty. This may bring spirituality out of its often closed monastic setting and make it more widely accessible. Catholic ashrams are essentially open communities, constituted by the temporary and lay visitor, more than by the permanent religious members. The Catholic guru may be a priest, a monk, or a nun, but also a lay person.

The emphasis on spiritual authority in the Hindu tradition is a challenge to a more spiritual understanding of authority, not only beside, but also within the official hierarchy of the Church. Catholic ashrams have been given considerable freedom to experiment with the adoption of a purely spiritual authority structure. This has led women and laymen to rise to the same authority as ordained ministers within the context of Catholic ashrams. It also brings about a spontaneous decentralization of authority within the church. To merely copy the Hindu model where the guru is the final authority in the ashram would lead to a total dispersion of authority, to disunity and schism. By remaining in a dynamic relationship with the official hierarchy, the leaders of Catholic ashrams may fulfill a reinvigorating and innovative function within the church. The church hierarchy is, moreover, challenged to move from an administrative and hierarchic to a more spiritual conception of authority. The awareness that Indian Christianity calls for a conception of ministry different from that developed in the history of the Church is steadily growing. Felix Wilfred argues that the ministry is one of the areas in most urgent need for inculturation. He calls for a shift from a legalistic to a spiritual understanding of authority:

> the ministers of the Church would deserve respect not so much because of the juridical title they have and the formal authority they possess as because they are persons who are truly enlightened as the

arhat or guru and have a deep experience of the mystery at the heart of the Church.[1]

The experiments which take place in the margin of the church may then serve as model for a radical transformation within church structures.

The purpose of inculturation is to adopt forms of worship and thought which are congenial to a particular culture, with which people belonging to that culture resonate. In becoming Indian, however, the Catholic ashrams and gurus have paradoxically come to appeal to people from the West, more than to Hindus and Indian Christians. The attempt at inculturation in India through the Hindu model of religious community and master-disciple relationship may thus be seen to have as yet missed its mark. This need not discredit or invalidate these attempts at inculturation. Many Indian Christians still feel that Christianity needs to distinguish itself from Hinduism by a difference in dress, lifestyle and language. While the West has believed the spiritual tradition to be representative of Indian religiosity, in actuality it has been the concern of a small minority in India, as everywhere else. It is not so much the abstract philosophy and the ascetic discipline of Advaita Vedanta, but popular devotion as usually referred to under the general noun of Bhakti, which is the dominant form of religiosity in India. The main preoccupation of the majority of Indians is, moreover, not with a return to a natural and simple life, but with overcoming the oppressive simplicity of misery and poverty.

In appealing to Westerners, Catholic ashrams fulfill a need and represent a message to the church. They represent a bridge between East and West, a channel of dialogue between Hinduism and Christianity, a spiritual refuge from Western materialism, and the spiritual authority and guidance which appears to be

---

[1] F. Wilfred, "Inculturation as a Hermeneutical Question," *Vidyajyoti* 52 (1988) p. 428. He adds that "a claim to authority without deep spiritual experience has, in the Asian view, little to do with religion and religiosity."

lacking in the Church. In "The Christian ashram: a model for the West," Vandana argues that a new form of religious life is needed today and that "the signs of the times point towards open Christian communities."[2] She calls these communities "cells of dissent" where people of all ages, races, sexes, and religious affiliations may meet in a common spiritual quest. Several such Christian ashrams have recently come to emerge in the West. They may be seen as an exponent of what has been called "New Age Religion." As the fruit of the inculturation of Christianity in the Indian spiritual tradition, the ashram has become, according to Jyoti Sahi, "India's gift to humanity as a whole."

[2] *The Tablet*, November 18, 1989, pp. 1332-1334.

Selected Bibliograpy on Christian Ashrams

Amaladoss, M. "Ashrams and Social Justice," *Word and Worship* 15 (1982) 205-214.

Amalorpavadass, D.S. "Ashram Aikiya: Whence and Whither?" *Word and Worship* 17 (1984) 303-308, 340-346.

Appasamy, A.J. "Christian Ashrams, An Indian Tradition in the Service of the Church," *Frontier* 4 (1961) 281-285.

Bagumiziriza, N., *et al.* "Spiritual Direction in Major Seminaries in India and Africa," *Vidyajyoti* 51 (1987) 330-337.

Beaver, R.P. "Christian Ashrams in India," *Christian Century* 82 (1965) 887-889.

Chenchiah, P., Chakkarai, V. and Sudarisanam, A.N. *Ashrams, Past and Present.* Madras: Indian Christian Book Club, 1941.

Goel, S.R., *Catholic Ashrams.* New Delhi: Voice of India, 1988.

Grant, S. *Lord of the Dance.* Bangalore: Asian Trading Corporation, 1987.

—, "The Ashram Movement and Social Justice," *Vidyajyoti* 46 (1982) 460-462.

—, "Ashrams and Ecumenism," *Word and Worship* 17 (1984) 170-175.

—, "Towards a Practical Indian Ecclesiology," *Vidyajyoti* 49 (1985) 39-35.

—, and von Loesch, B. "The Eucharist, Ecumenism and Dialogue," *Vidyajyoti* 59 (1988) 234-236.

Griffiths, B. *Christian Ashram.* London: Longman & Todd, 1966.

—, "Kurisumala Ashram," *The Eastern Churches Quarterly* 16 (1964) 226-231.

—, "The Monastic Order and the Ashram," *The American Benedictine Review* 30 (1979) 134-145.

Jesudason, S. and Paton, E.F. *Ashrams, Ancient and Modern.* Velloor: Sri Ramachandra Press, 1937.

—, *The Christakula Ashram.* Madras: N.M.S. Press, 1940.

—, "The Ashram and its Contribution to the Christian Life," *National Christian Council Review* 59 (1939) 573-584.

Kaipanplakal, P. "Siluvaigiri Ashram, The First Benedictine Monastery in India," *Indian Missionary Bulletin* 1 (1952-3) 156-158.
Kavumkal, J. "Christian Ashram: A Study of the Ashram in the Context of the Basic Communities," *Verbum SVD* 20 (1979) 68-78.

Lederle, M. "Ashrams and Dialogue," *Word and Worship* 17 (1984) 108-113.

Mahieu, F. *Kurisumala Ashram.* Tiruvalla: St. Joseph's Printing House, 1958.
—, "Kurisumala Ashram, An Experiment in Monastic Life," *The Clergy Monthly Supplement* 4 (1958-9) 202-204.
—, *Kurisumala: A Symposium on Ashram Life.* Vagamon: Kurisumala Ashram, 1974.

O'Toole, M. *Christian Ashram Communities* (revised by Ishvani Kendra). Pune: Satprakashan Sanchar, 1983.

Paton, E.F. "Christian Ashrams and the Building of God's Kingdom," *The Christian Ashram Review* 1 (1965) 11-12.
—, "The Inter-Ashram Conference, Tadagam, Coimbatore, 17 to 21 Feb. 1969," *The Christian Ashram Review* 5 (1969) 31-35.
Philip, P.O. "The Place of Ashrams in the Life of the Church in India" *International Review of Missions* 35 (1946) 263-270.

Ralston, H. *Christian Ashrams: A New Religious Movement in Contemporary India.* New York: Edwin Mellen, 1987.
Rodrigues, A. "The Guru-Sisya Model of Formation," *Indian Theological Studies* 20 (1983) 308-326.
Rogers, M. "Hindu Ashram Heritage: God's Gift to the Church," *Concilium* 9 (1965) 73-75.
—, "Jyotiniketan Ashram," *The Easter Churches Quarterly* 16 (1964) 232-238.

Sahi, J. *Stepping Stones: Reflections on the Theology of Indian Christian Culture.* Bangalore: Asian Trading Corporation, 1986.
"Statement of the All India Consultation on Ashrams," *Vidyajyoti* 42 (1978) 383-385.

Taylor, R. "From Khadi to Kavi: Toward a Typology of Christian Ashrams," *Religion and Society* 24 (1977) 19-37.
—, "Christian Ashrams as a Style of Mission in India," *International Review of Mission* 68 (1979) 281-293.
—, "Ashrams and the Kingdom of God," *Vidyajyoti* 54 (1990) 19-29.

Theerthan, J.D. *Christian Ashram in India (non-Roman)*. Kottayam, New Model, 1952.

Theobald, R. "The Role of Charisma in the Development of Social Movements," *Archives de Sciences Sociales des Religions* 49 (1980) 83-100.

Thomas, P. "Christian Ashrams and Evangelization of India," *Indian Church History Review* 11 (1977) 204-221.

Vandana. *Gurus, Ashrams and Christians*. London: Darton, Longman and Todd, 1978.

—, *Social Justice and Ashrams*. Bangalore: Asian Trading Corporation, 1982.

—, *Waters of Fire*. Madras: The Diocesan Press, 1981.

—, "The Ashram Movement and the Development of Contemplative Life," *Vidyajyoti* 47 (1983) 179-192.

—, "The Guru as Present Reality," *Vidyajyoti* 39 (1975) 127-130.

—, "Ashrams," *Word and Worship* 11 (1978) 15-22.

—, "Ashrams, Some Illusions and Fears," *Word and Worship* 17 (1984) 33-40.

—, "News and Comments: Ashramites Satsangh," *Indian Theological Studies* 15 (1978) 358-366.

—, "The Christian Ashram: a Model for the West," *The Tablet*, November 18, 1989, 1332-1334.

Weckman, G. "The Ashram, a Different Kind of Religious Community," *American Benedictine Review* 23 (1972) 98-112.

Glossary of terms

No diacritical marks have been used in the text. The transliteration of the Sanskrit words is kept as closely as possible to the English pronunciation. The palatal and the cerebral "s" are both transliterated as "sh;" the palatal "c" appears as "ch," and the short vowel "r" as "ri." The long vowels, the anusvara, and the guttural and cerebral "n" are not indicated. This glossary gives a transliteration with diacritical marks.

acharya (ācārya): teacher, preceptor, instructor

Advaita Vedanta (Advaita Vedānta): philosophical school of non-dualism, founded by Shankara in the ninth century C.E. The ultimate and only reality is that of Brahman without qualities, *nirguna Brahman (nirguṇa Brahman)*, which is not different from the Self, *atman (ātman)*. All perception of differentiation is based on *maya (māyā)*, illusion.

ahamkara (ahaṃkāra): egoism, selfishness.

antaryamin: inner mover, inner controller.

ashrama (āśrama): one of the four major stages of life.

atman (ātman): Self, ground of individual being. The term *paramatman* may be used to emphasize the notion of "highest Self."

avatar (avatāra): "descent," usually referring to one of the ten earthly manifestations which the god Vishnu took to save the world from disaster or corruption. The term *manusha (manuśa) avatar* is used to emphasize the "human" avatar.

avidya (avidyā): ignorance.

bhakti: loving devotion.

bhajan: hymn, song expressing love and longing for god.

Brahma: absolute Being, or the ultimate ground of existence in the Upanishads and Advaita Vedanta. In the theistic tradition, it refers to the creator god.

brahman, brahmin: belonging to the sacred *varna (varṇa)*, or social class of the priests.

Brahmanas (Brāhmanas): priestly lore of the Veda, ritual manual used to perform the Vedic sacrifice.

brahmacharya (brahmacarya): studentship, one of the four stages in life, or *ashramas (āśramas)*, which every twice-born Hindu must pass through. The person in this stage is called *brahmacharin (brahmacā-rin)*. *Brahmacharya* also came to mean celibacy, which was a strict requirement of the student.

dakshina (dakṣina): gift, offering to the priest in return for a ritual performance.

Dakshinamurti (Dakṣinamurti): the south-facing form (of Shiva.)

darshan (darśan): seeing, looking, showing, exhibition. It usually refers to the grace-bestowing vision of the godhead, manifested in an idol or in a living person.

diksha (dīkṣā): initiation.

guru: "heavy," "weighty," usually referring to a person who by virtue of his or her spiritual weight is regarded as a holy teacher, a spiritual master. The exceptional or authentic nature of a guru may be emphasized by the use of prefixes: *sadguru*, or real, true guru, *param-guru*, or highest guru; *jagad-guru,* or world guru; and *tevya guru*, or divine guru. The term may also be qualified or nuanced through adjectives: *upaya guru* or *karana (kāraṇa) guru* refer to the (merely) instrumental function of a human guru, and the term *upaguru* emphasizes that the human guru is near and under the real guru.

guru puja: worship of the guru

Ishvara (Īśvara): the Lord.

jivanmukta (jīvanmukta): emancipated while alive.

jñana (jñāna): gnosis, knowledge, insight. The one who has gained this sacred knowldge is called a *jñani (jñāni)*.

karma: deed, action, the law of action and reaction.

kavi (kāvi): the saffron robe worn in India by those who have renounced the world, the *sannyasis (sannyāsis)*.

Krishna (Kṛṣṇa): manifesting himself as the human avatar of Vishnu in the Bhagavadgita, he has become the fountainhead and the most popular god of the Bhakti tradition.

mahavakyas (mahavākyas): the great sayings of the Upanishads.

manana: reflection.

Manavadharmashastra (Manavadharmaśāstra): "Manu's treatise on dharma," India's book of law and societal structure.

matha: hindu monastery.

marga (mārga): path, way, road.

moksha (mokśa): release, emancipation, liberation.

mulagarbha: cosmic womb.

namarupa (nāmarūpa): name and form, matter, material form.

neti...neti...: neither this, nor that.

nididhyasana (nididhyāsana): deep meditation

paduka: wooden sandal.

parampara: lineage.

pradakshina (pradakṣiṇa): moving to the right, circumambulation.

puja (pūjā): worship, offering, ritual. The one who administers the ritual is called *pujari (pujāri)*.

purusha (puruśa): cosmic person, person, spirit. The term *satpurusha* is used to emphasize the true, ultimate or absolute nature of the inner person.

rishi (ṛṣi): seer, sage.

saccidananda (saccidānanda: sat, or Being, *citta*, or consciousness, and *ananda (ānanda)*, or bliss, are the three supreme "qualities" or "aspects" of the divine, and the way in which, according to the tradition of Advaita Vedanta, the absolute is experienced.

sadhana (sādhana): religious discipline, spiritual practice. The one doing *sadhana* is called a *sadhaka (sādhaka)*.

samdhya (saṃdhya): gathering for common celebration.

sampradaya (saṃpradāya): teaching tradition.

samsara (saṃsāra): transmigration, circle of eternal return.

sannyasa (sannyāsa): the fouth or ultimate stage in life which is that of total renunciation to the world. The one who has taken the vow of complete renunciation is called a *sannyasi (sannyāsi)*.

satya: truth.

shishya (śiṣya): disciple (the term *chela* may also be used).

Shiva (Śiva): successor to the stormgod Rudra in the Rig-Vedic pantheon, the god of creation and destruction, of the reconciliation of all opposites, patron of yogis.

shravana (śravaṇa): learning through listening.

shruti (śruti): what is "heard" or revealed.

smriti (smṛti): what is remembered, transmitted.

sutra (sūtra): thread, string, string of verses.

taraka (tāraka): boatman.

upanayana (upanāyana): puberty initiation.

Upanishad (Upaniṣad): sitting down under and near (a teacher); sacred teaching. The term is usually applied to the philosophical, mystical treatises which form one part of the Veda.

vidvat sannyasa: learned renouncer.

vividishu (vividiṣu) sannyasa: learning renouncer.

vanaprastha: the third stage in life which is that of the forest dweller, hermit.

yoga: discipline, psycho-somatic technique for self-realization.

INDEX OF NAMES

ORIENTALISTE, P.B. 41, B-3000 Leuven